The Spectacle of Ourselves

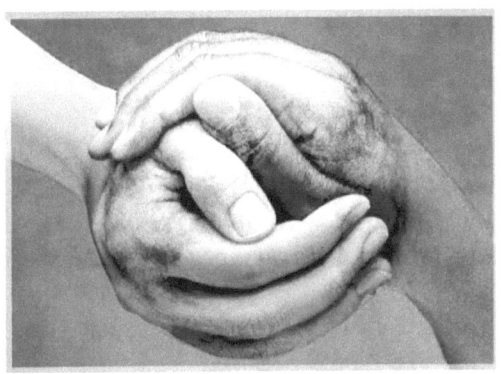

A CHRONOLOGY OF KEY
EVENTS IN WORLD HISTORY
FROM
BIG BANG TO 2012

Craig Chalquist

World Soul Books
114 Addison Street
Berkeley, CA 94702

Copyright @ 2013 by Craig Chalquist.

All rights reserved.
Printed in the United States of America.

No part of this book may be used or reproduced in any manner whatsoever without written permission except in the case of brief quotations in critical articles or reviews.

Printed in the United States of America
ISBN ISBN: 978-0-9826279-4-5

Visit the author's web site at Chalquist.com.

Table of Contents

Preface: Telling Our Tale 1

In The Beginning 7

Prehistory: Eradigm Mother Nature 15

Ancient History to Premodernity: Eradigm Heavenly City 17

    Common Era 42

    Middle Ages 53

    Late Middle Ages 69

    Renaissance 84

Modernity: Eradigm Big Machine 99

Information Age: Eradigm Earthrise 207

Epilogue for a Pale Blue Dot 245

Appendix I: Forty Lessons from History 251

Appendix II: Countries and Regions of the World 255

DEDICATION

To Mitrochondrial Eve, mother to us all.

Preface:
Telling Our Tale

Only the study of the past can provide us with a standard by which to measure the rapidity and strength of the particular movement in which we live.
— Jacob Burckhardt

If, after all, men cannot always make history have a meaning, they can always act so that their own lives have one.
— Albert Camus

Fellow citizens, we cannot escape history.
— Abraham Lincoln

"A chaotic pile of rubbish." That was cranky old Heraclitus's summation of human history.
And yet Time spins out an ever-lengthening tale, *our* tale, one not always told, or lived, by idiots. A tale without a predetermined plot externally imposed, surely, but woven even so through occasions of poignant encounter, head-splitting absurdity, uproarious confusion, and transient grandeur. Shakespeare came closer than Heraclitus: "All the world's a stage."

Over years of noting down and reflecting on historical events I have formed impressions that guided the compilation of this book. One is that Carlyle was full of wind when he offered the heroic view that "the history of the world is but the biography of great men." Most of the greatest never make it into history books because their greatness shines on a plane of being far above that of the normal run of generals, bankers, rebels, or gurus. As Albert Schweitzer pointed out in his autobiography, opportunities for great-spirited action are abundant rather than rare; most stay out of public view; and humanity's very survival depends on them every day even though most go uncelebrated.

Much of the perennial storehouse of courageous decisions, soulful encounters, loving moments, deep realizations, kind actions, loyal friendships, lessons learned, witty protests, and awe-inspiring creations remains lost forever to written history and always will. Its neglected treasures receive mention here as both memorial and corrective. What we study is public history copied down through countless layers of distortion. The fact that so much of it features males of European ancestry tells us that right off. The lack of early written records in non-Western areas of the world plants additional obstacles for the historian. All cultures are literate in the sense that all read the signs and portents of the natural world, but not all equally value the written word, and some came to it later than others.

This collection, then, must be at best a partial one. Each event herein reveals a little of who we are as one of many species inhabiting a blue-green planet circling an undistinguished star tucked away in a short arm of a galaxy lost among billions of others adrift in universes stretching far away beyond human comprehension. We matter, I suspect, not for our importance but for our uniqueness. The Epilogue at the end has more to say about that.

However partial, it's a story worth telling and retelling, even if most of its best-known players have hogged the stage of world affairs. Beyond their cumulative effect, the intersections of people, places, actions, and events mentioned in this book loosed startling forces in human affairs, opening possibilities for turning our human potential for self-becoming into actuality. Who can gauge the impact of Siddhartha Gautama? Of Moses, Zoroaster, Muhammad, Joan of

Arc? We will never be done with them. They still impact us and always will, as do the paintings of Van Gogh and the speeches of Martin Luther King Jr. and the hymns of St. Hildegard and the Mount of Olives and a Renaissance that even now announces far more than one of many cultural flowerings.

Included are well-known historical turning points and others less overtly political, financial, or military—cultural events, for example—that partake of the flavor of their time. Repetitious events like battles, earthquakes, regime changes, plane crashes, train wrecks, elections, market crashes, and terrorist attacks have largely been passed over unless they seem novel or unusual for when and where they occur. The chronology is organized by century and year but not by month or (usually) by day. My hope is that the reader moving through the chronology gets the feel of a complicated story unfolding in many places at once. Our story, the story of our global family.

While studying history I've often been struck by four scene changes in our story: immense archetypal images that rise from collective human consciousness, draw to themselves a wealth of invention, reflection, and devotion from all over the world and every level of civilization, enjoy their day in the sun, and, losing their numinosity, give way to what comes next. As far as I can tell, we have encountered, as a species, four of these *eradigms*, these worldview-shaping images that stamp entire eras: Mother Nature (from prehistory to the Agricultural Revolution), the Heavenly City (the rise of cities through feudalism and ancient history), the Big Machine (starting up with the Scientific and Industrial Revolutions), and Earthrise (from 1968 and still unfolding). Mother Nature feels local, with Here the center of Everything. The Heavenly City turns vertical, hierarchical, and dualistic, with the gods and chiefs above and ground and peasantry below. By contrast, the Big Machine, which views everything as parts of a cosmic apparatus, reaches out horizontally: think of the Age of Exploration. Earthrise underlines trans-border unity in geographic, cultural, and ecological diversity, with our planet taking center stage in human concerns.

Overall, this long movement of eradigms is not a progression, but a pageant, with past eradigms lingering to inform the present. I like to think of them as colorings-in of the collective soul.

Eradigm Mother Nature
Historical span: prehistory to 10,000 BCE.
Parallel names: Paleolithic/Mesolithic.
Primary collective fantasy: containment.
Direction: center.
Developmental task: appreciation.

Eradigm Heavenly City
Historical span: 10,000 BCE to 1500.
Parallel names: Ancient/Feudal.
Primary collective fantasy: height.
Direction: vertical.
Developmental task: ascension.

Eradigm Big Machine
Historical span: 1500-1968.
Parallel names: Modernity.
Primary collective fantasy: breadth.
Direction: horizontal.
Developmental task: expansion.

Eradigm Earthrise
Historical span: 1968 to ?
Parallel names: Information Age, Postmodernity.
Primary collective fantasy: conjunction.
Direction: depth (omni).
Developmental task: participation.

These, then, provide our primary demarcations of human history: transitions in the plots of our life as a species. The sections of the book delineate this four-part schema.

Even when incomplete, our knowledge of history teaches us to appreciate our greatness, laugh at our shortcomings, guide us through uncertainties, and, if we are willing, learn from our follies. As Janet, Freud, Santayana, Joyce, Hesse, DuBois, Campbell, and so many others have claimed with unfailing accuracy, we repeat what we fail to remember and learn from, and usually at great cost: the true lesson of unlucky King Oedipus. As United States troops moved into Iraq and Afghanistan, there to let blood, take lives, and leave behind an entirely predictable failure, the political leaders who had ordered them in were watched unawares by the unblinking ghosts of Sun Tzu, Captain Cook, T.E. Lawrence, Che Guevara, George Pickett, Louis XVI, and George Armstrong Custer. The First World War should have destroyed our "Enlightenment" faith in ever-expansive Progress, but enough of the delusion lingered to bring a Second World War and a Cold War after that. We've heard from elites for ten thousand years that their wealth trickles downward, yet billions today go without water, food, or shelter. Perhaps the most urgent unlearned lesson is that allowing the ambitious, grandiose, and emotionally immature among us access to power always results in disaster.

Beyond lessons, significant events and epochal individuals also remind us to make creative use of the protean present because it only lasts, historically speaking, for a moment. "All formations are impermanent," observed the Buddha and so many of our greatest teachers of life. And the poets: "Living is moving," wrote Annie Dillard; "time is a live creek bearing changing lights." Perhaps the generative idea here is not so much to guess their brilliance as to be illuminated by it. For a moment.

In the Beginning

....*is a cosmically resonant "Word"* as the Big Bang unrolls the fabric of space-time 13.81 billion years ago. Having expanded faster than the speed of light, the universe cools, and the four fundamental "forces"—capacities? gestures?—grow distinct; they are gravity (actually a space-time curve rather than a force), electromagnetism, and the strong (holds atomic nuclei together) and weak (e.g., radioactive decay) forces. As particles and antiparticles shift back and forth between states of matter and energy and settle down into materiality, two elements, hydrogen and helium, spread out as an ionized gas. Soon universe is a dim, opaque place clumped together by the pull of dark matter.

That matter forms into *quasars* (from *quasi-stellar radio source*), the most luminous objects there are: bright, black-hole-powered centers radiating within now-distant galaxies. When they switch on, they blast hydrogen back into its ionized state. Stretching unevenly across the universe, it coalesces into lumps: stars, planets, and galaxies. Stars begin to shine two hundred million years after the Big Bang.

10.8 bya (billion years ago):
Our Milky Way Galaxy swirls into being.

4.7 bya:
Gases collect to form our sun.

4.6 bya:
Planets of our Solar System coalesce. At first there are about twenty.

4.55 bya:
Earth forms.

4.53 bya:
A Mars-sized planet called Theia after the mother of Selene the moon goddess strikes Earth and breaks up, tilting it 23.5 degrees, and the resulting disc of volatilized material gathers in a hundred years into Earth's moon. One Earth day is six hours because the planet spins faster, the moon circles only fifteen thousand miles away, and enormous storms sweep the planet. The moon pulls mightily on new oceans fed by water released within Earth and by ice brought by comets, raising huge tides that race hundreds of miles an hour to erode shorelines, mix massive amounts of dirt and rock, and drop nutrients and minerals into the oceans, brewing a primordial soup of proteins and amino acids.

4 bya:
The tides slow Earth's spin by creating friction when they meet continental edges, days lengthen, and the gravity of the mountainous tides slings the moon farther and farther away from Earth (it still recedes 1.5 inches a year). The tides calm, and the weather dies down, down enough for life to organize.

3.8 bya:
Early life: simple cells in microbial mats left by shallow, gentle seas. These mats, composed of oceanic bacteria, form the foundations of all later forms of life.

3.6 bya:
Formation of Vaalbara, Earth's first supercontinent.

3.4 bya:
One branch of cyanobacteria (the blue-green type) learns how to photosynthesize sunlight into chemical energy, also changing carbon into oxygen, eventually giving Earth a breathable atmosphere. The bacteria evolve eventually into plants and animals.

3 bya:
The supercontinent Ur forms, then breaks up.

2.7 bya:
The supercontinent Kenorland.

1.8-2 bya:
The supercontinent Nuna or Columbia. Each of these supercontinents is larger than the previous.

1 bya:
Bacterial life spreads across the world. The supercontinent Rodinia gathers south of the equator.

750 mya:
Rifting runs through Rodinia and breaks it up into three huge continents.

650 mya:
Because weathering—carbon dioxide mixing with water vapor to make acid rain—removes CO_2 from the atmosphere, joins it with minerals in rocks, and locks it into the ocean, and because this occurs more rapidly in dry regions, AND because Earth's continents at this time all float near the equator, insufficient heat is trapped in the atmosphere to keep the planet warm, and the entire surface freezes ("snowball Earth") under thick slabs of ice several thousand feet thick that reflect even more heat back into space. Cynobacteria beneath the slabs adapt. Ultraviolet rays from the sun react with

water in the ice to make hydrogen peroxide, which stays locked up in ice.

635 mya:
Thousands of erupting volcanoes spew greenhouse gasses into the atmosphere, and Earth rewarms. Stored hydrogen peroxide breaks down, and the oxygen level of the atmosphere jumps to 21%. To adapt, single-celled microbes adapt into multicellular life. Manifestations of it grow larger and larger all over Earth.

570 mya:
The supercontinent Pannotia stretches a V shape across Earth. The Cambrian Period explodes with life that fills out into all extant phyla.

540 mya:
Pannotia breaks up into four continents.

505 mya:
Fish, and the first amphibians.

320 mya:
Reptiles.

300 mya:
The supercontinent Pangaea forms, surrounded by Panthalassa, a global sea.

250 mya:
The End Permian Extinction, in which smoke-belching volcanoes in Siberia cool the Earth, and then, through emitted CO_2 and methane hydrate released from the oceans, they raise the global temperature twenty degrees F, wiping out 95% of life on the planet. Cynodonts survive underground, and one branch evolves into mammals.

208 mya:
Mammals (class Mammalia, phylum Chordata, kingdom Animalia).

200 mya:
Volcanoes in Morocco, Nova Scotia, and New Jersey erupt to trigger a massive Triassic–Jurassic extinction that kills half of all life on Earth. Rise of the dinosaurs.

180 mya:
Underlying tectonics split Pangaea into Laurasia (North America, Europe, and Asia) and Gondwanaland (South America, Africa, India, and Australia). It then splits further into other continents.

140 mya:
Angiosperms (flowering plants).

65 mya:
The dinosaurs and 70% of living things die out from a comet strike. Animals that lay eggs out in the open are especially vulnerable. The way is clear for the ascendency of mammals (generalized rather than specialized eaters; young develop inside and not outside the mother) and other highly adaptive species.

50 mya:
A vast island, India collides with Asia and the resultant buckling raises the Himalayas.

35 mya:
A bubble of magma rises from two thousand miles below Ethiopia to burst on the surface and rupture the land and open the Rift Valley, the cradle of humanity, in east Africa. For several million years the rupture moves southward, opening like a zipper until it hits a kraton and is forced to split into eastern and western branches. Earthquakes and volcanoes twist the eastern branch; the western contains deep lakes that now hold a quarter of the world's fresh surface water. (An old story told by Pliny the Elder links "Ethiopia" to Aethiops, a son of Hephaestus; the word means "I burn" and "face." Ethiopia was also called Abyssinia.)

7-6 mya:
Mountains rise in central East Africa, bringing rain to the west; on the east the rain shadow gradually kills the forest. Sahelanthropus tchadensis walks upright east of the Rift Valley as, possibly, the earliest humanoid biped. Like that of the later humans, its brain takes years to mature (other apes acquire most of their brain development by age three), but it is still the size of a chimp's. Walking is increasingly necessary because the tropical rainforest canopy is shrinking and walking on two legs requires less energy than going about on all fours.

5.3 mya:
A plug of rock wedged at the Strait of Gibraltar gives way before the push of the Atlantic, and over the next four thousand years the dry basin of the Mediterranean fills with seawater.

4.4 mya:
In Ethiopia, Ardipithecus ramidus moves through the remaining forests of the Rift Valley with a helpful and unique big toe that aids in climbing. AR walks upright when not in the forest canopy.

3 mya:
A gene that controls production of sialic acid disappears from the human repertoire, possibly making for greater brain elasticity. Australopithecus afarensis swings from trees but has feet evolved for walking. Lucy, the skeleton was uncovered in 1974, is a member of this species. (The researchers were fond of the Beatles, whose famous song was inspired by a nursery school picture drawn by John Lennon's young son. An apt song for a find in the cradle of humanity.) So is Selam, discovered in 2004. An Ice Age begins.

2.4 mya:
A mutation in the MYH16 gene turns off a jaw muscle protein in humans but not other apes. Result: smaller jaws but bigger brain capacity.

2 mya:
Homo habilus survives a period of highly variable African climate and emerges a competent tool-user with an enlarged brain and a generalist capacity for surviving many climates.

1.9 mya:
Homo erectus in the Rift Valley: greater ability to run upright, less body hair to allow the body to cool itself better by sweating, use of fire. Cooking means more calories, more leisure to socialize, and selection potential for social traits. Interaction with each other probably makes their brains even bigger. Driven by the cyclical drying out of the Sahara, Homo erectus migrates out of Africa over the Levantine corridor and Horn of Africa into Eurasia. This migration is followed by that of Homo antecessor into Europe around 800,000 years ago, followed by Homo heidelbergensis around 600,000 years ago, and the latter species evolves to become Neanderthals capable of art, fire, tool use, and burial of their dead with implements presumed to help in the life to come.

Prehistory:
Eradigm Mother Nature

200,000 BCE:
Mitochondrial Eve, the early human to whom we are all related. Other humans were around then, of course, but only the offspring of this one black woman in east Africa survived in the long run.

140,000 BCE:
Y-chromosome Adam.

125,000 BCE:
The first wave of modern humans migrating from Africa reaches the Near East.

77,000:
In Blombos Cave on the southern Cape coast somebody leaves behind a piece of ochre decorated with a delicate geometric pattern. It could be as much as 100,000 years old.

64,000 BCE:
The Toba volcano in Sumatra blasts with such force that the world

goes into global winter. Humans, some still in east Africa and some as far as Asia, are thinned down to roughly three thousand survivors. (To this day a group of thirty chimps show more genetic diversity than all of humanity.)

40,000 BCE:
Animal images and human handprints decorate El Castillo cave in Spain. They might have been left by Neanderthals.

38,000 BCE:
Proto-Mongols cross the Bering Strait, the ice covering it having been soaked up by the growing polar cap. They reach Patagonia, the tip of South America, by 6000 BCE. There is genetic evidence that these people were related to the Jomon and the Ainu in present-day Japan.

24,000 BCE:
Venus of Willendorf, the first known deity image, found in Austria in 1908 near Krems.

17,000 BCE:
The very first indications of early settlements.

11,5000 BCE:
The Pleistocene Epoch gives way to the Holocene Epoch.

Ancient History to Premodernity:
Eradigm Heavenly City

10,000 - 8,000 BCE:
The Earth shifts less than a degree on its axis, drying the Sahara and making the Nile and Tigris/Euphrates areas more lush. The ice-sheets which had periodically covered much of northern Europe and North America melt. Invention of the bow and arrow now, if not earlier, as the first truly abstract machine not to be found anywhere in nature. As the Quaternity Extinction Event ends, many large animals die off. Beginnings of settled agriculture. Earliest pottery, in Japan. The Danes settle Jutland. By 5500 BCE, a sea-going people leave traces in Norway. Stone Age migrants settle the North China Plain and build settlements around the Yellow River. Towns and villages dot the countryside in Mesopotamia.

9500 BCE:
The oldest known temple goes up on top of a hill at Göbekli Tepe in southeastern Turkey. The Younger Dryas cold period ends.

8000 BCE:
Jericho ("City of the Moon") established. Walls around it by 6800 BCE.

7400 BCE:
Agriculture and settlement at Catalhoyuk in central Asia Minor.

7000 BCE:
Settlement of rice and millet farmers along the Yellow River in China.

6000 BCE:
Wine is made in Persia. Maize cultivated in Mexico.

5500 BCE:
Villages, herding, copper, and pottery and other craft work in Egypt along the Nile at the earliest known center of post-horticultural civilization. Farming in the Faiyum.

5400 BCE:
Near the Persian Gulf, and between the Tigris and Euphrates, Eridu ("Mighty Place") founded as a small temple around which will gather the great empires of Mesopotamia. Here was Eden, whose name means "wild grassland of the south," now withered, a desert in our time. Sumerian myths say the arts of civilization fashioned here, where urbanization concentrates human forces and desires into combinations never previously glimpsed, will create for humanity both joy and sorrow.

5000 BCE:
The Chinese develop a pictogram alphabet. Sumerians move into Mesopotamia, possibly from near the Caspian Sea.

4600 BCE:
Early metalwork in southeastern Europe, whee the plow also arrives. The Neolithic Period (last phase of Stone Age) begins there.

4000 BCE:
Rise of Uruk (possibly "River City" or just "City"; later: al-Iraq, now Warka), a fabled city of alluring Inanna, aerial An, and heroic Gilgamesh. Uruk stands in the center of Sumer and east of the Euphrates River where agriculture flourishes, where "alcohol" is a locally derived word, and where writing and the potter's wheel are invented: people write to please the gods and to keep trade accounts, and writing is a sacred business. Urbanization and civilization stir, and with their many benefits come hierarchy, possessiveness, and limits on human freedom. City heads called *ensi* control the Sumerian city-states. The wheel is invented in Mesopotamia for making pottery. In three hundred and fifty years wheels are attached to carts for transportation. Over in Egypt engineers build dikes and sluices to contain the Nile, which floods periodically. The standards of the city of Ur contain scenes of both peace and war. According to Sumerian myth, Inanna obtained the techniques of civilization from the trickster Enki, who said: With these arts of delight and craftsmanship, music and rejoicing must go the kindling of strife, plundering of cities, lamentation, fear, pity, terror, and death: all this too is civilization, and you must take it all with no argument; and once taken, you cannot give it back.

3800 BCE:
The City of Ur ("abode of Nanna" the moon god; modern Tell el-Muqayyar), which the Bible says is the home of the patriarch Abraham, founded by Ubaidians of Sumer originally from southern Mesopotamia.

3600–3100 BCE:
The Botai people domesticate the horse in what is now Kazakhstan.

3500 BCE:
Kurgan Indo-Europeans from the northern Caucasus (Ukraine) sweep on domesticated horses into Old Europe, where matriarchal idols and images give way to patriarchal. Beginnings of Harappan civilization in what is now Pakistan.

3200 BCE:
Egyptians use the sail.

3000 BCE:
Minoan civilization in Crete, but destroyed by volcanic Thera around 1650 BCE. The first numerals quantify things in Egypt. Start of the Bronze Age, and a shift from agricultural innovation (leading to centralized power, writing, city-states) to conquest at the behest of rulers equipped with the accoutrements of divinity. The Phoenicians (indigenous Canaanites) settle at Tyre and Sidon. Caral, the oldest city in the Americas, rises in Peru. Fertile Crescent farming methods reach as far as China. Troy founded. World population: roughly 30 million.

2900 BCE:
Menes, first king of Egypt, unites the nation by force. A 365-day calendar in Egypt.

2700 BCE:
Merit Ptah, earliest known woman doctor; her image is found on a tomb in Egypt's Valley of the Kings. Reign in China of the legendary first emperor Huang Ti (the Yellow Emperor), who learns wisdom from dreams and who reorganizes a fabulous kingdom to conform to its imaginal counterpart. A book on Chinese energy medicine is attributed to him. "Methuselah," a bristlecone pine tree, germinates in California; it is still standing. Stonehenge under construction.

2600 BCE:
The Indus ("River") settlement in India grows and complexifies. Harappan civilization in the Indus Valley spans a million square miles and employs irrigation and writing, but a shift in the climate halts the moist monsoons, dries up the Indus River, and ends the great empire. Pyramids and Sphinx built; the Pyramid Texts are the oldest religious text in the world. One states, "Live, that you may go to and fro every day; be a spirit in your name...be strong, be effective, be a soul..."

2570 BCE:
Great Pyramid at Egypt built. Queen Nefertari, "God's wife," rules in Egypt.

2500 BCE:
Metalworking Bell Beaker folk (called so because of their pottery) arrive from Spain, farm southern England, and fan out through parts of Europe. The city of Mohenjo Daro in the Indus Valley is founded; the city contains a sophisticated drainage system, houses have bathrooms, and water and sewage run through earthenware pipes. Excavations of these Indus works reveal male figures standing in meditative postures; their chants continue today, spoken by Brahmins, in a language no one now recognizes. First traces of domesticated cats, from Egypt. In Sumer, the Zeus-like father god Enlil takes over as the chief god in his heavenly city. Survivors of intercity Sumerian wars are made slaves. The goddesses vanish from Mesopotamian image and script. The Great Sphinx.

2400-2350 BCE:
Former cupbearer Sargon I conquers Sumer and, founding his capital at Agade, builds the Akkadian Empire and its library, roads, and postal system. According to legend, Sargon's mother abandoned him as an infant by sending him off in a cradle of reeds. Gutians, a hill people, eventually overrun the Akkadian Empire and are themselves overrun by Ur-Nammu (Utu-hegal), who introduces the first known codified system of law and order: a prologue describing Ur-Nammu as a divine king and seven laws to obey. Shulgi, his son, transfers the cities' powers to his government, thereby eroding the traditional city-state form. But at the end of the third millennium, this third dynasty is plundered by a marauding band from Elam, and Sumerians believe that Ningal, their moon goddess, has deserted Ur. Most cities wind up in Amorite hands. Aryan ("noble, civilized") from central Russia nomads invade Old Europe, but patriarchy sprouts elsewhere as well, serving hierarchy and warfare by replacing intrafamily and clan-based ties with loyalty to an army. A long Era of Empire begins that persists even into the twenty-first century.

2300 BCE:
Mycenae Greeks conquer southern Greece. They meet the Minoans and acquire writing and sea craft. Enheduanna, a Sumerian priestess and the earliest known female poet, composes the *Exaltation of Inanna*. First dynasty in Korea.

2200 BCE:
Sumerian political power shrinks as salt brought forth by irrigation chokes the once-fertile fields of Mesopotamia, and Sumer becomes the first demonstration of the inherent fragility and nonsustainability of empires. Indo-Europeans called Hittites overrun Asia Minor. Sumerian Gilgamesh tales come together into one big poem about the hubristic hero-king who seeks but loses the Herb of Immortality; he is also an early example of how the hero always constellates the antihero. Queen Semiramis constructs the first tunnel built below a river to link the Babylonian royal palace with the Temple of Jupiter. Maize cultivated in Central America. A worldwide century of aridity coincides with the collapse of the Akkadian Empire in Mesopotamia and the Old Kingdom in Egypt; in China a cooling sets in that displaces Longshan culture.

2100 BCE:
Abraham, father of three religions, worships the Canaanite father god El ("God"), husband of the goddess Asherah, above all others, as will Isaac and Jacob. El is the Canaanite counterpart to Enlil and will evolve into the god of Moses: "I revealed myself to Abraham, to Isaac, and to Jacob as El Shaddai ("God Almighty") but was not known to them by my name, YHWH" (Exodus 6:3). The Canaanites live in the eastern Mediterranean strip of land between Asia Minor and Egypt; the Israelites came originally from the highlands of Canaan but were monotheists rather than polytheists. The son of an idol-maker, Abraham leaves Ur as its early civilization falls and heads for Palestine.

2070 BCE:
Rise of the Hsia/Xia family in China—its first kings.

2000-1800 BCE:
Metal money used in China, the value determined by weight. Elamites destroy Ur (2004 BCE). Early Latin tribes in Italy. Ethiopians settle in Kenya. Glass is made.

1900 BCE:
Rise of Babylon, founded by Amorites, a Semitic-speaking people of Syria. After two centuries of instability and rebellion, Egypt unites under the Theban Amenemhet I (Twelfth Dynasty). As a devotee of Ma'at, the goddess of justice, he promotes a participatory form of government.

1890s BCE:
Hebrews in Egypt.

1800 BCE:
Hammurabi, king of Babylon, in control of Sumer. He draws up a complex legal code and may have begun building the Tower of Babel (possibly the Babylonian tower Etemenanki). First version of Gilgamesh tale written down; a later version is called *He Who Saw the Deeps*.

1700s BCE:
In ancient China the priests write their prophecies in a language now called the Shell-bone Script, a forerunner to the modern Chinese script. Fortunes are cast by heating bones or tortoise shells and interpreting the cracks (forerunner of the *I Ching* or Book of Changes). Shang aristocrats that displace the Xia believe their ancestors live in heaven. Leavened bread baked in Egypt. The Indus Valley civilization falls, possibly because of deforestation, erosion, and flooding.

1600 BCE:
Bronze work in Europe. The Oracle at Delphi; the priestesses will be referred to with respect by Plato, Aristotle, and many others, and Socrates will confirm its motto "Know Thyself." The Hyskos, a band of Indo-Europeans on chariots, swing down from Central Asia into the Nile Delta (1630 BCE), followed by the Hittites penetrating

Mesopotamia (1595 BCE). Sea Peoples from the Aegean raid around North Africa, Anatolia, and the eastern Mediterranean. Babylonians make a twenty-one-year chart of the appearances of Venus. Hittites under King Mursili I sack Babylon (1595), taking down one of the two ancient superpowers (the other is Egypt).

1500 BCE:
Pastoral Aryan Indo-European tribes move eastward from central Asia prior to settling the Indus Valley. Earliest hymns of what will become the *Rig Veda*. Aryans establish the four-level forerunner of the later Indian caste system. Their gods include Indra and Agni. Early Mayan civilization at Belize. Intensive agriculture and plain but intricate pottery in Korea.

1460 BCE:
Kassites mounted on chariots descend from the Zagros Mountains to take over Babylonia for more than five centuries.

1353-1336 BCE:
Akhenaton (also: Ikhnaton), ruler of Egypt's eighteenth dynasty. He institutes monotheism in Egypt by requiring everyone to worship Aton, the sun god with hands. After his death Egypt reverts to polytheism, but scholars speculate that his monotheism might have shaped that of the Hebrews.

1300 BCE:
According to the Old Testament, Moses encounters a God beyond word, imagery, or definition, a living God of liberation and justice. Moses brings the Hebrews out of Egypt, leads them across a desert wilderness, brings them Ten Commandments, one of which is "Thou Shalt Not Kill," and establishes them in Palestine. In Egypt, a woman can own her own property and can sue for divorce. Assyrians, who originated with the city of Assur, control all of Mesopotamia. Bronze casting develops in China, later than elsewhere but more advanced than any in the world. The story "King Neferkare and General Sasenet" suggests a homosexual relationship between the two.

1274 BCE:
After the Battle of Kadesh in Syria, Hittites and Egyptians sign the first known peace treaty. Soon both powers will be overrun by the rising Assyrians.

1200 BCE:
As northern Dorian Greeks invade the rest of Greece, their sky god Zeus marries indigenous Hera. The Greek dark ages. The Olmec culture rises in Mesoamerica.

1100 BCE:
The Assyrian Empire expands rapidly under Tiglath-Pileser I. King David secedes King Saul of the Israelites. King Wu topples the Shang Dynasty and founds the Zhou (1046 BCE).

1000 BCE:
Germanic tribes migrate southward from southern Scandinavia, Denmark, and lands between the Oder and Elbe Rivers.

900 BCE:
Chavins unite Peru. Mayans populate the Yucatan. In India, the later *Vedas* and early *Upanishads* are written down. "Liberated from the grip of egoism, like the moon (after the eclipse), full, ever blissful, self-luminous, one attains one's essence." —Adhyatma Upanishad

957 BCE:
Solomon finishes the first Temple of Jerusalem.

815 BCE:
Phoenicians found Carthage in North Africa. Etruscan civilization in Italy. The Bronze Age gives way to an Iron Age; writing grows in influence and complexity in India, Babylonia, and China. Time of Elijah the prophet.

800 - 200 BCE:
During the Axial Age, a term coined by philosopher Karl Jaspers, revolutionary word and thought in religion surfaces in Asia, the

Middle East, and the West. In this threshold period a line of great teachers challenge the waxing influence of imperial hierarchy, conquest, and force. The Nok people work with tin and terra cotta in what is now Nigeria.

753 BCE:
According to legend, Rome is founded by the orphaned twins Romulus and Remus, the first of whom kills the second, a motif that will echo there in perpetuity. A third of Athenians are slaves.

700 BCE:
Aryans begin to build cities and to trade with Assyrians and Arabs. The *Odyssey* and *Iliad* ascribed to the blind poet Homer undergo revision and transmutation from older tales. They will set the pattern for Greek conceptions of heroism as the age of Classical Antiquity opens with the rise of Rome and the expansion of Greece. Isaiah becomes a prophet: "What mean ye that ye beat my people to pieces, and grind the faces of the poor?" Hesiod's *Theogony* and *Works and Days*. In Hallstatt, Austria the early Celts mine salt; trade spreads their culture all over northern Europe. They are described as chatty, decorative, skilled at farming, and fond of telling stories.

689 BCE:
King Sennacherib's Assyrian army ravages Babylon. Under a different king they will also hit the Arabs and take Egypt, but Egypt will revolt.

636 BCE:
Birth of Thales of Miletus (636-546), first of the Greek "pre-Socratic" philosophers. He will teach that "all things are full of gods."

628-551 BCE:
Zoroaster (Persian name Zarathustra), founder of Zoroastrianism, the first world religion. He sees the universe as a battleground of good and evil, with the good god Ahura Mazda (or Ormuzd) fighting against the evil Ahriman; those who help Ahura Mazda find the realm of light, those who do not land in a fiery hell of molten metal.

Beginning of the *Avesta* ("Law"), the holy Zoroastrian book.

650 BCE:
A cooling climate pushes Scandinavian tribes south into northern Europe.

612 BCE:
The Assyrian capital at Nineveh falls to vengeful Medes (from west Iran) and Babylonians, making space for a century of the Neo-Babylonian (Chaldean) Empire. In Ashurbanipal's wrecked library sits a copy of the story of *Gilgamesh*.

610 BCE:
Birth of Sappho (610-580), devotee of Aphrodite and greatest of the early Greek lyric poets, on the island of Lesbos. Plato refers to her as the tenth Muse. "Although they are / only breath, words / which I command / are immortal."

600 BCE:
Lao Tzu ("old philosopher"). Perhaps a curator of the dynastic archives, he pauses on his way to retire in the K'un-l'un Mountains long enough (in 604) to give a border guard an account that becomes the *Tao Te Ching* (The Way and Its Virtue), the core text of Taoism: "Nature does not hurry, yet everything is accomplished." More than a dozen kingdoms reign in India, where Panini devises a Sanskrit grammar, the first in the world for any language.

597 BCE:
Having built the famous Hanging Gardens, Nebuchadnezzar II captures Jerusalem, taking a large number of people captive to Babylonia. Jeremiah laments. The Hebrews pray for a delivering messiah. Solon (in 594) is archon in Athens and begins numerous reforms.

582 BCE:
Pythagoras (582-507), who teaches the transmigration of souls, the equality of the sexes, the intelligibility of the world, the greatness of

Apollo, and the constitutive nature of numbers; he might also be the first to use the term *philosophy* (Greek "love of knowledge"). For him science and spirituality have not yet separated. He probably traveled through Babylonia and Egypt. "Consult and deliberate before you act, that you may not commit foolish actions. For it is the part of a miserable man to speak and to act without reflection."

586 BCE:
The Babylonians under Nebuchadnezzar II absorb Judah and destroy the original Temple of Jerusalem. Beginning of the Babylonian Captivity (to 538).

563 BCE:
Prince Siddhartha Gautama (563-483), later known as Tathagata and the Buddha. He is born into the noble Sakyamuni clan, finds enlightenment under a tree, and goes about teaching the value of reflection, mindfulness, right action, and freedom from harmful attachment. His First Noble Truth: "Living means suffering." According to an old story, when asked who he is—King? God? Demon?—he replies, "I am awake."

560 BCE:
Peisistratus, a popular leader, brings an army into Athens accompanied by a tall village woman he claims is Athena. The leaders of the aristocrats flee. Unlike so many of Solon's, his reforms actually work, and prosperity returns, some of it based on transferring land owned by the rich to the poor. He orders the beautification of Athens, mints coins with Athena's owl symbol on them, and has the *Odyssey* and *Iliad* copied out and distributed. He is exiled but returns. Croesus, fabled for his wealth, is king of Lydia.

551 BCE:
Kung Fu-Tzu (Confucius) is born (551-479) in Lu. Calling for filial piety and a return to the classics, he will teach that humaneness matters more than fire and water. "If there is righteousness in the heart, there will be beauty in the character. If there is beauty in the character, there will be harmony in the home. If there is harmony in the

home, there will be order in the nation. If there is order in the nation, there will be peace in the world."

550 BCE:
Claiming the sanction of the god Marduk, Cyrus overthrows King Croesus and the Median Empire and makes himself King of Persia. Thus rises the Persian Empire. Carthage starts its imperial ambitions by conquering Sardinia, Corsica, and Sicily.

545 BCE:
Xenophanes becomes a wandering poet and minstrel and postulates a single supreme God.

539 BCE:
Cyrus the Great of Persia adds Babylon to his kingdom. He also permits a captive named Zerubbabel to lead forty thousand Hebrews back to their homeland. Cyrus's son Cambyses will eventually end the rule of pharaohs in Egypt and supplant their Egyptian idols with his Persian ones.

540 BCE
Some Jews return from Babylon and begin work on the Second Temple. Wall paintings in the Etruscan Tomb of the Bulls depict homosexual love.

535 BCE:
Heraclitus (535-475), who emphasizes change and polarity and the unity of all opposites in an underlying Logos (thought, speech, word, Reason) symbolized by universal fire. His idea of a rational order feeds into the Greek conception of the universe as an orderly *kosmos*.

525 BCE:
Persia conquers Egypt.

522 BCE:
Greek lyric poet Pindar (522–443).

515 BCE:
Parmenides is born; he will found the Eleatic school and teach that change and becoming are illusions and that intellect should be trusted over the senses, doctrines that influence Plato. (In general the Eleatics favor the contemplation of eternal verities, whereas the Ionians take a more empirical approach in understanding life, self, and world.)

510 BCE:
Anaxagoras (510-428), who teaches that Nous (Mind) founds the order of the cosmos; the science he brings from Ionia whets the Greek thirst for natural explanations of how the world works. He conceives of the sun as a fiery ball of matter and the moon as a receiver of solar light.

508 BCE:
A resurgence of hard feelings against the Athenian aristocratic oligarchy results in the first mob revolt in recorded history. The people put exiled Cleisthenes into power, a leader whose reforms—including a constitution, elections, and theoretical equal rights for all citizens—give rise to the Greek enthusiasm for democracy. In the shadow of the Acropolis he starts by collecting votes from citizens in a vase: white pebbles for yes, black for no. Raped by Sextus, son of Tarquinius Superbus, Lucretia, wife of Tarquinius Collatinus, stabs herself after telling her husband; this leads to a successful uprising against the Tarquins, the Etruscan family that ruled Rome. Romans under Lucius Junius Brutus revolt, driving out Tarquin the Arrogant. The Roman Republic is founded, ruled by a Senate of patricians. In 502 the Latin League beats the Etruscans, but future Roman authorities, including the early Church, will take over Etruscan trappings and titles.

500 BCE:
The Indian *Ramayana* (story of Rama) written about now, perhaps by Valmiki. The *Mahabharata* written, perhaps by Vyasa and others. Birth of Phidias (500-432), Greece's greatest sculptor; he fashioned the *Athena Parthenos* at Athens and the *Zeus* in the temple of

Olympia. The Persians rule the eastern Mediterranean and the Carthaginians the western side. Bantu-speaking people settle in what is now Uganda.

496 BCE:
Sophocles (496-406), general, priest, and playwright. Greek tragedy increasingly reflects the decline of, and a new suspicion toward, the reality of the traditional gods.

495 BCE:
The pre-Socratic Empedocles (495-435) is born in Sicily and becomes leader of its democratic faction. He teaches that everything is composed of four elements: earth, air, fire, and water; and that all apparent changes in an object are actually changes in the particles constituting it (as later physicists discover). "For they two (Love and Strife) were before and shall be, nor yet, I think, will there ever be an unutterably long time without them both."

490 BCE:
Another Persian army invades Greece and is beaten by the Athenian army at Marathon, where two hundred Athenians and sixty-four hundred Persians die; Western civilization takes on a Greek rather than Persian cast after this. Zeno of Elea born (490-430); he invents the method of dialectic argument employed by Socrates and carries on the work of Parmenides. Protagoras (490-420) is among the first Sophists: young men's teachers of rhetoric, debate, and applied reason, a faculty more dependable than either tradition or mystical epiphany, both at bottom merely human constructions. Truth for the Sophists is relative rather than absolute, and virtue a matter of utility and practicality.

480 BCE:
Greek playwright Euripides (480-406). Xerxes I of Persia leads his armies against the Greek Hellenic League to punish them for aiding the Ionian cities against Persia in 499 BCE; at the Battle of Salamis, he is aided by Queen Artemisia I, ruler of Halicarnassus and Cos and commander of a flotilla of warships. At Thermopylae, King

Leonidas and the Spartan defenders holding the pass are betrayed by a traitorous Greek and, attacked from the rear, die to the last man while their Theban allies surrender. The Athenians flee from Athens, which is then burned by the Persians. However, the Persian army is defeated at the Battle of Plataea, and again through the loss of its navy at Salamis. Xerxes I retires to Asia and is killed by the captain of his royal guard. These victories greatly swell the pride of Athenians in their potential for grand accomplishment.

469 BCE:
Socrates (469 BCE-399 BCE). He will counter both traditionalism and Sophistry with a dialectic whose goal is to uncover the divine foundations of human conduct, with capabilities like Goodness, Beauty, Truth, and Justice treated as absolute entities. Wisdom appears in dialogue, and happiness in living in accord with one's soul: a soul that reflects the presence of the World Soul (*anima mundi*) of the kosmos. In the hands of Socrates and his student Plato, the gods are reimagined as archetypal Forms behind the visible world. Some Socratic dialogue from Plato's *Republic*:

"Well, there is another question: By friends and enemies do we mean those who are so really, or only in seeming?" - Socrates
"Surely...a man may be expected to love those whom he thinks good, and to hate those whom he thinks evil." - Polemarchos
"Yes, but do not persons often err about good and evil: many who are not good seem to be so, and conversely?" - Socrates
"That is true." - Polemarchos
"Then to them the good will be enemies and the evil will be their friends?" - Socrates
"True." - Polemarchos
"And in that case they will be right in doing good to the evil and evil to the good?" - Socrates
"Clearly." - Polemarchos
"But the good are just and would not do an injustice?" - Socrates
"True." - Polemarchos
"Then according to your argument it is just to injure those who do no wrong?" - Socrates

"Nay, Socrates; that doctrine is immoral." - Polemarchos
"...But ought the just to injure any one at all? And will not men who are injured be deteriorated in that which is the proper virtue of man?" - Socrates

460 BCE:
Hippocrates (460-377), the doctor who invents Hippocratic Oath that includes the promise to "never do harm to anyone."

449 BCE:
Herodotus starts the discipline of documenting, and occasionally exaggerating, history by completing his famous *History*. Earliest date of the Book of Ecclesiastes: "To everything there is a season, and a time to every purpose under heaven...."

448 BCE:
Aristophanes (448-388), an Athenian playwright who composes comedies and satires. Aeschylus wins a prize for writing the *Oresteian Trilogy*. Construction on Athena's Parthenon begins, overseen by builder Callicrates and designer Iktinos, to be finished in 432 BCE on the site of an old temple burned by the Persians. Part of the building will hold tax money collected by the extortionist Delian League, an Athens-controlled association of Ionian city states dedicated to looting the remains of the Persian Empire. Around this time the hetaera Aspasia of Miletus becomes the lover of Pericles; renowned for her wisdom and her rhetorical gifts, she might have helped Pericles compose his famous speeches.

442 BCE:
Sophocles writes *Antigone*.

438 BCE:
The Parthenon finished. In three years the statue of Zeus at Olympia, one of the Seven Wonders of the World, is done. (The seven wonders are: the Great Pyramids, the Hanging Gardens of Babylon, the mausoleum at Halicarnassus, the Artemis at Ephesus, the Colossus of Rhodes, the Zeus, and the Pharos lighthouse.)

431-421 BCE:
The Peloponnesian War between Sparta and Athens begins as Sparta, upset by the Athenian habit of intervening elsewhere to encourage democracy, invades Athens. The imperialistic Athenians welcome it, not guessing it will eventually ruin Athens. Thucydides will write a famous account of this war. Euripides writes *Medea*.

430 BCE:
Sophocles' *Oedipus the King* is staged for the sorrowful figure who leaves Thebes to rid it of the plague whose origin is his own actions.

427 BCE:
Shortly after Pericles suggests that Athens pay for its fight with Sparta by stripping the gold from the huge Athena statue within the Parthenon, a plague kills Pericles and a third of Athens. Aristocles, a wrestler known as Plato (427-347), is born. In his written dialogues he develops the implications of the thought of his teacher Socrates into a spacious philosophy centered on contemplation of the eternal Forms. The virtues of these are made visible in the changeless-seeming, luminous, and orderly heavens, abode of the gods, realm of inquiry for Babylonian astronomy, and primal pattern of earthly happenings. Plato also guesses correctly that the planets, "wanderers" whose orbits do not conform to the regularity of celestial motion, must elicit their own kind of orbital consistency, and he calls for science to study this further in order to comprehend the mind of the divine. "The price good men pay for indifference to public affairs is to be ruled by evil men."

415 BCE:
Bold and brash Alcibiades and friends vandalize sacred herms in Athens before sailing to Sicily, where they are soundly beaten in battle.

404 BCE:
Athens surrenders to Sparta.

400 BCE:
Democritus, who believes that the gods represent a supernatural explanation for what is actually natural, works with his teacher Leucippus on the idea of the atom, and with it a materialist philosophy and cosmology. Goths destroy the temple complex at Eleusis.

399 BCE:
Socrates is ordered to drink hemlock after being found guilt of subverting the Athenian youth with philosophy. He turns down a chance to escape. His last words refer to the god of healing: "Crito, we owe a rooster to Asclepius," presumably for curing him of life. "Please don't forget to pay the debt."

389 BCE:
Followers of Theophilus of Alexandria destroy the Serapeum, Alexandrian temple to the god Serapis, an Osiris-like deity of abundance, transformation, and resurrection.

384 BCE:
Aristotle (384-322), philosopher, naturalist, teacher, and the son of a physician. Believing that with the Forms Plato took categories for substances, Aristotle changes the static being/becoming dichotomy inherited from Parmenides and Socrates into a potential/actual process model whereby the essence of things strives for self-realization (example: a seed essence growing into a tree actuality). The universal derives from the particular, not the reverse as in Plato, with the sole exception of the Prime Mover that gets it all going. Aristotle's ideas of science, category, and logic shape all later Western thought, as does his emphasis on grasping the tangible world instead of gazing toward its archetypal foundations. From the *Nichomachean Ethics:* "...Love is like activity, being loved like passivity; and loving and its concomitants are attributes of those who are the more active."

387 BCE:
The Gauls (or Celts, from "Keltoi" used later by Caesar and his men) sack Rome. Plato founds his Academy in Athens.

372 BCE:
Confucian philosopher Meng Tzu (Mencius)(372-289), whose *Meng-tzu* is a classic of Chinese philosophy. "He who exerts his mind to the utmost knows his nature. He who knows his nature knows Heaven. To preserve one's mind and to nourish one's nature is the way to serve Heaven."

369 BCE:
Taoist philosopher Chuang Tzu (Zhuangzi)(369-286): "Once upon a time, I dreamt I was a butterfly, fluttering hither and thither, to all intents and purposes a butterfly. I was conscious only of my happiness as a butterfly, unaware that I was myself. Soon I awaked, and there I was, veritably myself again. Now I do not know whether I was then a man dreaming I was a butterfly, or whether I am now a butterfly, dreaming I am a man."

360 BCE:
Plato writes *The Republic*. Failing to recognize its satirical qualities, readers forever after mistake it for a blueprint for civilization.

354 BCE:
St. Augustine (354-328), who gives Christianity its emphasis on original sin, hatred of the flesh, redemption in the world to come, and the Church as the vehicle of salvation.

352 BCE:
Artemissa II, Queen of Caria, an ancient region in the southwest of Asia Minor, takes over after her husband King Mausolus dies. A botanist, medical researcher, and political leader, she suppresses a revolt by the inhabitants of Rhodes. The temple she builds at Halicarnassus to commemorate her dead husband lends its name to all later such monuments.

338 BCE:
Philip II of Macedon conquers Greece.

335 BCE:
Aristotle founds the Lyceum, his academy and research center, at Athens.

331 BCE:
Having destroyed the Persian Empire, Alexander the Great, son of Philip II and former student of Aristotle, inaugurates Hellenism (and a check on Carthaginian power until the Romans destroy it) by spreading Greek language, culture, and learnings across Europe and by founding Alexandria, diverse city and cultural, scientific, and intellectual center of antiquity. Its lighthouse, the Pharos, is one of the seven wonders of the ancient world. The city's crowning achievement is the Alexandrian Library and an associated museum devoted to the Nine Muses from whom it gets its name. The Library, where ancient manuscripts are stored and where the Old Testament will be translated into Greek, receives ongoing support by the Ptolemys, the Greek kings who will inherit the Egyptian part of Alexander's empire after his death.

322-185 BCE:
Founded by political and religious reformer Chandragupta Maurya, who embraces Jainism, the Mauryan Empire overthrows the Nanya Dynasty and stretches westward to unify India for the first time. Buddhism and Jainism take hold in India, where the arts and trade flourish. Patanjali composes the *Yoga Sutras*.

312 BCE:
Seleucus I Nicator founds the empire named after him in Babylon.

306 BCE:
Epicurus founds the Epicurean School of philosophy to promote forms of quiet enjoyment. Skepticism brought by Pyrrho of Elis and Sextus Empiricus calls for a retreat from all conviction and judgment—any argument to prove something requires further arguments, which requires further—into a "nothing is certain, not even that" stance of perpetual, contented non-belief. In part such philosophies—and astrology, Stoicism, and Neoplatonism should be includ-

ed as time goes forward—reveal an attempt to reorient as provincialism gives way under Hellenistic influence to a new cosmopolitan awareness in Europe of how large and complex the world really is.

300 BCE:
A warming trend accompanied by plentiful rain nourishes crops throughout Europe and vineyards in England, and the Roman Empire spreads out. This Roman Warm Period will persist until 400 CE. Zeno of Citium organizes the Stoic philosophers. Aesara of Lucania argues in her *Book on Human Nature* that the soul has three parts: the mind which performs judgement and thought, the spirit which shows courage and strength, and desire which gives love and affection. This tripartite schema will reappear in Plato and, as a result, in Freud.

295 BCE:
Euclid writes the *Elements*, a primer on geometry still in use.

284-277 BCE:
Rule of Bartare, first of the ruling queens of Meroe in Nubia (northern Sudan and southern Egypt near the Nile River).

280 BCE:
The Colossus of Rhodes built, and the Pharos lighthouse.

270 BCE:
Aristarchus argues that the Earth and other planets circle the sun.

268 BCE:
Asoka ascends to the Mauryan throne in India and becomes a Buddhist and humanitarian.

264 BCE:
Because of a strategic dispute in the city of Messana, the Romans and the Carthaginians ("Punics" in Roman) send in bigger and bigger forces. They clash eventually—so much for the notion of peace

through military buildup—and the First Punic War breaks out. At this time Rome owns most of Italy, and Carthage owns northwest Africa and the islands and the commerce of the western Mediterranean; these wars will eventually ruin Carthage. First Roman gladiator games (from *gladi*, a short sword).

250 BCE:
Scholars at the Alexandrian Library translate the Old Testament into Greek.

230 BCE:
In China the Qin defeat the Han and take over. In 221 BCE the Qin will unify China politically.

221 BCE:
The magnetic compass is invented in China. End of Warring States period in China as the Ch'in dynasty conquers the state of Ch'i. The Great Wall of China is built during the Ch'in reign to keep out the northern nomads. It doesn't.

218 BCE:
The Second Punic War starts over a quarrel over Saguntum. During the war Archimedes, the seventy-five-year-old thinker who had grasped the secret of the lever, the pulley, and the principle of mechanical advantage, is run through by a sword-wielding thug. Eager to avenge Carthage over the First Punic War, Hannibal gives the Roman army the slip and crosses the Pyrenees almost before the Romans know what happened. He has visions of rebelling Roman citizens but starts a slash-and-burn campaign that does not make him popular in Italy.

216 BCE:
Hannibal beats the Romans at Cannae.

209 BCE:
The mighty Xiongnu clan in Mongolia threatens China until they are defeated in 89 CE (at the Battle of Ikh Bayan) and move instead into

Europe as the Huns.

202 BCE:
The Han dynasty rises in China. Roman commander Scipio defeats Hannibal at Zama. Rome wins the Second Punic War and expands aggressively through North Africa and the Mediterranean.

168 BCE:
Rome defeats Macedonia at the Battle of Pydna.

165 BCE:
The Jews successfully revolt against the Seleucids (Babylonia) who had outlawed Judaism. Simon Maccabaeus founds Hannukah to celebrate the rededication of the Temple of Jerusalem.

146 BCE:
The Third Punic War ends with Carthage burned to the ground and half a million of its soldiers dead. Greek revolts against Roman authority prompt the Romans to burn Corinth, the city of Aphrodite/Venus, and conquer Greece. In 129 BCE the Seleucid Empire also falls.

100 BCE:
Teotihuacan ("where people meet the gods") and its pyramids built in Mexico; it grows into the largest city in the Americas. Having been on the move since around 200 BCE, when they forced Celts west to the Rhine, Germanic tribes migrating southward and westward enter Gaul and are halted by Julius Caesar and Gaius Marius. Other Germanics migrating since 600 BCE from Scandinavia to the Vistula near the Carpathians include the Cherusci, Hermunduri, Chatti, and Tencteri at first, then the Franks, Alemanni, Frisians, Saxons, and Thuringians.

73 BCE:
Outlaw gladiator Spartacus takes control of Mount Vesuvius and is joined by many other rebels. They are eventually captured piecemeal and crucified; going forward, fewer slaves are kept in Rome.

63 BCE:
Caesar's rival Pompey deposes the last of the Maccabees, Aristobulus II, and captures Jerusalem, Syria, and lands south of Egypt, including Judea, where the constant power plays had annoyed the Romans. No free Jewish homeland until 1948.

60 BCE:
Lucretius composes *On the Nature of Things* to explain philosophy and science to the Roman public.

57 BCE:
Rise of the Silla kingdom in eastern Korea as one of the Three Kingdoms along with Goguryeo and Baekje.

49 BCE:
Julius Caesar leads an army across the Rubicon River and takes over Rome.

44 BCE:
Mark Antony shares consulship with Caesar. On the way to the Forum to ratify use the old title of King when outside Italy, Julius Caesar is stabbed twenty-three times, assassinated by a conspiracy led by Gaius Cassius. Caesar's worried wife had warned him not to go.

42 BCE:
Virgil's *Eclogues*, the second of which is an early example of homo-erotic literature.

29 BCE:
The Pali Canon of Buddhist scriptures written down in Sri Lanka.

27 BCE:
Having attacked Alexandria, where Mark Anthony and Cleopatra commit suicide, forced her son Caesarion to be put to death, and annexed Egypt, Octavian, the adopted son of Caesar, claims to have

"transferred the State to the free disposal of the senate and the Assembly," appearing to preserve a republican form of government. In return, the Senate, packed with his supporters, calls him Augustus Caesar and he becomes the first Roman emperor. End of the Roman Republic.

23 BCE:
Horace writes his *Odes*. "Carpe diem."

19 BCE:
Virgil's *Aeneid*, written to glorify Rome.

4 BCE:
Herod dies, his rule divided up among three sons, one of whom, Herod Antipas, will later order Jewish prophet John the Baptist executed for protesting his marriage to the former wife of his half-brother. At the edge of the Roman Empire, Jesus born in Bethlehem ("House of Bread"), the northwestern Jordan town where King David had been born. He will grow up in the town of Nazareth, which lies within the district of Galilee in northern Israel, and will be crucified after opposing religious hypocrisy, casting bankers out of the Temple of Jerusalem, chastising the wealthy for not aiding the poor, and exhorting his followers to "love your enemies" and "love your neighbor as yourself."

COMMON ERA:

1:
In northern Guatemala, El Mirador, perhaps the greatest early Mayan city, is at its height. The burgeoning city of Teotihuacan in the Valley of Mexico contains a population of over forty thousand. Having grown slowly throughout a million years of prehistory, the Earth's human population is around three hundred million; by 1820, it will pass one billion, double a century later, and double again within fifty-five years...

8:
Roman poet Ovid's *Metamorphoses*.

20-50 BCE:
Philo of Alexandria, whose work involves synthesizing ancient Greek and Jewish thought.

33:
The Kushan Empire of tribes pushed out of China by the Han Dynasty rules north India and parts of Central Asia until fracturing around 375 under pressure from Sassanids (Persia) to the west and Guptas (India) to the south and east. Falsely arrested, tried, and banished by the Emperor Tiberius, who feared her influence over the Praetorian Guard, Agrippina the Elder, wife of Germanicus, and the first Roman woman to travel and live with the army, starves herself to death. Jesus is crucified by Roman soldiers and entombed. His followers claim that his empty tomb signifies his ascent to heaven. Despite his message of joy and liberation, the dominant image of Christianity to come will be the crucifixion, a bloody image of the dismemberment of innocence by ignorance and worldly power.

40:
Rome annexes Mauritania (now northern Morocco and northwestern Algeria). In Vietnam, the Trung sisters Trung Trac and Trung Nhi lead eighty thousand in a revolt against Chinese domination, and Trung Trac is made ruler. The sisters will commit honorable suicide after defeat in battle.

41:
Having cut down the sacred groves of Artemis to obtain lumber for his warships, Roman Emperor Caligula is assassinated, possibly with the help of the Praetorian Guard, and Caligula's introverted historian uncle Claudius is made over by the Guard into Emperor Claudius. His wife Messalina will do much of the actual leading, but he will have her killed after she stages a mock wedding with her lover.

47:
England becomes the Roman province Britannia. Having undergone conversion on his way to persecute Christians in Damascus, Saul the Pharisee (strict literalist and legalist), now Paul, formerly of Tarsus, joins with others to organize Christianity. His charisma, Roman conditioning, and Platonist learnings will transform the radical and liberatory teachings of Jesus into a world religion.

50-60:
Letters written by Paul to outposts of the early church.

52:
Thomas the Apostle arrives in India.

54:
Men can marry each other in Rome.

60-61:
Rebellion of Boudicca, queen of the Iceni, against the Romans in Britain. Unwisely attacking the Ninth Roman Legion, she is captured and poisoned, but only after almost convincing the Romans to pull out of Britain.

70-80:
Gospels of Matthew and Mark written, with Luke and John later. "A new commandment I give to you, that you love one another, even as I have loved you, that you also love one another. By this all men will know that you are My disciples, if you have love for one another."
— John 13:34-35

73:
After surviving a year-long siege under Flavius Silva, nine hundred and sixty Zealot Jews at Masada commit mass suicide by the sword rather than give up their freedom and submit to Roman mistreatment.

79:
At the place where the African Plate slides under the Eurasian, Mt. Vesuvius erupts. The cities of Herculaneum and Pompeii are buried. Later researchers uncover in the ruins many examples of erotic art, some of it queer.

96-180:
Under the Five Good Emperors—Nerva, Trajan, Hadrian, Antonius Pius, and Marcus Aurelius—the Roman Empire reaches its full extent and power before subsiding into gradual decline.

100s:
A century of movements and beginnings: Iron Age Japanese push into northeastern Honshu and absorb the native Ainu, an aboriginal people of Jomon-period culture (Mesolithic or early Neolithic). The Anasazi migrate into Arizona. The Moche civilization on the Peruvian coast flourishes at Sipan. Hopewell culture on the upper Mississippi. The Kingdom of Aksum emerges in Eritria; positioned between the Roman Empire and India, it expands through trade to be a metropolitan empire until its decline in 940 because of the influence of Islam. Mogollon culture develops in the southwestern United States and produces intricate painted pottery. Aksum becomes a capital in Eritrea, northern Ethiopia. In Jerusalem, Judaism, Roman religious cults, and Christian worship circles compete for audiences. Many gospels circulate.

105:
Paper invented in China, perhaps by Cai Lun. Roman Senator Publius Cornelius Tacitus writes the *Histories*.

110:
Plutarch's *Parallel Lives*.

132:
Hadrian's Wall is built across Britain to keep out the native Britons. It doesn't.

140:
At the Alexandrian Library Ptolemy classifies and publishes ideas from astrology, geography, and astronomy. He also writes about optics and music.

150:
Justin Martyr attempts to integrate Christianity and Platonism and identifies Christ with the Logos, a move to be taken up later by Augustine and many other leaders of the early Church.

161-166:
Expansive Rome fights in Armenia, Syria, Media, and Mesopotamia and wins against the Parthian Empire of ancient Persia.

167:
The Marcomannic Wars: fighting between the German tribes and the Romans. Stoic Roman Emperor Marcus Aurelius writes his *Meditations*. "When you arise in the morning think of what a privilege it is to be alive, to think, to enjoy, to love ..."

171:
To ease conflict around the Danube, the Roman authorities permit marauding Germanic tribes to settle in the Roman Empire.

177:
According to the Christian historian Eusebius, the slave Blandina is publicly tortured for days in Lyon for her Christian refusal to sacrifice animals to the Roman gods. Such acts of courage arouse the public's curiosity about the values involved.

180:
Emperor Marcus Aurelius dies of the plague, and his passive son Commodus becomes emperor; end of the Pax Romana, the enforced Peace of Rome. Roman glory has reached its height. Bishop Irenaeus of Lyon writes *Against Heresies* to attack the Gnostics, who are spiritualists who eschew dogma to pursue direct knowledge of the sacred. They irritate him because they revere Eve and Mary

Magdalene, allow women to lead worship services, explore dreams, and engage (it is said) in erotic ceremonies. They also maintain that Magdalene was specially trained by Jesus to receive the "inner teachings" but had her authority taken away by Peter and the other disciples after the death on the cross. Irenaeus throws out all gospels—including Mary Magdalene's—but the now-traditional four. He is one of a band of believers who call themselves "orthodox," meaning "straight-thinking" (not to be confused with the later Greek or Russian Orthodox Churches). He also emphasizes the virginity of Mary. (The word "bishop" comes into the early church from a word that means "watcher" or "overseer.")

184:
The three Taoist Zhang brothers lead the unsuccessful Yellow Turban Rebellion against the Hans, who win but are weakened.

200s:
The *Corpus Hermeticum* of Hellenistic wisdom writings is compiled in Alexandria. Alchemist Maria Prophetissa invents the double boiler. When the Emperor Diocletian orders all Egyptian books on alchemy and "occult" sciences destroyed, alchemical manuscripts are smuggled into Arabia, where the mystery tradition develops further and receives its modern name. The first sections of the Talmud written down: "Not even the angels stand higher than the man who took the wrong way and then returned."

220:
The Three Kingdoms (and Six Dynasties) period in China.

224:
Ardashir I consolidates the Sassanid Empire (224-651) in Persia.

228:
After a Parthian prince in the Mesopotamian city Seleucia attempts but fails to restore Parthian rule, Mani claims a command from God to to leave the religious community to which he belongs. He is also

told to keep aloof from impurity and to avoid proclaiming his revelation publicly for now because of his youth. He later declares himself a prophetic successor to Zoroaster, Buddha, and Jesus and founds Manichaeism.

247:
Death of Pimiku (Himiko), first known female ruler of Japan and reputed to have built the Shrine of Ise, the most important Shinto temple.

250:
The classic period of Maya civilization opens in Guatemala, Honduras, and eastern Mexico. In Rome, agricultural lands go unused, and trade with China and India falls off. With the economy declining steadily, people move from cities and towns to rural areas in search of food. Cities shrink to a fraction of their former size, some occupied only by administrators. Yet Roman officials ignore the gathering warning signs and go on with business as usual.

260:
Forces of the Sassanid Empire under Shapur I defeat those of Rome at Edessa and the Emperor Valerian is captured and imprisoned for life by the Persians.

270:
Porphyry collects the writings of Neoplatonist philosopher Plotinus, his teacher, and publishes them as the *Enneads*: "We are not related to Spirit, we are in it." Neoplatonism expands Platonic thought by sketching a cosmos of emanations from the One into Nous, the World Soul, and the material realm at the bottom. The philosopher seeks to escape the prison of flesh and materiality to return to the One. These doctrines work their way into Christianity.

300s:
Early eastern Polynesian culture. Rise of the Toltecs in Mesoamerica. Bantu cereal cultivators in southeast Africa begin to herd cattle. At Alexandria, Gnostic mystic Zosimos of Panopolis

describes the rudiments of alchemy: the search for the Philosopher's Stone that dispenses healing and wisdom. Like many later alchemists, he links this search to finding the wisdom goddess Sophia.

305:
Canon 36 of the Synod of Elvira, southern Spain prohibits images in churches, "lest that which is worshiped and venerated be depicted on the walls." This is the first of several attacks led by the early Christian church against imagery and, by extension, against the imagination.

312:
Anti-Christian Emperor Diocletian martyrs future saints Rhipsime, Gaiana, Marianne, and their thirty-five companions. Having defeated all opposition, Constantine arrives in Rome with his troops bearing the Christian monogram on his battle standards. To get the increasingly influential Christians on his side, he claims he'd seen a luminous cross in the sky and received the message, "By this sign you will triumph." He did, beating Maxentius in a battle before the Milvian Bridge. Once marginalized and radical, Christianity congeals into a militarized state religion.

313:
Constantine and his colleague Licinius publish the Edict of Milan to promote freedom of worship and the restoration of all property seized from Christians.

320:
In the Ganges Valley, rise of Gupta Empire under Chandragupta I. Gupta paintings adorn the caves of Ajanta, sculptures fill the temples of Ellora, and mathematics and metaphysical speculations flower.

322:
The stirrup is invented in China.

324:
Constantine wages war in the east and becomes sole Emperor. He founds a capital called New Rome at the ancient Thracian city Byzantium (in Turkey), named after Byzas, a Greek told by the Oracle at Delphi to found a city "opposite the blind." It is later called Constantinople, then Istanbul, but the references to "Byzantium" and "Byzantine" remain. Eusebius writes the first history of the Christian Church.

325:
Constantine holds the ecumenical First Council of Nicaea to settle the dispute over Arianism (the belief that Jesus and God were separate beings) and to make over the pagan spring festival of Eostre into Easter. The bishop of Alexandria receives papal authority over the eastern half of the empire, and the bishop of Rome authority over the western half. Constantine also allows masters to beat their slaves to death and orders his son and stepmother executed for reasons unknown. He relies on heavy taxes, terror, and secret police. Christians in the western half of the empire celebrate the pagan holiday December 25th as Christmas; Christians in the east disagree and choose January 6th; but both originate as pagan holidays. Once Constantine dies, his three Christian sons go to war with each other over the Empire. Throughout the coming schisms, judgments, excommunications, wars, and other Church conflicts, few will bear 2 Corinthians 3:6 in mind: "...For the letter kills, but the Spirit gives life."

350:
The Sassanid Empire of Persia is attacked by oncoming Huns who then ravage parts of Europe (until 453) and take over Kazakhstan. Their viciousness, hit-and-run tactics, and use of the metal stirrup make them a fearful cavalry. Their raiding of the Goths and other Germanics pushes the refugees into the Roman Empire, where they are forced into slavery, soldiery, or concentration camps.

361:
A secretly pagan relative of Constantius in charge of operations in

Gaul, Neoplatonist Julian the Apostate orders his troops to rebel against the emperor and place Julian in charge. He tries but fails to counter Christianity by reviving paganism. Constantius dies of a fever. Julian will die while fighting the Persians, and Jovian takes over. An incompetent Christian commander, he makes peace with the Persians by giving them all the territory that Diocletian had previously gained.

376-380:
Reign of Chandragupta II; the Gupta golden age. In the Ganges Valley tolerance, business, wealth, and culture flourish. The Huns attack the Vandals, Franks, Goths, Slavs, Ostragoths, Alans, and other Germanic tribes, pushing them westward toward the Roman Empire.

378:
The Romans lose the Battle of Adrianople to rebelling Goths on horseback, once-peaceful farmers who, made starving refugees by the Huns, hadn't gotten the food they'd been promised and whose wives and sisters were being ravaged by Roman soldiers; Emperor Valens dies in the fighting. Foot soldiers will be deemphasized in battle for centuries because of the impressive performance of Visigoth cavalry.

383:
The Battle of Fei River keeps South China independent of the Qin for the Jin.

390:
Greek poet Nonnus of Panopolis writes the forty-eight-book *Dionysiaca,* the longest poem from antiquity, larger than the *Odyssey* and *Iliad* combined. It celebrates the life of Dionysus and includes homoerotic poetry in Homeric hexameter.

396:
An army of Christian Visigoths led by former Roman soldier Alaric sacks the temples of Eleusis and of the ancient Delphic Oracle.

400s:
The Gupta Empire grows until it stretches across the north and width of India. Romantic dramatist and poet Kalidasa, whose life is largely a mystery, is retained by the Gupta court and rises to the stature of the greatest figure in classical Sanskrit literature. The Zapotec state with its capital at Monte Alban expands in southern Mexico. Use of iron throughout eastern Africa. Christianity infiltrates the empire in Aksum in what is now northern Ethiopia. Augustine begins the autobiographical genre in all its self-absorption by writing his *Confessions*. As the Roman Warm Period ends, and as the Huns, Avars, Bulgars, Alans, and Slavs push the Goths, Vandals, Angles, Suebi, Frisians, and Franks westward toward Britain, storm surges and a changing climate drive the Saxons, who had been raiding the Romans, out of their homeland on the German north coast. Saxon mercenary brothers Hengest and Horsa fighting under Vortigern in Britain hire more Saxons to fight the native Picts, and soon boatloads of Saxons arrive and deposit settlers resolved to stay.

408:
As the Franks and Vandals assail the northern frontiers of the Roman Empire, Alaric's army enters Italy and quickly attracts other tribes oppressed by the Romans. Alaric demands gold from General Stilicho in exchange for halting the invasion, but Emperor Honorius refuses. Stilicho fails to turn back the resulting Germanic attack and is arrested and murdered by the order of a misinformed Honorius, who wrongly considered him a traitor. Emboldened by this, Alaric and his Visigoths move north through Italy toward Rome.

410:
Alaric attacks and the hungry Visigoths sack Rome. In three years Augustine writes *City of God*, where he blames Rome's fall on its spiritual decadence. In 455 Vandals will invade Rome. The unified tribes from the Visigoth Empire stretch across southern France and Spain. Saxons, Angles, Jutes, and other tribes enter Britain. The loss of Empire ushers in Dark Ages (the term invented by Petrarch) until around 750 (early Middle Ages). Farmers and settlers pick stones out of what's left of Roman structures, and the early Church rushes

into the power and culture vacuum in the West, erects a Greek/Zoroastrian/Judaic/Roman blend of eschatology, offers a salvific creed as antidote to the gaping cosmopolitan rootlessness opened up by Alexander and Rome, brings the sacred down into concrete history, replaces subtle philosophical explorations and mythic metaphors with absolute, literalized, and ritualized doctrines, invokes a father God who loves personally and unconditionally, endows the individual with a new sense of personal worth, and makes the new emperor of the universal kingdom Jesus.

MIDDLE AGES (fall of Rome to Renaissance):

415:
On her way to work, Hypatia, chief librarian of the Alexandrian Library, is flayed to death with abalone shells swung by a mob of parishioners of Cyril, Archbishop (and later Saint) of Alexandria, who hated her sex, her friendship with the Roman governor, and her "pagan" learnings in mathematics and Neoplatonic philosophy. The Alexandrian Library is burned down soon after, an incalculable loss of knowledge across so many fields of endeavor.

416:
Prompted by Augustine, an African church council brands the English monk Pelagius a heretic for proclaiming the innocence of children and the body, the unreality of original sin, the primacy of free will over predestination, and the evil of wealth. Pelagius also believes that faithful pagans got to heaven before Christ came around. He is exiled to Egypt, where he dies. "Those who are unwilling to correct their own way of life appear to want to correct nature itself instead."

431:
First Council of Ephesus under Emperor Theodosius II. Under urgings from Cyril, Nestorianism, the doctrine of the difference between Christ's divinity and humanity, is declared heretical, and Nestorius is removed from his see. Some of the churches go with him into exile.

The Council also rules that Mary is the mother of God.

432:
The nomadic Huns from Asia, whose hordes had pushed the Goth tribes into Europe, have power enough that they collect an annual tribute from Rome. St. Patrick lands in Ireland. The new story of salvation he brings will accomplish what centuries of Roman force could not: an isle-wide change of piety and culture.

439:
The Vandals, loose in North Africa, overrun Carthage and make it the capital of their kingdom. Forces from East and West will try to retake this key trade city but will fail until Justinian succeeds.

445:
Attila the Hun rides into western Europe, murders co-king Bleda, and takes supreme command. These attacks push the Visigoths farther west across Europe. Denied the marriage she wished, Honoria, sister to Roman Emperor Valentinian III, hits back by sending her ring to Attila, who claims her and half of the Western Empire as dowry. Denied tribute money from Byzantine Emperor Marcian, Attila attacks but is defeated in Gaul by Roman General Aetius, who commands a Visigoth-Roman army near what is now Châlons-en-Champagne.

451:
At the Battle of the Catalaunian Plains, a Roman-Visigoth coalition beats the Huns, stopping Attila from taking over Gaul. In 454, a Germanic army ends Hun incursions into Western Europe (Battle of Nedao).

455:
Vandals vandalize Rome.

470-536:
Bodhidharma, the traveling monk (place of origin unknown) who brings Ch'an (Zen) Buddhism to China and train monks at the

Shaolin Monastery.

476:
The revenge of Remus: having been refused land grants and federal status for his Ostrogoth troops, Germanic invader Odoacer expels boy emperor Romulus Augustus, the last western Emperor of Rome, kills his father Orestes, and takes control of the city. (According to legend, Romulus had founded Rome and killed his brother Remus. And Orestes had been chased by the Furies...)

481:
Having overthrown the Roman governor of Gaul, Clovis I (also known as Chlodwig, grandson of Merovech) of what will become France succeeds his father Childeric as king of the Salian Franks and in 496 converts to Catholicism. He begins his conquests and founds the Merovingian Dynasty, which sets the stage for the French monarchy and the conquests of Charlemagne (Charles the Great).

500s:
The world's population is a hundred and ninety million. India's population is fifty million. The Ghanaian empire becomes the most important power in West Africa. The Hopewell culture in northern America constructs elaborate burial mounds, makes pottery, and uses iron weapons. Originally from Southeast Asia, Polynesians settle in the Hawaiian Islands and Easter Island. Indian mathematicians introduce the zero. The Battle of Badon Hill includes a commander named Artorius (Arthur), a Romano-Celtic who tries to fight off incoming Jutes, Angles, and Saxons. Ultimately, however, this effort does not succeed, and the Germanics overrun Britain in waves and breed with the native Celts. The Irish migrate into Scotland. The Hindu book of sculpture and architecture *Shilpa Shastras* circulates in India. The Huns destroy the Gupta Empire.

524:
Boethius writes *The Consolation of Philosophy*. "Human perversity, then, makes divisions of that which by nature is one and simple, and in attempting to obtain part of something which has no parts, suc-

ceeds in getting neither the part—which is nothing—nor the whole, which they are not interested in."

525:
In Rome Scythian monk Dionysius Exiguus the Small invents the Anno Domine calendar.

526:
Along the Silk Road the continuing influx of Buddhism into China will also bring a Hellenistic influence and the realization that China is not the center of the world.

527:
Justin I dies and his Christian nephew Justinian becomes ruler of the Byzantine Empire (Eastern Roman Empire based in Constantinople). He outlaws paganism and Plato's old academy and persecutes philosophers, Jews, and homosexuals. His codification of Roman law, the *Corpus Juris Civilis* (Body of Civil Law, also known as the Justinian Code), gives unity to the centralized state and greatly influences all subsequent legal history. Byzantine law, culture, pageantry, and force fill some of the gaps left by the defunct Western Roman Empire until Byzantium falls to the Ottoman Turks in 1453.

529:
After surviving several poisoning attempts by fellow mendicants, St. Benedict founds his monastery at Monte Cassino south of Rome. Justinian blames problems in Rome, even bad weather, on queer people.

532:
The Nika Riots destroy half of Constantinople as Senate-backed rioters who hate Justinian swarm through the Hippodrome after a chariot race.

535:
A cooling period, possibly the result of a tropical volcano, brings

cold weather to Europe and drought to Central America, where Teotihuacan declines in part because of the dryness.

538:
His authority having been saved by his courtesan wife Theodora just as he prepared to flee the rebellion, Justinian embarks on a grand plan to reunite the Roman Empire from the east, but as his troops hack their way through Italy, Turkey, Greece, Palestine, and North Africa, a cargo ship lands in Constantinople with the bubonic plague aboard (542). The plague lays him low and kills half the populace in the cities of continental Europe. He survives but is sleepless and paranoid after. New outbreaks occur periodically. As cities depopulate and centralized power fragments, monasteries grow in importance as centers of culture, commerce, and learning.

550-600:
Mayan city Chichen Itza founded in central Yucatan.

552:
Buddhism enters Japan.

563:
The Irish St. Columba, "Apostle of Caledonia," leaves Ireland and lands on the island of Iona on the west coast of Scotland, where he founds a monastery to Christianize northern Scotland.

570:
Muhammad, the Prophet of Islam, born in Mecca. He is orphaned soon after birth and brought up by his uncle Abu Talib.

580:
Wen-ti, the first Sui emperor, reunites the Chinese empire. The Sui period won't last long but it carries through many public works and lays the foundation for further consolidation under the T'ang dynasty. Under the Sui the Grand Canal, built to link the Huang He and Chang Rivers, opens up the lower Chang valley and facilitates

national reunification. In the Roman Forum the future Pope Gregory I sees a group of Angle slave children for sale and, according to Bede, asks about them. Told they are Anglii, he replies with a joke: "It is well, for they have an angelic face, and such people ought to be co-heirs of the angels in heaven." With this he decides to convert England.

587:
The first Buddhist monasteries in Japan are founded.

590:
When Gregory becomes pope, he standardizes plainchant, teaches that Mary Magdalene had been a prostitute, and launches the conversion of England via Augustine of Canterbury.

600s:
Mutually weakening of the embattled Sassanid and Roman Empires permits the spread of Islam, which is aided by mounting dislike of the oppressive policies of Constantinople, Roman Catholicism, and the Zoroastrian priesthood. Early Middle Ages. A key period of art and literature in Ireland. Tiahuanaco civilization begins in Bolivia. Height of Mayan civilization. Rise of Huari in Peru.

610:
Heraclius becomes Emperor in Constantinople as the Sassanid Empire attempts to dominate Byzantine civilization. While praying on Mt. Hira, Muhammad hears the voice of the angel Gabriel call out, "Recite!" *Qur'an* means "Recital," and in it God's grand presence, which lights the heavens and the earth, is said to be "closer than the vein in your neck." In one *hadith* (saying) the Prophet responds to the question of how to be saved by stating, "Do not become angry"—not "feel," but "become"—and each time he is asked, he repeats, "Do not become angry."

614:
Sassanid armies defeat Jerusalem, take the Jerusalem cross, and destroy the Church of the Holy Sepulchre.

618-907:
The T'ang dynasty unifies China. A dynasty known for poetry, painting, and literature, it is founded by Li Yuan and his son Li Shih-min with the aid of Turkish allies and builds on the communications and administration systems established by the Sui. Civil service exams are established to test knowledge of the Confucian classics. In 626 the T'ang court will adopt Buddhism.

622:
Muhammed's *hijra*—flight from Mecca to Medina to escape assassination—and the start of the Islamic calendar. In 628 his army captures Mecca. Entering the Kaaba, he smashes its idols and establishes monotheism in the city.

632:
Buddhism becomes the state religion in Tibet. Muhammad dies and Abu Bakr is named Caliph ("successor"). Arabs carrying the Islamic faith expand across northern Africa until 711. In 642 they burn what remains of the Alexandrian Library. Wars rage between Muslim Arabs and the Byzantine Empire until 976.

634:
Abu Bakr dies and is succeeded by the great Caliph Umar I. Rise of the Islamic Empire and of a period of high culture, political reform, support for the poor, Islamic jurisprudence (*fiqh*), and tolerance of Jews and Christians. Queen Sonduk rules the Korean kingdom of Silla. She keeps the kingdom intact, extends its relations to China, and builds the Tower of the Moon and Stars, the first known observatory in the Far East, in Kyongju, South Korea.

651:
End of the Sassanid Empire as it falls to the Islamic sword. Muslims conquer Palestine, Armenia, and Egypt.

656:
Muslims from Kufa and Egypt march to Medina and call for Ali, husband of Fatima, to become the Caliph after the Caliph Uthman is

killed. However, Aisha, the widow of the Prophet Mohammad, supports Ali rival Muawiya's claim to be Caliph. Those who share this view become Sunnite Muslims, and those who support Ali become Shi'ites. In 661 Caliph Ali is assassinated by *Khawarijis*, ex-supporters; his son, Hasan, abdicates to Muawiya, who founds the Umayyad dynasty.

657:
St. Hilda teaches England's first vernacular poet, Caedmon, to write.

663:
The Kingdom of Silla takes over Korea. Expansion of the T'ang Dynasty in China.

668:
Silla captures the other two kingdoms of Korea.

677:
The Arabs (or Saracens) attempt to conquer Constantinople but fail when beaten back by Greek Fire, a kind of napalm projected by bronze tubes fastened to the prows of Byzantine ships.

680:
Caedmon's Hymn, the oldest English poem by a known author. Bulgar tribes from near the Volga cross the river and settle in what is now Bulgaria (formerly Moesia and Thrace). The first Bulgarian Empire rises and will eventually threaten Byzantium.

690:
Empress Wu Zetian rules China; throughout her reign Buddhism attains its Chinese peak, peasants are treated better than previously, literature and Taoism receive state support, and aristocrats are replaced at court by scholars. She also contributes to construction of the Longmen Grottoes containing thousands of intricate Buddhist statues carved into caves.

691:
Buddhism becomes China's official religion.

700s:
Easter Islanders erect stone platforms that support giant statues. Polynesians settle in the Cook Islands. *Beowulf* is written in northern Europe. Rise of Mound Builder culture in the Mississippi river basin; their flat-topped mounds serve as temple bases. Benedictine missionaries complete the conversion of England begun by St. Gregory the Great. Chinese warrior Nie Yinniang reputed to have been a one-woman Robin Hood.

700-900:
In eastern Arizona, the Pueblo people live in houses above ground.

701:
Komyo (701-760), Buddhist member of Japan's Fujiwara family; she marries Emperor Shomu, gives birth to Empress Koken, and founds temples and charitable institutions throughout Nara, capital of Japan.

711:
The Omayyads conquer Sind and found the first Muslim state in India. A Muslim invasion of Spain under General Tarik ibn Ziad is met with welcome by oppressed peasants and Jews and puts an end to Visigoth rule under Roderick as only the mountainous north, home of the Basque people, remains independent. (*Gibraltar* means "Gabal-Tariq": Mount of Tarik.) Spain remains under Muslim rule until 1492.

717-718:
Byzantine Emperor Leo III the Isaurian deposes Theodosius III, then counters the Umayyad Arabs seeking to conquer Byzantine Asia Minor with Greek Fire and military strength, beating them with Bulgarian help. Asia Minor and Greece are the seat of Byzantine civilization for several centuries and, after that, of the Ottoman Empire. The *Kojiki*, or "Record of Ancient Matters," the earliest chronicle of

history and myth in Japan, is written at the request of the Empress Gemmei.

721:
Persian polymath Abu Mūsā Jābir ibn Hayyān (721-815), known in Europe as Geber, invents the scientific method and conducts research in chemistry, alchemy, astronomy, astrology, metallurgy, engineering, geology, medicine, and philosophy. He will also invent at least twenty types of lab equipment, some of it still in use.

732:
The wealth of the church of St. Martin draws a Muslim cavalry-equipped army of fifty thousand from North Africa, but when a rumor goes around that the Franks are stealing their loot from the rear, the army begins to fall apart and is hammered by Frankish king Charles Martel at the Battle of Tours (it actually happened between Tours and Poitiers) in France, putting an end to the Muslim advance northward through Europe and laying territorial and political groundwork for Charlemagne and French feudalism. Martel forms an alliance with the Church that enables the Merovingian Dynasty, and Christianity, to expand into Germany.

735:
As violence and chaos reign in Dark Age Europe, Venerable Bede, an Anglo-Saxon Benedictine scholar, writes the pivotal five-volume work *History of the English Church and People* in which he dates events from the birth of Jesus. Monks in monasteries copy and translate (and mistranslate) the pre-Christian classics.

739:
The Great Berber Revolt against Umayyad Arab rule starts in Tangier and runs through North Africa.

750:
Irish monks propagate early medieval art like the *Book of Kells*, an illuminated Gospel. The Caliphate moves to Baghdad as the Abassids take over. The Ghana Empire rises in west Africa.

751:
Muslim soldiers win the Battle of River Talas in central Asia; Islam comes to China. St. Boniface makes Pepin the Short, first Carolingian king and son of Charles Martel, a divinely sanctioned king, and the Frankish monarchy is integrated into the papal order. Having forced Childeric III into a monastery, Pepin strengthens the interdependency between Benedictine missionaries and Frankish expansion. Pepin will be crowned by Pope Stephen II for invading Italy to protect him against the Lombards.

760:
Caliph Harun al-Rashid founds the House of Wisdom in Baghdad. It starts with the study of Persian texts and eventually adds Greek philosophy, Indian science, zoology, and cartography. It will grow to include the largest collection of scholarly works in the world.

772:
Having disinherited his dead brother Carloman's sons and seized his territory, Charlemagne defeats the Saxons during the Saxon Wars (772 – 804), and his troops destroy replicas of the Saxon sacred tree Irminsul (based on Yggdrasil the World Tree).

789:
Idris I rules Morocco.

793:
Vikings sack Lindisfarne and the monastery at Jarrow, opening their long terror campaign against Britain (until 1100). They rely on the feared longship, a craft that speeds through the water, reverses course without turning, and carries troops right to an enemy shore and far inland along rivers.

794-1185:
Heian period in Japan: more independence from Chinese influence and modification of ideas and institutions imported from there. Buddhism and Taoism thrive. Heian-kyo (Kyoto) becomes the capital of Japan. The Fujiwara family exerts control.

800s:
Hokokam people in Arizona expand settlements and enlarge houses. The first castles rise in western Europe.

800:
Knowing that Charlemagne believes he has revived the office of Western Emperor of Rome, the pope crowns him thus on Christmas Day in St. Peter's Church. Charlemagne's system of government divides his realm—most of western Europe except Spain and Portugal-into regions ruled by local counts. Within his realm he orders the heads cut from everyone who refuses to convert. To aid expansion and administration of the kingdom, he promotes what will be called the "Carolingian Renaissance." Before it, most of the realm (with the exception of Benedictine England) is illiterate because of the decay of the Roman Empire. The director of this renaissance is Anglo-Saxon Benedictine Alcuin, who receives his own education from a student of Bede. Alcuin sets up schools, sees to the copying of classical Latin texts, and develops a new type of handwriting. He also writes unabashedly passionate love letters to fellow monks. As France and Byzantium are menaced by Islamic armies, Charlemagne institutes feudalism: chief tenants, who are usually barons, provide armored knights in exchange for portions of land (feuds) worked by peasants, with everyone obedient to their lord.

805:
Kassia the Nun is the most famous hymnographer, abbess, and poet of the Eastern Orthodox Church.

806:
Hien Tsung is the Emperor of China. During his reign a shortage of copper leads to the distribution of paper money.

814:
When Charlemagne dies, Louis I of the Holy Roman Empire (Louis the Pious) becomes Emperor and king of France and Germany. Louis will divide his own inheritance between his three sons, who squander it by fighting each other. The realm is invaded by Vikings,

Hungarians, and Muslims during these civil wars and, broke because of tribute payments to the Vikings, it disintegrates.

815:
The Treaty of 815 ends decades of fighting between the Byzantines and Bulgaria.

820s:
Persian mathematician Musa al-Chwarazmi develops algebra.

841:
The Vikings found Dublin on the east coast of Ireland.

843:
Kenneth MacAlpin unites the kingdom of Scotia and is crowned first king of Scotland.

850s:
Mayan civilization in the southern lowlands of Mexico collapses as its cities lie abandoned. Arabs perfect the astrolabe.

859:
Vikings attack as far south as the Mediterranean but are stopped there. The University of al-Karaouine in Fez, Morocco, is the world's first university.

861:
Iceland is discovered by the Norse. Russian Norsemen sack parts of France.

865:
The alchemist Ar-Razi, known as Rhazes, devises an empirical classification system that anticipates modern chemistry. "One book opens another."

866:
John Scotus Erigena attempts a synthesis of Christianity and

Neoplatonism in *The Division of Nature*.

868:
The *Diamond Sutra* is printed on Chinese woodblocks.

878:
Alfred the Great defeats Vikings under Gudrum at Ethandune, after which the Treaty of Wedmore divides England between them. The Danes get control of Eastern and Northern England. This treaty also saves the English language from being replaced by a Scandinavian tongue.

884:
Fujiwara Mototsune becomes the first *kampaku* (chancellor with a regent's powers) of Japan. The classical age of Japanese literature.

889:
Khmers start on their capital city at Angkor, Cambodia. 889–1434: the Golden Age of Khmer civilization displays unsurpassed architectural, sculptural, and Sanskrit literary achievements. The Italian city of Forlí becomes a free republic, starting a trend that carries into the early Renaissance.

891:
Monks write the history of England in early English in the *Anglo-Saxon Chronicle*.

900s:
Kasar Hausa (Hausaland), a fertile region on the lower Niger River in West Africa, prospers because of increasing trade and industry. Ancestors of the Maoris reach South Island, New Zealand. The Toltecs build a capital at Tula, Mexico. Magyars, a nomadic people from central Asia, invade Europe.

907-960:
Chinese calligrapher Lady Li Fu-jen is probably the first expert anywhere on bamboo painting.

909:
Abdullah al-Mahdi Billah (Ubayd Allah) founds the Shi'ite Fatamid Caliphate (named after Ali's wife Fatima) that rises in Tunisia and extends over much of North Africa, with Cairo founded as its capital. The religiously tolerant Caliphate endures until the Abbasids under Saladin take over in 1171.

911:
Making a treaty, Viking chief Rollo settles in Normandy ("land of the Northmen"), France.

918:
Koryo dynasty founded by Emperor Taejo in western central Korea, setting it apart culturally and politically from the rest of the East. In Korea the *Tripitaka Koreana*, a revered collection of Buddhist scriptures, are carved into wood blocks. A hunter in central Germany discovers a huge load of silver-lead ore that will enrich the kingdoms of Saxony and Bohemia.

931-999:
St. Adelaide, Empress of the Holy Roman Empire when Otto the Great is crowned in Rome (962), founds and restores monasteries and labors as a peacemaker.

935-1002:
German nun Hrosvitha in Lower Saxony becomes one of the first to adapt classical dramatic forms to Christian narrative poems and epics. She also writes comedies.

948:
The Kingdom of Nri (948—1911) in Igboland, West Africa is a homeland for exiled peoples. Ruled by a priest, its peaceful solidity derives from ritual and agreement rather than from force.

950-1050:
Igbo-Ukwu farming culture thrives in eastern Nigeria.

960:
The Sung dynasty in China (960-1279).

962:
Otto defeats the Hungarians and is crowned Holy Roman Emperor by Pope John XII. He is a self-appointed successor to Charlemagne.

963:
Mieszko I founds the kingdom of Poland and is succeeded by Boleslav I, who greatly expands its territory.

973:
Persian polymath Abū al-Rayhān Muhammad ibn Ahmad al-Bīrūnī (Alberonus) (973-1048), who will write a hundred and forty-six learned books on topics from astronomy to geography to natural science.

980:
Ibn Sina (Avicenna)(980-1037); this Persian doctor and interpreter of Aristotle is a philosopher of medieval Islam whose Neoplatonic angelology will be attacked by Averroes. He writes about the World Soul and, centuries before Descartes, surmises that a man suspended and blinded would still know he possessed a soul.

982:
Faced with manslaughter charges, Eric the Red leaves Iceland to go exploring. He establishes the first Viking colony in the place he euphemistically names Greenland to attract settlers.

983:
A thousand-chapter encyclopedia, *Taiping Yulan*, is produced in China. Earliest possible date of the written *Poetic Edda* of Norse mythology.

989 BCE:
To deal with hordes of knights who, having mustered out to fight off Vikings and Muslims and other Dark Ages threats in Europe, where

local chiefs now pillage at will, the Roman Catholic Church issues two edicts to curtail violence: the Peace of God to bar peasants and widows from attack by knights, and then, in 1027, the Truce of God, prohibiting violence on Sundays and holy days. Neither works very well, but as the church attempts to enforce them, and as Europe's climate warms, eyes begin to turn to the Muslim-held Middle East, where Crusades will break out in 1095.

LATE MIDDLE AGES:

1000:
Throughout Europe run millennial rumors of second comings, visits by messiahs, final judgments, and various Revelations-style end-of-the-world scenarios that panic lots of people, but nothing universally catastrophic happens, and earthly life goes on pretty much as it did before. The Chinese invent gunpowder and use it in warfare. Farmers in Peru grow sweet potatoes and corn. Polynesians build stone temples. Using the perfected longship, Leif the Lucky and his Vikings explore the New World after Bjarni Herjolfsson spots North American on a trip out from Greenland, but they fail to colonize it. They name North America "Vinland." Bantu-speaking people set up kingdoms in southern Africa. The kingdoms of Takrur and Gao flourish in West Africa thanks to the gold trade. In Europe agriculture, trade, literacy, and urbanism all increase, guilds form, and universities are founded. Ibn Yunus of Egypt records precise astronomical observations and calculations in the Hakemite Tables (*Al-Zij al-Hakimi al-Kabir*).

1008:
Japanese author Lady Murasaki Shikibu writes *The Tale of Genji*, a three-part novel of romance. "You that in far-off countries of the sky can dwell secure, look back upon me here; for I am weary of this frail world's decay."

1014:
Anawrata takes power in Burma and builds a large empire, strength-

ens his army, and founds a dynasty of relatively able rulers. Brian Boru, High King of all Ireland, defeats the Vikings at Battle of Clontarf but is murdered in his tent afterwards. His victory breaks the Norse power in Ireland forever, but Ireland falls into anarchy.

1021:
Contradicting Aristotle, Ptolemy, and Euclid, who thought vision relied on rays streaming from the eye like light from a lamp, Ibn al-Haytham (Alhazen) introduces an accurate theory of vision in his *Book of Optics*.

1026:
Danish Cnut (Canute) the Great rules England, Scotland, and much of Scandinavia. Viking attacks cease under his rule, perhaps because he is himself a Viking.

1027:
The Book of Healing by Avicenna (Ibn Sina): an encyclopedia with articles on earth science, astronomy, philosophy, psychology, mathematics, and logic. He also wrote *The Canon of Medicine* (1025) and hundreds of papers on various topics.

1135:
Italian monk Joachim of Fiora (1135-1202), who writes that an Age of the Father (Old Testament) and an Age of the Son (New Testament) will be followed by an Age of the Holy Spirit in which having a direct relationship with God will transcend the scriptures and the church.

1138:
Byzantine princess and physician Anna Comnena writes the *Alexiad*, a fifteen-volume historical work about the reign of her father, Emperor Alexios I Komnenos of Byzantium. She is educated in science, mathematics, geography, classical history, astronomy, philosophy, theology, medicine (which she taught and practiced), grammar, literature, Greek language, rhetoric, and history. She also ran a hospital and an orphanage.

1040:
Pi Sheng of China invents block printing that uses movable type made of baked clay. The epic *Poem of the Cid* composed in Spain.

1044:
Theravada Buddhist Anawrahta Minsaw founds the Pagan Empire that unifies all Burma.

1050s:
The Yoruba people of Ife prosper in Nigeria in West Africa. The first agricultural revolution of Medieval Europe develops in 1050 with a shift to the northern lands for cultivation, a period of warmer climate (from 700 to 1200) in western Europe, and the widespread improvement of farming machines, some first discovered by the Carolingians and the Romans. These innovations include the heavy plow, the three-field system of crop rotation, mills for processing cloth, beer breweries, pulp for paper, and employment of iron and horses in the fields. With all this, western towns and trade grow exponentially. Dominance of Western Europe and papal authority.

1054:
When Michael Cerularius, the Patriarch of Constantinople, orders the Latin churches of that city closed, the Christian church divides into Eastern and Western branches (the Great Schism) that develop into the Eastern Orthodox Church and the Roman Catholic Church.

1058:
Sufi mystic and philosopher Abu Hamidi Muhammad Al-Ghazzali (1058-1111), whose work bridges orthodox and Sufi Muslims. "Knowledge exists potentially in the human soul like the seed in the soil; by learning the potential becomes actual."

1065:
Seljuk Turks invade Asia Minor. A branch of the Tatars, the Seljuks descend from a tribal chief named Seljuk, who came from the area near the Aral Sea. They are Sunnite Muslims.

1066:
William, Duke of Normandy, had previously obtained his cousin Edward the Confessor's agreement that William would inherit the throne of England, but as Edward dies, he makes Harold, Earl of Wessex, king instead. With the agreement of Pope Alexander II, William invades England and with his Normans wins the Battle of Hastings, the first and most decisive battle of the Norman Conquest. After Harold dies in battle, William is crowned king on Christmas day. As the Norman Conquest fuses French and English culture, Old English evolves into Middle English, with its English syntax and grammar and heavily French vocabulary. French art and literature prevail, and the French language eventually dominates politics. William achieves political stability by blending the Norman feudal system with the English monarchical system. Philip I of France takes over from his mother and uncle.

1071:
At the Battle of Manzikert, Alp Arslan leads his Seljuk Turks to defeat the Byzantine Empire, after which Turks flood into Anatolia.

1075:
Pope Gregory VII ignites the Investiture Controversy by claiming that only the pope can invest high church officials, not the nobility. The result is a series of wars in Germany until the Concordant of Worms in 1122.

1076:
Seljuk Turks capture Jerusalem.

1079:
Scholasticism emerges as an attempt to reconcile classical philosophy (primarily Aristotelian) with Christianity. Peter Abelard, who unlike Al-Ghazzali believes in that logic can be applied to faith, and analysis to Christian truth, contributes to this movement with his theological work *Sic et Non*: "The first key to wisdom is defined, of course, as assiduous and frequent questioning." The Third Lateran

Council decrees excommunication for anyone who commits sodomy.

1185:
André le Chapelain's *Art of Courtly Love*.

1086:
William the Conqueror orders that all landlords swear an oath of loyalty to him (the Oath of Salisbury). A survey is taken by William and the *Domesday Book*, a census, is written. She-tsung, Emperor of China, nationalizes agricultural production and distribution.

1088:
Chinese polymath Shen Kuo writes the *Dream Pool Essays* to develop and reflect on several disciplines. He theorizes about climate change, geomorphology, planetary motion, eclipses, and archeology, and he experiments with an early camera and the marine compass.

1090:
The Serbian Grand Principality is founded; it will eventually lead to a kingdom (1217).

1095:
When Byzantine Emperor Alexius Comnenus requests help in reconquering the lost territory of Asia Minor, Urban II calls for the First Crusade—"God wills it!"—to free eastern Christendom from the Muslim Turks. Buoyed by the mythic goal of saving holy territory from invaders, the Crusade is a power play to strengthen the Gregorian papacy by bringing the Greek Orthodox Church under its authority while humiliating the antipope-creating Holy Roman Emperor Henry IV, who had forced Urban to flee Italy after being excommunicated by him for supporting Clement III as rival pope. Robert II mortgages Normandy to William II of England in exchange for money to finance the crusade.

1098:
A monastery founded at Citeaux in France starts up the Cistercian

order of monks. Multitalented mystic Hildegard of Bingen (1098-1179) born; a visionary abbess, she will write a medical encyclopedia, liturgical music, poetry, lives of saints, and other works. "The Word is living, being, spirit, all verdant greening, all creativity. This Word manifests itself in every creature."

1099:
Crusaders take Jerusalem after a forty-day siege and spend three days raping, looting, slaughtering Muslim families, and burning Jews in their synagogues. They then divide the territory into four principalities. The oldest epic poem in French, *The Song of Roland*, is written by an unknown author to highlight differences between Christianity and paganism.

1100:
The Katanga in Zaire founded. Rise of Incas in Peru; they are farmers led by warrior chiefs. Construction begins on the Chartres Cathedral in France.

1118:
Temple of Solomon Order (Knights Templars) founded by knight Hugh de Payens to protect pilgrims on the road to Jerusalem.

1120:
The Chinese play with painted playing cards.

1122:
With the Concordat of Worms in Germany the Papacy and the Holy Roman Emperor come to a power-sharing agreement that paves the way for the rise of nation-states and for secular education.

1122-1204:
Eleanor of Aquitaine, duchess and countess and queen of France, powerful, wealthy, and patron to art, literature, and troubadour ideals of courtly love.

1132:
St. Denis Abbey, the first Gothic church, is built by Abbot Suger in Paris. They are called "Gothic"—Goth-like—as a disparagement of their soaring structures.

1135-1153:
The Anarchy period bursts throughout England after Henry I's son dies, initiating a long fight over succession until the Treaty of Winchester stops the raiding, skirmishing, plotting, and sieging.

1144:
The *Risalat Mariyanus*, translated from Arabic into Latin under the title *Liber de compositione alchimiae*, reintroduces alchemy, transmuted and enlarged, into Western Europe.

1147-49:
The Christian armies of a Second Crusade called for by St. Bernard are defeated in Asia Minor and forced to abandon the siege of Damascus and go home. Inspired by puritanical Islamic teacher Ibn Tumart, who claimed to be the *mahdi* (messiah), Almohad Berbers sweep down from the Atlas Mountains of Morocco through North Africa and into Spain. The Almohads gradually lose their conservatism and fade.

1150s:
The Zagwe dynasty rules the Ethiopian highlands. Universities of Paris and Oxford founded.

1154:
Al Idrisi publishes a world atlas.

1160:
After another civil war, the Taira clan takes control of Japan away from the Fujiwara.

1161:
Sung Dynasty boats prevail against Jin Dynasty boats in the East

China Sea and on the Yangtze River by using gunpowder projectiles flung by catapult.

1165:
Frenchman Chretien de Troyes combines tales of Arthur and his knights into the Arthurian Romances, setting the stage for the appearance of the modern novel. He also proposes the ideal of romantic love within marriage. Chivalry, another popular ideal, includes the defense of honor, combat in tournaments, and the virtues of generosity and reverence. Its code exalts noble life and the status of noblewomen. Troubadours wander Europe singing about feudalism and romantic love. Sufi mystic Abu Bakr Muhammad Ibn al-'Arabi (1165-1240) born: "Understand then who you are, understand what your selfhood is, what is your relation with the Divine Being; understand whereby you are He and whereby you are other than He...."

1167:
Most of the cities of northern Italy form the Lombard League to stand up to Frederick I, Holy Roman Emperor, from controlling them. They are supported by the pope.

1168:
English scientist Robert Grosseteste brings Byzantine translators to England to render Aristotle's *Ethics* and other works. Arab scholars are also hard at work on translations of Aristotle. They have preserved classical culture and science throughout the European Dark Ages.

1169:
The Normans invade Ireland.

1170:
Having excommunicated those who crowned Henry II without church permission, Archbishop Thomas á Becket is murdered by four of the king's knights in the cathedral at Canterbury. Leonardo Fibonacci born (1170-1240); he will have a hand in Arabic numer-

als replacing Roman ones, which starts bookkeeping and finance in Europe, and will discover the Sequence named after him by which ratios show up in the patterns of the natural world.

1171:
Salah al-Din (Saladin), Kurdish Muslim warrior and commander in Egypt, overthrows the Fatimid dynasty; rise of the Ayyubid dynasty.

1175:
Mu'izz-ud-Din Muhammad (Muhammad of Ghur) embarks on the conquest of northern India. Honen Shonin founds Pure Land Buddhism.

1176:
The Battle of Legnano, won by the Lombard League, forces Frederick I (Barbarossa) to bow to the pope's sovereignty. At the Battle of Myriocephalum what's left of the Byzantines fail to take Anatolia from the Seljuk Turks.

1180:
Philip Augustus becomes ruler of France. He recaptures most of the western French territory previously taken by William the Conqueror from England and installs royal officials in the conquered regions. All this lays the foundations for modern France. The Minamoto leader Yoritomo leads an uprising in eastern Japan against the Taira, forces them from their capital, and becomes the first shogun.

1181:
St. Francis born (1181-1226). He will collide with Pope Innocent III by insisting that Francis's order imitate the poverty of Jesus. "Lord, make me an instrument of Your peace."

1184:
Tamar the Great rules Georgia, where commerce, culture, and industry proliferate.

1187:
Saladin defeats the Christians, who run out of water, at Hattin and takes Jerusalem. The Third Crusade is ordered and will be led by German Emperor Frederick Barbarossa (until he drowns while bathing in a shallow river), French King Philip II Augustus, and English King Richard the Lionheart. In 1192, Richard and Saladin sign the Treaty Ramla, agreeing that Muslims keep control of Jerusalem but that Christians can make pilgrimage there.

1200s:
Cahokia, a city of temple mounds, at its height in North America. The Tui Tonga monarchy builds coral platforms for ceremonial worship on the island of Tonga in the South Pacific. Incas in Peru settle around the growing settlement of Cuzco. As a consequence of the Concordat of Worms, European students with no intention of becoming priests can go to school, and education is offered in languages other than Latin. Literacy rises, and cathedral schools change into liberal arts universities. In Europe the cult of chivalry reveals its shadow in one Crusade after another.

1202:
Start of the Fourth Crusade (1202-1204), launched by Pope Innocent III and led by French and Flemish nobles. Leonardo Pisano writes the *Liber Abbaci*, the first popular treatise on mathematics, and popularizes the counting of numbers.

1204:
The Latern Edict decides against the Church Fathers in favor of "realists" who maintain that bread is literally turned into Christ's body: literalism takes hold of Christian thought and food becomes spiritualized. The fourth Crusade starts for Jerusalem but wrecks Constantinople instead.

1207:
Shota Rustaveli of Georgia writes *The Knight in the Panther's Skin*. Persian poet and mystic Jelalaldin Rumi (1207-1273) born. "Dance, when you're broken open. Dance, if you've torn the bandage off.

Dance in the middle of the fighting. Dance in your blood. Dance when you're perfectly free."

1208:
When Papal legate Peter de Castelnau is murdered, probably by an aid of Albigensian noble Raymond VI of Toulouse, Pope Innocent III proclaims a crusade against the Albigenses (ascetic Cathari spiritually descended from Gnostics and Manichaeans) near Albi in Southern France. This crusade, which continues until 1229, is led by Simon de Montfort, who when asked how to tell the heretics from the true believers says, "Kill them all. God will know his own."

1210:
Wolfram von Eschenbach writes *Parzival*, and Gottfried von Strassburg *Tristan und Isolde*.

1212:
Alfonso VIII of Castile beats the Muslim Almohades at the battle of Las Navas de Tolosa (Battle of Al-Uqab), weakening the Moors on the Iberian peninsula. The Children's Crusade; led first by Nicholas of Germany and later by Stephen of Cloyes, a French boy seeking to correct the mistakes of the corrupt elder Crusaders, thirty thousand believers of all ages wind up enslaved or in brothels.

1215:
The abusive King John Lackland is forced by revolting barons to agree to the Magna Carta at Runnymede to stop royal money demands made without the barons' consent and to require that all men be judged by a jury of peers in public courts rather than in courts privately owned by the Crown. An old story says King John was so angry he fell down and chewed on the carpet. The University of Paris receives a charter from the Vatican, marking the rise of universities as centers of knowledge increasingly under their own control.

1217:
The fifth Crusade heads toward Jerusalem, veers toward Cairo, runs

out of steam, dissipates, and retires.

1220:
Roger Bacon (1220-1292); he predicts powered transportation, calls for and performsexperimental science, and is the first Westerner to discuss gunpowder, a substance that will eventually make moats and thick city walls obsolete. "All sciences are connected; they lend each other material aid as parts of one great whole, each doing its own work, not for itself alone, but for the other parts; as the eye guides the body and the foot sustains it and leads it from place to place." Snorri Sturluson composes the *Poetic Edda*.

1223:
Rampaging Mongols engage in the longest cavalry raid in history—from Central Asia to the Caucasus—to defeat the Rus (people of Viking and Slavic blood: eventual Russians) at the Battle of the Kalka River.

1225:
Thomas Aquinas (1225-1274), the most influential Scholastic theologian. He believes along with Albertus Magnus in the contemplation of God through the natural order and not through disembodied revelation, thereby opening a road to the coming Scientific Revolution, although ultimate truths are revealed only by studying the revelations of the Bible. His two greatest works are the *Summa contra Gentiles* and the unfinished *Summa Theologica*, both of which attempt to justify Christian faith on rational principles. His philosophy emphasizes human reason, personal salvation, the perpetuation of Adam's sin via reproduction, the mutual influence of Plato and Aristotle (whose works now reemerge in Western Europe thanks to Arab scholarship), the compatibility of Aristotle and Catholicism. "Beware the man of a single book."

1228:
The sixth Crusade.

1233:
The "Excommunicamus" of Pope Gregory IX ignites the Inquisition, which will be first employed mainly in southern France, northern Italy, and Germany. Here is how it plays out: Ferdinand and Isabella establish the Spanish Inquisition (1478). Tomas Tourquemada, Grand Inquisitor, forces Spanish Jews to convert or be expelled (1492). Forced conversion of Moors (1499). Inquisition in Portugal (1531). Protestants burned at the stake in Spain (1543). Spanish Inquisition finally abolished (1834).

1235:
After defeating King Sosso, warrior leader Sundiata (Sunjata) Keita founds the Mali Empire to liberate the Mandinkas in West Africa. This empire will extend from the Atlantic to Nigeria and will regularly host tribal representatives at its meetings. He also creates an oral but binding constitution, parts of which still exist in the written constitution of Mali.

1240:
Russian Alexander Nevsky defeats the Swedes at a great battle on the Neva River. However, Mongols enter the state of Kiev and create a new state on the Volga River, from where they rule Russia for two centuries. The Grand Duchy of Moscow will eventually emerge (early 1300s) and defeat the Mongol Khans (1480). Sundiata controls the Ghana Empire (Wagadugu) until the Mali Empire absorbs it.

1241:
Hansa (guilds) in Lubeck and Hamburg associate for trade and mutual protection after Henry the Lion rebuilds Lübeck: origins of the Hanseatic League that will dominate trade in coastal northern Europe until the 1600s. Marauding Mongols defeat the Germans in Silesia, invade Poland and Hungary, and then withdraw from Europe when their leader Subetai gets word that Mongol leader Ogodai has died. They never again enter central Europe.

1244:
The Muslims recapture Jerusalem. This time is not taken back until 1917, not even during the seventh Crusade of 1248.

1250:
Her husband having died, Shagrat al-Durr takes upon herself the title of Sultan and regroups the Egyptian army to take Damietta back from Frankish Crusaders. Throughout Europe, homosexuality and bisexuality, once tolerated everywhere, are now treated as capital crimes because of Christian influence. This repressive agenda coincides with Roman Catholic consolidation of control over reproduction.

1258:
Henry III of England is forced to agree to the Provisions of Oxford by which he will share his power with a council of barons instead of extorting money from them. The Great Council formed to monitor this will evolve into Parliament. With support from the pope Henry breaks the agreement, and the barons go to war against him under Simon de Montfort. They capture Henry and place him under house arrest, but his son Prince Edward rallies a force to beat Montfort and free his father. Mongols under Hulegu sack Baghdad and put an end to the Abbasid Caliphate and wreck the canal system that kept the Tigris-Euphrates valley agriculturally rich for five thousand years. They also level the House of Wisdom. "You ask me about the sack of Baghdad," writes a survivor; "it was so horrible there are no words to describe it. I wish I had died earlier and not seen how these fools destroyed these treasures of knowledge and learning. I thought I understood the world, but this holocaust is so strange and pointless that I am struck dumb. The revolution of time and its decisions have defeated reason and knowledge."

1260-77:
German mystic Meister Eckhart (1260-1328), who will be done to death by the Inquisition. "Spirituality is not to be learned by flight from the world," he writes, "or by running away from things, or by turning solitary and going apart from the world. Rather, we must

learn an inner solitude wherever or with whomsoever we may be. We must learn to penetrate things and find God there." He also writes that an earnest prayer is worth all the works in Christendom.

1270:
Louis IX of France leaves for the Eighth Crusade when Jafa and Antioch fall to the Muslims, but he dies in Tunisia. Edward I leads a Ninth Crusade on the heels of the failed Eighth. Having some respect for the barons' rights and influence, he establishes Parliament as a feudal court for the king but not yet an organ of representative government. The Church forbids alchemical research.

1274:
Thomas Aquinas finishes the *Summa Theologica*. It includes five reasons why God exists.

1275:
Marco Polo is in the service of the Great Khan of the Mongol Empire until 1292. His reports will inspire Spanish attempts to hunt for an Asian land of gold: hence Columbus.

1276:
Architect and painter Giotto di Mondone (1276-1337), the most important painter of the later Middle Ages, begins the modern style in painting. He is a naturalist whose works include depictions of Christ's entrance into Jerusalem and of the death of St. Francis.

1281:
A Mongol fleet is driven away from Japan by the *kamikaze*, "the divine winds" (typhoons). Eyeglasses invented in Italy.

1285:
William of Occam (or Ockham) (1285-1349); anticipating Martin Luther and disagreeing with Aquinas, he denies any inherent connection between faith and reason, undercutting the rationalistic assumptions of the twelfth and thirteenth centuries, and he also denies any archetypes or Ideas beyond human-invented categories

(Nominalism). "Occam's Razor" declares that when a simple scientific explanation competes with a complex one, then, all else being equal, the simple one is probably the better one. The Razor severs science and religion so completely that the two develop separately, especially once the Renaissance starts.

1291:
Muslims take Acre and end the Crusades, all nine of which have accomplished nothing constructive while wasting lives, fortunes, and cities.

1300s:
Osman I founds the Ottoman dynasty in Turkey. The Incas expand their empire throughout the central Andes. Hawaii develops class structure as a result of economic growth from agriculture. The spinning wheel is invented.

1300:
Duns Scotus delivers lectures that will be published as the Ordinatio; he emphasizes the particularity or "thisness" (*haecceity*) of things apart from their higher reality as Platonic forms. The Ife culture of West Africa produces unique bronze, stone, and terracotta sculptures (since 900 CE); the Yoruba people here form art guilds that provide economic and philosophical hubs of culture. "The king's palace that got burnt added beauty to it" - Yoruba proverb.

RENAISSANCE:

1304:
Italian man of letters Francesco Petrarca (Petrarch) (1304-1374), devotee of "learned piety"and first man of the Renaissance. "I wish to go beyond the fire that burns me." The classical manuscripts he collects, some translated by Arab scholars and some culled from Byzantium as its scholars fled the rampaging Turks, combine with the resurrected arts of poetry and rhetoric and sculpture to feed a new liberal humanism loosed throughout Europe.

1307:
Jealous of their power and wealth, Philip IV of France has Grand Master Jacques de Molay of the Knights Templars arrested and forces the pope to suppress their order.

1309:
Under Clement V, the papacy moves from Rome to Avignon, beginning the Church's "Babylonian Captivity." For most of the fourteenth century the papacy remains subordinate to French authority, and the majority of cardinals and popes are French. Dante's White Guelph party falls out of power after calling for more freedom from the rule of the Papacy and he is exiled for life from his native Florence. During this exile writes the *Commedia* (later called *The Divine Comedy*), a beautifully complete picture of the Christian-Aristotelian worldview, finishing it in 1321 and dying two months later. "In the middle of the journey of our life, I came to my senses in a dark forest, for I had lost the straight path...."

1314:
At Bannockburn, Edward II's deployment of his army blocks his archers and their longbows, allowing Robert the Bruce to defeat the English at the Battle of Bannockburn ("Let us do or die!") and promote Scottish independence from England.

1315:
Bad weather, crop failures, and a Great Famine sweep northwestern Europe, and unsanitary conditions and malnutrition increase the death rate. Even after the revival of farming weather disasters recur. This bitter mixture of war, famine, hunger, and plague in the Late Middle Ages reduces the population of Europe by half.

1325:
The Aztecs found their capital city of Tenochtitlan (now the site of Mexico City) on an island in Lake Texcoco. Peak of Islamic culture in Spain.

1336:
The Vijayanagar Empire in India founded by Harihara I resists incursions by Islam. On Mont Ventoux, Petrarch has a revelation of inwardness while going through Augustine's *Confessions:* "People are moved," he reads, "to wonder by mountain peaks, by vast waves of the sea, by broad waterfalls on rivers, by the all-embracing extent of the ocean, by the revolutions of the stars. But in themselves they are uninterested." Signaling the opening of both modernity and humanism, Petrarch concludes, "Nothing is admirable but the soul." This call to introspection runs forward through pietism and Romanticism to the birth of psychology, existentialism, and process philosophy.

1337:
France comes to the aid of Scotland against England, so Edward III of England declares war on Philip VI of France, and the Hundred Years War begins. The three greatest battles of the war are fought at Crecy (1346), Poitiers (1356) and Agincourt (1415). The French are defeated in most of the battles.

1340:
The Songhai in Gao, West Africa, gain independence from the declining Mali Empire and begin their own thousand-year empire.

1346:
Probably for the first time in Europe, gunpowder is used (in bombards fired to scare horses) by the English during the Battle of Crecy, where Edward III of England and his son Edward the Black Prince swarm into Normandy. This battle also demonstrates the longbow's superiority over the crossbow and the uselessness of armor: unknown to most, the days of armored chivalry have ended.

1347-1349:
The Little Ice Age, until 1850. The Black Death, a combination of bubonic and pneumonic plague, arrives in a Genoese trading vessel from Crimea and ravages economically depressed Europe. Flagellants whip themselves to appease divine wrath. About forty

million people die of the plague anyway: roughly a third of Europe. Clothes left from the dead are made into rag paper to feed the printing press, literacy, and, ultimately, the Renaissance.

1348:
Giovanni Boccaccio (1313-1375) begins writing the *Decameron*, a collection of stories about love, sex, adventure, and trickery told by seven ladies and three men embarking on a journey into the country to escape the Black Death. Boccaccio's work is the first realistic rather than moralistic English literature written in narrative prose. Between now and 1400 an anonymous monk writes *The Cloud of Unknowing*.
"Let that meek darkness be your whole mind and like a mirror to you. For I want your thought of self to be as naked and simple as your thought of God, so that you may be with God in spirit without fragmentation and scattering of your mind."

1356:
At the Battle of Poitiers, where the longbow prevails again, John II of France is captured by the Black Prince and held captive in England. His son Charles (later Charles V), who acts as regent, is called the Dauphin due to the recently obtained Dauphine area of France. The homes of French peasants are pillaged and burned. The Golden Bull promulgated by Charles IV of the Holy Roman Empire states that the "king of the Romans" is to be elected only by a majority vote of seven primogeniturely entitled princes, a claim that nullifies papal claims to intervene in elections. Furthermore, the Bull encourages the prince-electors to combine their holdings into sovereign states and gives them regalian rights over mining, coinage, and the courts. All this will encourage the organization of nation-states.

1357:
The Treaty of Berwick ends the Wars of Scottish Independence.

1358:
Economic hardship in France and the king's captivity in England trigger an uprising of the "Jacquerie" (in honor of French peasant

Jacques Bonhomme) north of Paris. The peasants burn castles, murder their lords, rape their lords' wives, and take advantage of the political confusion by attempting to reform the government. Aristocrats then massacre the rebels.

1360s:
Bonds are invented in Florence to help pay for the ongoing wars between Italian cities.

1368:
After the Battle of Lake Poyang (1363), where the Yuan, allied to the Mongols, fought the Wu, Han, and Ming, in over a hundred fighting ships sailing near Nanchang, the Mongols are driven out of China by Zhu Yuanzhang, the peasant warlord. He founds the Ming Dynasty known for restoring trade between the new capitol, Beijing, and the south; magnificent Ming pottery; a Forbidden City complex; an enormous multi-volume encyclopedia; and transoceanic voyages by huge junks that open transoceanic trade routes centuries before Columbus (most of this happens under the Emperor Yongle).

1369:
Tamerlane (Timur the Lame) overthrows the Khan and takes control of the Mongols.

1377:
William Langland takes a poke at the aristocrats with his poem "Piers Plowman."

1378:
Elected by French cardinals threatened by a Roman mob, the Italian pope Urban VI, who might have been insane, makes himself so difficult to get along with that the cardinals change their minds and elect the French antipope Clement VII, who removes himself to Avignon and initiates a Western Schism.

1380s:
Foundation of the Kingdom of Kongo in Zaire in central Africa.

Organized by villages and larger provinces, it observes matrilineal descent, communal land ownership, choice of the "king" by senior electors, a tax on trade, and shells used for currency. Despite occasional uprisings, invasions, and civil war, the kingdom endures until 1914, when Portugal abolishes native rule.

1381:
In one sense the Black Death in England helps the peasants economically—those who survive it, anyway—by causing a shortage of labor, a freeing of serfs, a rise in salary, and a decrease in rent. But the aristocratic class passes legislation that lowers wages to the pre-plague level and levies a tax for every person in England, thereby causing the Peasants' Revolt. The peasants, led by Wat Tyler, march into London, murder the lord chancellor and treasurer, and are met by Richard II, who promises the abolition of serfdom and a lower rent. After they disperse, Richard has them followed and killed. Tamerlane takes Persia.

1382:
Ignoring protests by the clergy, John Wyclif and his followers translate the Latin Bible into English.

1387:
Using clever battle tactics, Sir John Hawkwood and his White Company of condottiere (mercenaries) stop ambitious Milanese Duke Gian Galleazzo Visconti, who has rolled up most of northern Italy, from taking Florence, which helps preserve the political freedom that breeds humanism and the Renaissance ("rebirth") fed by the cultural and financial diversity of the unconquered Italian city-states. Margaret I rules Denmark and Norway (and Sweden in 1398).

1393:
Christian mystic Julian of Norwich completes her *Revelations of Divine Love*. "If there is anywhere on earth a lover of God who is always kept safe, I know nothing of it, for it was not shown to me. But this was shown: that in falling and rising again we are always kept in that same precious love."

1400s:
The Engaruka community farms in Tanzania. The Kingdom of Great Zimbabwe in southern Africa profits from the gold trade. The Tonga build a major ceremonial center at Mu'a on the largest island in the Tongatapu Group (South Pacific Ocean). Widespread cultivation of wet taro on the Hawaiian Islands. German scholar and visionary Nicholas of Cusa (1401-1464); he makes spectacles with concave lenses, regards the pulse as an indicator of health, believes that the Earth spins on its axis and circles the Sun, and regards stars as other suns. Chaucer completes the Canterbury Tales. An unknown author writes the *Aurora Consurgens*, a conversation between the alchemist seeking wisdom and the goddess Sophia.

1404:
Vergerio's *Concerning Liberal Studies*, the first such treatise.

1405:
Supported by the Yongle Emperor, Admiral Zheng He of China voyages around Southeast Asia and, eventually, out to India, Arabia, and Africa. He commands three hundred and seventeen ships.

1409:
Cardinals meet in Pisa to try to end the Western Schism. They elect Alexander V as pope, but because current popes Gregory XII of Rome and Benedict XIII of Avignon refuse to be deposed, there are now three rivals for the papacy instead of two.

1415:
Inspired by Wyclif, John Hus travels to the Council of Constance to propose reforms for the Church. Despite a promise of safe passage, he is tried for heresy and burned. To claim what he regards as ancestral lands, Henry V of England goes to war against France, winning Harfleur and then the Battle of Agincourt with the assistance of the longbow and a cavalry-drenching rain. Richard the Earl of Cambridge (grandson of Edward III through his fifth son, Edmund Duke of York) is executed by Henry V for plotting to put Edmund

Mortimer on the throne.

1417:
The Council of Constance, the largest Church meeting in medieval history, boots out the current three popes and elects Martin V. It also replaces the papal monarchy with a conciliar government that recognizes a frequently convening council of prelates as a papal authority. Henry V executes Sir John Oldcastle, the leader of the Lollards, and, in Shakespeare's plays, the humorous core of the character Falstaff. Henry begins a conquest of Normandy; he will make a peace treaty with Charles VI of France and marry his daughter Catherine of Valois, events idealized in Shakespeare's play *Henry V*.

1418:
Portugal's Prince Henry "The Navigator" sponsors the exploration of Africa's coast. His captains will return with slaves and gold and set a precedent for the institutionalized slavery of Africans. The Portuguese invention of the carrack, a vessel fitted with square sails for downwind sailing and lateen sails for tacking, will open the entire world to exploration by sailing ship. (Columbus's ships are carracks.)

1419:
The Hussite Wars begin as a religious struggle between Hussites outraged over Hus's murder and the Roman Catholic Church, a national struggle between Czechs and Germans, and a social struggle between the peasant and the landed classes. John Zuzka will equip the Hussites with cannon-carrying armored wagons: a forerunner of the tank.

1419-50:
Korea prospers under King Sejong, who introduces an official Korean script.

1420:
The artist Filippo Brunelleschi begins work on the Duomo in Florence. Realizing that if ships could get around Africa to the Far

East (harder to reach since the demise of the Mongol Empire) they could avoid the Ottoman Empire, Henry (John's son) "The Navigator" of Portugal orders a navigation center built at Sagres. This will oversee the Age of Exploration.

1427:
Thomas á Kempis writes *The Imitation of Christ*, a manual for living a spiritual life of the interior. Written originally in Latin, it is translated into other European languages for the lay audience. The only sacrament suggested to the reader is the Eucharist. "Wherever you go, there you are."

1431-33:
Zheng He embarks on his seventh and final voyage, sailing out to Africa's east coast. The voyages end because the Xuande Emperor does not see their value.

1431:
Joan of Arc is condemned as a witch—voices of dead saints had told her to kick the English out of France and restore the Dauphin to power—and burned at the stake at Rouen by the English. Having been put on the throne by her military prowess, French King Charles does nothing to help her.

1434:
The Medici banking family runs the government of Florence. Cosimo Medici, who encourages scholarship, also has the novel idea of taxing those best able to pay. Once the Medicis make banking respectable by moving it out of the Jewish ghetto (for religious reasons Jews could lend with interest but strict Christians could not), their money will fund some of the greatest works of the Renaissance. Having discovered a new people south of the Sahara, Portugal brings black slaves to Lisbon. Columbus will see some of them but only his eyes will bleed.

1435:
Leone Alberti writes *Della Pictura*, in which he applies the laws of

mathematics to painting and thereby creates linear perspective. He also writes the first book on cryptography.

1436:
Sultans of Kilwa on the East African coast initiate a grand building program. German metal worker Johannes Gutenberg experiments with printing with moveable type. This, the first attempt anywhere to apply mass production with standardized and interchangeable parts, will also break down the traditional confinement and hoarding of what should be public knowledge. Unfortunately, Gutenberg enters into a partnership with a man named Faust who loans him the money to set up the printing press but then sues to recover his money and the press.

1438:
Pachacuti founds the Inca Empire in Peru.

1440:
Nicholas of Cusa's *On Learned Ignorance*.

1444:
Portuguese sailors reach Senegal.

1448:
Christian I establishes the Oldenburgs in Denmark.

1450:
At the Battle of Formigny in Normandy, English longbowmen face the French artillery of Charles VII's reorganized army and take heavy losses. In England, Jack Cade leads a band of farmers in a brief rebellion to protest taxes levied to pay for the Hundred Years' War. (In *Henry VI*, Shakespeare will make fun of Cade by having one of his followers suggest, "First thing we do, let's kill all the lawyers.")

1450s:
Building in Great Zimbabwe, southern Africa, at its height. Inca city

of Machu Picchu founded on a high ridge above the Urubamba River in Peru. Florence is a center of Renaissance arts and learning under the Medicis. During this period of rebirth, classical manuscripts and future hopes of achievement, Copernican heights and Age of Exploration breadths, Shakespeare and Cervantes, Magellan and Michelangelo, printing press and magnetic compass, music and poetry, sculpture, painting, linear perspective, soaring architecture, and scientific achievement all come of age in Europe and beyond as Middle Ages and Modernity collide.

1452:
Engineer, inventor, and artist Leonardo da Vinci (1452-1519); he will paint, sculpt, make music, study plants, speculate about human flight, and design tanks and other military machines for the despotic Duke of Milan, although he suppresses the design for a submarine. "The greatest deception men suffer is from their own opinions."

1453:
With heavy cannon Muslim Turks (Ottomans) under Mehmed II smash down the walls of Constantinople and kill Constantine XI, ending the Byzantine Empire and the Middle Ages and inaugurating the Ottoman Empire and Islamic rule of the eastern Mediterranean for five centuries. The pope gets nowhere trying to rally another army. The idea of crusading finally dies. Nationalism begins to replace feudalism. In the Battle of Castillon, the French king Charles VII captures Bordeaux in the southwest of France and finally ends the Hundred Years War after the withdrawal of Burgundy from an alliance with England. All England has gotten from this long war is Calais.

1455:
The Portuguese reach Gambia. The Gutenberg Bible sees print. Henry VI of England recovers from madness long enough to reclaim his throne and start the Wars of the Roses between Plantagenets fighting for the throne. The two sides of the war are Henry's family at Lancaster (whose emblem is the red rose) and the House of York

(white rose). Yorkist Richard III gains the kingship for a short time. A huge temple dedicated to the Aztec war god Huitzilopochtli towers in Tenochtitlan. Henry of Portugal forbids the kidnapping of blacks from Africa.

1462-1505:
Reign of Ivan III (the Great) as the first Russian czar and Grand Prince of Muscovy. Over twenty-three years he annexes all Russian principalities between Poland-Lithuania and Moscow. The Portuguese visit and map Sierra Leone in West Africa.

1463:
Italian priest Marsilio Ficino finishes the first complete translation of Plato's writing into Latin. As Scholasticism degenerates into arid doctrinal arguments, Ficino founds the Plato Academy in Florence with funds provided by Cosimo de Medici.

1468:
The Songhai Empire is founded when Sunni Ali Ber takes Timbuktu from the nomadic Tuaregs.

1469:
Ferdinand of Aragon marries Isabella I of Castile, and the two Spanish kingdoms end their conflict but remain separate powers. Guru Nanak (1469-1539), the First Guru and founder of Sikhism; he will oppose idolatry and the caste system and blend Islamic and Hindu theology.

1470:
Sir Thomas Malory finishes *Morte d'Arthur*. Ficino finishes the first Latin translation of Plato's dialogues.

1476:
Printed texts appear thanks to William Caxton, who brings to England the German method of printing with movable type.

1478:
Egged on by Ferdinand and Isabella, Pope Sixtus V issues a bull authorizing kings and queens to appoint inquisitors to deal with offenders against the church, thereby launching the Spanish Inquisition to discover and punish converted Jews (and later Muslims) whose faith is insincere.

1482:
Girolamo Savonarola starts his preaching against paganism, worldly pursuits, and spiritual degeneration. Portuguese explorers find gold in Ghana and built a fort at Elmina ("The Mine") to trade ivory, gold, and slaves; by the 1800s other European powers will build similar forts there for similar reasons.

1483:
After he retires, eighth shogun Ashikaga Yoshimasa promotes the Higashiyama Period of Japanese high culture, which includes the Noh play, the tea ceremony, flower arrangement, and the Silver Pavilion Temple (Ginkakuji) in Kyoto.

1485:
The War of the Roses ends when Lancastrian Henry VII, aided by alienated Yorkists, becomes the first Tudor king of England and Wales after defeating Richard III at the Battle of Bosworth. He marries Elizabeth (thereby joining the houses Lancaster and York), reestablishes royal power over the aristocracy, ends the funding of foreign wars, and reforms finances. Parliament becomes a stable part of the government system. Botticelli paints *Birth of Venus*.

1486:
Inquisitor Heinrich Kramer writes *Hammer of the Witches* (*Malleus Maleficarum*) as a guide for prosecuting and punishing the thousands of women condemned to death for witchcraft. Pico della Mirandola's *Oration on the Dignity of Man* compares human energy and worth to that of the god Prometheus.

1490:
Da Vinci sketches *Vitruvian Man*.

1492:
Spanish forces take Granada (in Spain) from the Muslims, after which Ferdinand and Isabella expel all Jews from Spain—with help from the Dominican monk and Grand Inquisitor Tomas de Torquemada—and seek overseas expansion. A day later, Isabella sends Christopher Columbus and three ships named after prostitutes to find a westward route to the Indies. Columbus lands in the Bahama Islands, Cuba, and Hispaniola, becoming the first European to reach the Americas since the Vikings. He discovers the American mainland during the last two of his four voyages: 1498 and 1502. During these voyages he subjugates the native Taino people, who starve, finds himself under arrest for swindling colonists onto Hispañola, and mails crazy letters to the Spanish Crown about how Earth is not round but shaped like a woman's breast. His two obsessions are gold and the coming end of the world. "...They are guileless," he writes about the indigenous, "and so generous of all they have that no one would believe it who had not seen it. They never refuse anything that is asked for. On the contrary, they even offer it themselves, and exhibit so much loving kindness that they would give their very hearts. Whether it be something of value or of little worth that is offered them, they are content." The flow of American gold and silver through Spain, the conquest of Mexico and Peru, and military superiority make Spain the most powerful state in Europe.

1493:
Alexander VI writes a bull that proposes to give the New World to Spain and India to Portugal. Adventuring nobleman Michele de Cuneo sees Taino mothers so frightened of being enslaved by Columbus that they take their infants from the breast, leave them on the ground, and flee in terror. Paracelsus (Philippus Aureolus Theophrastus Bombastus von Hohenheim)(1493-1541), physician, mystic, astrologer, and alchemist, who teaches that an *archeus* principle emanating from the World Soul animates all matter. Foreshadowing *Frankenstein*, he claims to have devised a homuncu-

lus and then destroyed it because it held no soul.

1494:
The Italian Wars (1494 to 1559) start as dynastic struggles in Italy and swell to include other countries.

1497:
Henry VII sends Giovanni Caboto (John Cabot) to explore North America, and he visits Newfoundland. Amerigo Vespucci (Americus Vespuccius) voyages to the West Indies and South America. Portuguese sailor Vasco da Gama rounds the Cape of Good Hope and locates India, from where he returns home with half his men dead of scurvy but with a ship laden with spices to sell.

1498:
Da Vinci finishes painting the *Last Supper*. Portuguese explorers reach Mozambique. They also try for Cameroon, but malaria resists colonization efforts until the 1870s, when an antidote is found.

1499:
Amerigo Vespucci names an island Venezuela ("Little Venice") and the name drifts to the mainland.

Modernity:
Eradigm Big Machine

1500s:
French exploration in Canada begins. Lead pencils scratch away in England. Plus and minus symbols appear in European arithmetic. Nilotic-speaking Luo people from eastern South Sudan establish Buganda. The Songhai Empire in West Africa enters its period of greatest expansion under Askia Mohammed Turré. Trade encourages the growth of the Hausa states in West Africa. The Portuguese visit Madagascar. Shaybani Khan unites the Uzbeks and conquers Samarkand, Herat, and Bukhara. Birth and career of Florentine artist, musician, goldsmith, painter, and sculptor Benvenuto Cellini (1500-1571), who will be tried repeatedly for sodomy.

1501:
The first black slaves in America arrive at the Spanish colony of Santo Domingo. The Safavid Dynasty rules Iran under Shi'a law and expands well beyond it into Iraq, Armenia, Pakistan, and Asia Minor (until 1736).

1503:
In southern Italy, at the Battle of Cerignola, a smaller Spanish force armed with arquebuses (primitive rifles) defeats a larger French force in the first battle won by force of gunpowder small arms.

1504:
Michelangelo completes the statue *David*.

1506:
Da Vinci paints the *Mona Lisa*. Tatars (Turkic people previously conquered by Mongols) emanating from the Crimean Khanate (1441-1783) invade Poland and are crushed.

1506-1612:
Construction of the basilica of indulgence-funded St Peter's in Rome.

1507:
After reading Amerigo Vespucci's descriptions of the New World, which he believed to be an unexplored continent (it was, by Europeans), German mapmaker Martin Waldseemüller names America in his honor. *Amerigo* goes back to words that mean "power," "universal," and "labor."

1509:
Desiderius Erasmus writes *In Praise of Folly*. "In the land of the blind, the one-eyed man is king."

1510
Safavid Shah Ismael I beats the forces of Shaybani Khan at the Battle of Marv, after which Ismael coats the skull of Shaybani with gold and uses it as a drinking goblet. Garci Rodríguez de Montalvo of Spain finishes *The Exploits of Esplandian*, a novel about the conquest of an island called California ruled by a powerful black-skinned queen dressed in gold armor. Although no European had set eyes on California, the name will stick there after Cortez tries unsuccessfully to land his men there. Having been warned in a dream by

one of the novel's characters that publishing the book would kill him, Montalvo publishes it anyway and dies soon after.

1512:
Michelangelo finishes painting the Sistine Chapel ceiling.

1513:
Spanish explorer Vasco Balboa sights the Pacific Ocean. Juan Ponce de Leon, Governor of Puerto Rico, discovers the coast of Florida during a slave-hunting trip. Machiavelli completes *The Prince*, a book of ruthlessly pragmatic power politics.

1516:
Sir Thomas More publishes *Utopia* ("Nowhere"), a book about a fictional community led by the principles of reason. The Ottoman Empire continues its expansion by forcing back the Mamluks from Arabia, Egypt, and the Levant.

1517:
In Wittenberg, Martin Luther unwittingly begins the Reformation by publishing his Ninety-Five Theses objecting to religious corruption and the selling of indulgences (documents guaranteeing remission of sins and relocation of dead souls from Purgatory to Heaven) to fund construction of St. Peter's Basilica. We are not saved by works, Luther storms, but through faith in God's grace. Luther's views will be spread all over Germany, a land of rebelling lords and knights, by the printing press. "Everything that is done in this world is done by hope."

1519:
Huldrych Zwingli begins the Reformation in Switzerland with his lectures on the New Testament. Stung by the Reformation, the Catholic Church turns away from Hellenized practice and thought and seeks a new world- and flesh-denying conservatism. Hernando Cortez lands in "New Spain" (Mexico) from Cuba and founds the city of Veracruz. He burns his own ships to keep his men from returning to Cuba. Then, boasting about his ruthlessness in letters to

King Charles of Spain, he enters the Aztec capital Tenochtitlan preparatory to bringing down the Aztecs and renaming their country New Spain. Portuguese explorer Ferdinand Magellan finds the Strait and names the Pacific Ocean and circumnavigates the world. He will die in the Philippines. Hernando de Soto charts the Gulf of Mexico.

1521:
Condottieri Prospero Colonna successfully defends Milan against French incursions; new city fortifications that take guns into account will force urban planners to build up instead of out. The Ming keep the Portuguese from swarming into China.

1524:
Peasants rise in revolt in German-speaking countries and are massacred by the aristocracy. Giovanni da Verrazzano explores the North Atlantic coast of North America.

1525:
Spain conquers "New Granada" (Colombia).

1526:
Armed with artillery, Zahir Muhammad Babur takes Delhi, then Agra, and establishes the Muslim-ruled Mughal Empire in India. As is the case with the Crimean Khanate, the Mughal rulers are descendants of Genghis Khan.

1528:
Castiglione's *The Courtier*.

1529:
During the first Siege of Vienna Ottoman forces under Suleiman the Magnificent, including elite janissaries, are thrown back by farmers, peasants, and residents of the city, who organize to halt a century of Ottoman aggression along the Danube. The Ethiopian-Adal war breaks out between the Ethiopian Empire and the Adal Sultinate of Somali, who sack and loot but who are finally routed.

1531-33:
As with Cortez among the Aztecs in Mexico, Spanish soldier Francisco Pizarro locates and levels the Inca Empire in Peru.

1532:
Michelangelo meets nobleman Tommaso Dei Cavalieri and writes thirty passionate poems about him. In Peru the Inca Empire at its height, but the Spaniards are coming.

1534:
French explorer Jacques Cartier discovers the Gulf of St. Lawrence; on a later voyage he will mishear a Native word—possibly *kanata*, "village"—and call a nearby region "Canada." He also claims Quebec for France. Determined to divorce even though it's against the pope's wishes, Henry VIII of England breaks with Rome: his Act of Supremacy separates the Church of England from the Roman Catholic Church. Thomas Moore, a Catholic, is beheaded for failing to recognize Henry's religious authority. The Ottomans take Baghdad. At the Münster Rebellion Anabaptists—Radical Reformers who restrict baptism to adults—try to take over and set up a religious government. Anabaptists are forerunners of the Amish and Mennonites.

1535:
Spanish ex-soldier Ignatius of Loyola's *Spiritual Exercises*. In 1540 he establishes the Society of Jesus (the Jesuits: "God's soldiers") to send men to remote places to make converts.

1536:
John Calvin establishes Reformed and Presbyterian versions of Protestantism in Switzerland, writes *Institutes of the Christian Religion*, and teaches that only a predestined elite will be saved. Calvin's call to use work in the world as a holy vocation eventually combines with puritanical strivings toward self-renunciation to serve the ends of capitalism: Max Weber's Protestant work ethic. Danish and Norwegian Reformations. Michelangelo's *Last Judgment*. Queen Anne Boleyn beheaded, supposedly for treason to England

but in actuality for not giving Henry VIII a male heir.

1541:
Francisco de Orellana charts and names the Amazon, where he sees tribes apparently led by women, reminding him of the Greek legend. The Ottomans eat Hungary.

1542:
A storm-driven Portuguese ship makes the first European visit to Japan, whose inhabitants study the sailors' firearms. The Spanish Crown makes Peru a viceroyalty, with Lima its capital. The French come to Madagascar.

1543:
Andreas Vesalius updates Galen with his illustrated anatomy book *On the Structure of the Human Body*. The Portuguese trade with the Japanese. In his *On the Revolutions of the Heavenly Spheres*, which he dedicates to the pope, Nicholas Copernicus demonstrates mathematically that the earth revolves around the sun. He is directly inspired by Neoplatonism's cosmos animated by simple and elegant forms overseen by a sunlike God and by the Pythagorean love of sacred numbers. Not realizing what Copernicus has done to wreck the traditional worldview, with the cosmos centered on humanity, the Church supports his work until the Reformation. "To know that we know what we know, and to know that we do not know what we do not know, that is true knowledge." On the day he dies he is shown the first published copy of *On the Revolutions*.

1545-63:
At the Council of Trent, Italy, the Catholics attempt to head off the Protestants by reforming the church from within, starting the Counter-Reformation led by the Jesuits. In time both Reformation and Catholic reform will turn against science, the flesh, and the feminine with ever more repressive strength until the obvious plurality of religions and perspectives deflates religious absolutism in all but the most fanatical.

1546:
Henry VIII launches the growth of England's naval power by ordering lots of ships built.

1547:
Ivan IV "the Terrible" takes power in Russia as its first tsar. Japanese pirates raid along the coasts of China, and in three years Mongols invade by land.

1550:
In Spain, former slaveowner Bartolomeo de las Casas stands up for indigenous rights. The church tries to figure out of Native people have souls. Vasari's *Lives of the Artists*.

1555:
In his Bull *Cum nimis absurdum*, Pope Paul IV (1555-1559) renews all previous anti-Jewish legislation, then installs a ghetto in Rome. Jews are forced to wear a special cap and forbidden to own real estate or to practice medicine on Christians. Communities aren't allowed more than one synagogue, and Jews in all the papal states must lock themselves in each night. French astrologer Michel Nostradamus begins writing his prophecies.

1556:
In *De Re Metallica* Georgius Agricola deals with the art of smelting and refining metals. Having embraced the Reformation and refused to recant, University of Padua student Pomponio Algerio is boiled in oil by the Inquisition.

1558:
Queen "Bloody Mary" I (called so for her burning of Protestants) dies, and Elizabeth I of England is crowned; under her reign Jesuit Priests and Catholics are oppressed. The word *Puritan* begins to circulate, referring to people who feel the Reformation won't be finished until the pope is rejected, the monasteries dissolved, Mass abolished, and the *Book of Common Prayer* imposed on everyone. Polymath Johann Battista della Porta's *Natural Magic*.

1562-98:
French Wars of Religion between Catholics and Huguenots (French Calvinist Protestants).

1563:
A plague outbreak in England.

1564:
William Shakespeare (1564-1616) born. Christopher Marlowe (1564-1593) born. Galileo Galilei (1564-1642) born.

1565:
Bernardino Telesio's *On the Nature of Things according to their Own Principles* argues ahead of the empiricist philosophers that the senses are the source of scientific knowledge.

1566-1648:
The Eighty Years' War, with the Netherlands revolting successfully against Spain.

1568:
Gerardus Mercator devises the Mercator map.

1568-1600:
A period of national unification in Japan when Oda Nobunaga captures the capital at Kyoto.

1569:
Polish-Lithuanian Commonwealth established as a prototypal monarchical commonwealth equipped with a legislature and laws for religious tolerance.

1570-1610:
The Kanem-Bornu kingdom in what will become Chad in western Central Africa at its most powerful after an alliance with the Ottomans brings it firearms, military training, and Arab camel troops.

1571:
Don John of Austria smashes the Ottoman fleet at the Battle of Lepanto. Invading Tatars of the Crimean Khanate fight the Russians, burning Moscow, but are eventually repelled by Cossacks, the cowboys of Ukraine and Russia. German astronomer Johannes Kepler (1571-1630) born.

1572:
Massacre of St. Bartholomew's Day in Paris, where thousands of Huguenots are killed by Roman Catholic assassins. The Peace of Constantinople ends Turkish attacks on Europe. Luís de Camões of Portugal publishes *The Lusiads*. Tycho Brahe notices a supernova whose presence disrupts the idea that the heavens are eternal. Theologian John Donne (1572-1631): "No man is an island, / Entire of itself. / Each is a piece of the continent, / A part of the main...."

1575:
In Mikawa Province, Takeda Katsuyori leads a force of samurai cavalry against Okudaira Sadamasa, whose firearm-equipped troops respond with continual volley fire, cutting Takeda's force to pieces and ending the age of chivalry in Japan.

1573-1620:
Reign of emperor Wan Li in China: a period of superbly executed paintings and porcelain-making. Imperial kilns at Jingdezhen disgorge vast quantities of china.

1576:
Setting out to find a northwest passage to China, English explorer Martin Frobisher reaches the Canadian coast, and Frobisher Bay is named after him. Mughal emperor Akbar conquers Bangladesh.

1577-1580:
English seaman Sir Francis Drake sails round the world. Teresa of Avila writes *The Interior Castle*. "It is foolish to think that we will enter heaven without entering into ourselves."

1579:
The northern Netherlands organize into the Union of Utrecht, and the southern Netherlands into the Union of Arras. Thomas North provides Shakespeare with play material by translating Plutarch into English. John of the Cross writes *The Dark Night of the Soul* while imprisoned by Carmelites who fear his reforms: "On a dark night, / Kindled in love with yearnings — oh, happy chance! —I went forth without being observed, / My house being now at rest...."

1581:
Finland is a grand duchy of Sweden. Akbar conquers Afghanistan. Influenced by the return of Skepticism in classical documents pouring into Europe, Montaigne's *Essays* published. "My life has been full of terrible misfortunes, most of which never happened." An age of declining belief in religion and its power structures will eagerly seize on Science as the new source of orientation and meaning.

1582:
Hideyoshi Toyomoti becomes Emperor of Japan. Advised by Father Christopher Clavius, Pope Gregory rolls out the Gregorian calendar, replacing the Julian calendar that had lagged behind the solar calendar. It also uses leap years to stay correct. John of the Cross completes the *Spiritual Canticle*.

1583:
Humphrey Gilbert establishes an English colony at Newfoundland.

1584:
Friar Giordano Bruno's *On the Infinite Universe and Worlds*. He believes the sun is a star, that points of light in the night sky are other stars, that the cosmos is filled with intelligently populated planets, and that all things are animated with their own kind of consciousness.

1585:
In retaliation for Spain's stirring up of the Irish, Sir Walter Raleigh establishes the first Virginia colony in North America in the hope it

will prey on passing galleons, but the attempt perishes. Natives begin to die of European diseases, and perhaps 90% of them will be killed by smallpox, measles, malaria, and yellow fever before and during the subsequent colonial fighting. However, a strain of syphilis originating in the New World ravages Europe. The disease is named after Sipylus, a son of boastful Niobe, whose children were all shot by the arrows of Apollo and Artemis.

1587:
Mary, Queen of Scots, is executed by order of Queen Elizabeth. The Portuguese establish Luanda and Benguela in Angola to capture slaves for sale in Brazil. Monteverdi's *First Book of Madrigals*.

1587-1629:
Reign of Shah Abbas I (the Great) of Persia, who consolidates and expands his territories.

1588:
The English defeat Philip II's Spanish Armada in the Battle of Gravelines just west of Plymouth. The battle promotes English nationalism, shows the weakness of the Spanish (Catholic) Empire, which now falls into decline, and helps secure Protestantism as a state religion. Tycho Brahe, Danish astronomer and alchemist, collects astronomical observations that will aid Kepler and Galileo and publishes *Introduction to the New Astronomy*.

1590:
El Greco's *St. Jerome*. Henri Bouget's *An Examen of Witches*. Spenser's *The Faerie Queen*.

1591:
Moroccan forces under Judar Pasha end the Songhai Empire at the Battle of Tondibi. Sir John Harrington of England invents the first flush toilet, the Ajax.

1592-98:
Korea staves off Japanese invasions with the help of two low-profile

ironclads, an idea thought up by the Korean admiral.

1594:
Scottish physicist John Napier discovers logarithms and their mathematically exponential power. The emphasis in Richard Hooker's *On the Laws of Ecclesiastical Polity* on scripture as a literal authority influences John Locke, the Anglican Church, and the Puritans.

1596:
Johannes Kepler's *The Cosmographic Mystery* draws parallels between the shapes of the five Platonic solids and the orbits of the six inner planets.

1598:
The Edict of Nantes offers religious tolerance to the Huguenots in France.

1600s:
In Tonga, political leadership passes from the Tu'i Tonga dynasty to the Tu'i Konokupolu dynasty. The Kalonga kingdom north of the Zambezi River grows rich through the ivory trade. Hausaland dominates trade routes to the Sahara. Great Zimbabwe is replaced by several regional capitals in Transvaal, Botswana, and Zimbabwe. Because much of its forest wood has been cut down, England turns to coal as a substitute for wood. English coal production will eventually fuel the Industrial Revolution.

1600:
Battle of Sekigahara, Japan; Tokugawa Ieyasu defeats his rivals to become shogun, and in 1603 he moves the imperial capital to Tokyo (Edo). Giordano Bruno is burned as a heretic in Rome, probably for supporting the Copernican theory, criticizing Christian literalizations of Biblical truths, teaching animism, recommending religious tolerance and cooperation, and suggesting that God is not separate from nature. Centuries ahead of Einstein, he writes, "There is no absolute up or down, as Aristotle taught; no absolute position in

space; but the position of a body is relative to that of other bodies. Everywhere there is incessant relative change in position throughout the universe, and the observer is always at the center of things." Bruno bravely mocks the Inquisitors who sentence him to death by fire: "Perhaps you, my judges, pronounce this sentence against me with greater fear than I receive it." William Gilbert writes *The Magnet* to theorize about magnetism and electricity; he also believes Earth's magnetic field to reflect the presence of a planetary soul.

1600-14:
Its profits enriched by Asian spices used as flavorings and preservatives, the Dutch East India Company forms in 1602 in response to Spain's closure of the Port of Lisbon to Dutch ships and becomes the first transnational company and the first joint stock company (in 1610, when it requires that deflated bonds be sold to other investors rather than redeemed). It monopolizes all trade from the Cape of Good Hope to the Straits of Magellan. Ten thousand soldiers and forty warships protect the Company's Asian factories and ports. The English, Danish, and French East India Companies also founded.

1601:
Severe famine depopulates Russia.

1602:
Caravaggio paints *The Inspiration of St. Matthew*.

1603:
Pierre Du Gua de Monts and Samuel Champlain found a colony in Nova Scotia. Shakespeare writes *Hamlet*: "To be, or not to be: that is the question: / Whether 'tis nobler in the mind to suffer / The slings and arrows of outrageous fortune, / Or to take arms against a sea of troubles, / And by opposing end them?"

1605:
The Gunpowder Plot, a Catholic plan to blow up James I in Parliament, falls through, and Guy Fawkes and other conspirators are arrested. Cervantes writes *Don Quixote* and ends up rooting for

the heroic windmill-fighting character he intended to satirize.

1606:
Dutch baroque artist Rembrandt Harmenszoon van Rijn (1606-1669). Captain Willem Janszoon and the crew of the East India Company ship *Duyfken* are the first Europeans to spot Australia.

1607:
The London Company establishes the first permanent colony on the James River in Virginia as three ships—*Susan Constant, Godspeed,* and *Discovery*—found Jamestown. The colony survives thanks to Captain John Smith's ingenuity, will, and guts; he in turn owes his life to Pocahontas. He's chosen as their president in 1608, although he does not carry out crazy English orders to make Powhatan King James' vassal, find gold mines, etc. Monteverde writes *Orfeo*, the first true Western opera.

1608:
Samuel de Champlain founds the village of Quebec.

1609:
The first regularly published newspaper, *The Relation*, appears in Germany. Kepler publishes Tycho's calculations of the orbit of Mars, including the first two of Kepler's Laws describing the movements of the planets around the sun (celestial mechanics). It is Kepler who realizes that planet orbits must be ellipses rather than perfect spheres. Imbued by Pythagorean notions of a cosmos composed of sacred numbers, Galileo points a telescope skyward, then writes *The Messenger of the Stars*. His scope reveals Jupiter's moons and the surface features of other planets: not divine essences but material structures open to empirical study. He confirms that the sun is the center of the solar system, for which he is arrested by religious authorities (made severe by the Reformation) and forced to recant. Nevertheless, he insists that science deal only in objective, measurable tangibles testable through experimentation. He also posits the idea of inertia: in a vacuum objects move forever unless a force prevents or deflects them.

1610:
Hudson Bay is explored by Henry Hudson before his crew mutinies. The Polish-Lithuanian Commonwealth defeats Russian and Swedish forces and conquers Moscow.

1611:
Jesuits arrive at Port Royal in Canada. Shakespeare finishes his career with *The Tempest* and then retires. "Our revels now are ended.... We are such stuff / As dreams are made on; and our little life / Is rounded with a sleep."

1611-32:
Reign of Gustavus Adolphus of Sweden, the Protestant leader who makes effective use of mobile musket-armed troopss. The King James Version of the Bible is finally published in England after much opposition by clergy. Rubens paints his *Descent from the Cross*. John Donne's "Anatomie of the World."

1612:
The East India ship *The Globe* visits Siam (now Thailand).

1613:
The Romanovs rule Russia.

1618:
Manchus (people from Manchuria) invade China; the Ming's days are numbered.

1618-48:
The Thirty Years War involves nearly all of Europe except Britain. It begins in Prague, where two royal Catholic officers are thrown out of a window by Protestant members of the Bohemian diet (the "Defenestration of Prague") and escalates into a revolt of Protestant nobles in Bohemia, which is under Hapsburg domination, against the Catholic king Ferdinand (later Holy Roman Emperor Ferdinand II) and takes fire throughout Europe because of the constitutional frailty of the Holy Roman Empire, the inability of the German states to act

in concert, and the ambitions of other European powers.

1619:
The first European representative political assembly in America—a House of Burgesses—is held in Jamestown. African indentured servants are brought to Jamestown by Dutch traders. Kepler proclaims the "harmonic law," the third law of planetary motion, in his *Harmony of the World*. Descartes dreams about being bent over sideways by a strong wind and somehow concludes that God wants him to unify all the sciences. His skepticism reflects that of a time of failing belief systems and religious corruption.

1619-28:
In London, William Harvey discovers the circulation of the blood. At first he is not believed.

1620:
The small merchant vessel *Mayflower* sails from Plymouth. Besides officers and crew, the ship carries a hundred and five passengers, thirty-five of them pilgrims. On November 9th they sight the tip of Cape Cod and look for a better spot, but wind and rocks force them into Provincetown harbor, and a party led by Bradford finds Plymouth harbor. The fur trade keeps the colony going. Attorney Francis Bacon, who calls for scientific study of the world without religious, Aristotelian, or Platonic explanations, an idea of immense influence on future Western science, writes the *Novum Organum*: "Toward the effecting of works, all that man can do is to put together or put asunder natural bodies. The rest is done by nature working within."

1620s:
Queen Nzinga of Ndongo and Mtamba fights the Portuguese in Angola. She leads men into battle well into her sixties. She also concludes a treaty with the Dutch and resettles returned slaves.

1621:
The Polish-Lithuanian Commonwealth holds off an Ottoman army

at Battle of Khotyn in Ukraine.

1622:
Margarite-Marie Alacoque, later sainted, suffers a series of visions on which are based the Catholic image of the Sacred Heart. An Anglo-Persian force takes Ormuz from the Portuguese to open Persia to English trade.

1623:
The First Folio of Shakespeare's plays includes all of them but the mediocre collaborations *Pericles* and *The Two Noble Kinsmen*. Jakob Boehme's *Mysterium Magnum*.

1626:
Dutchman Peter Minuit buys Manhattan for $24 and calls the area New Amsterdam. The joke about swindling the Native people forgets that they were visiting and didn't own the island to begin with.

1628:
William Harvey publishes a book identifying the heart as a pump.

1629:
Massachusetts Bay Colony founded.

1630:
The Taj Mahal is constructed in Agra, India, as a memorial to emperor Shah Jahan's favorite wife, Mumataz Mahal. Missionaries found schools in Canada.

1635:
Roger Williams is driven out of Massachusetts for believing that American land belongs to the Native people who live on it. He becomes their advocate as well as one of the first abolitionists in North America. He sets up Providence, Rhode Island as a haven for exiles with full permission from the native Narragansetts.

1637:
The Shimabara Rebellion in Japan: of Christian peasants agains the shogunate that raised taxes on them to build a new castle. After the revolt is put down Christianity is suppressed for the next two centuries. The first public opera house opens in Vienna. Descartes publishes *Discourse on the Method*: "I think, therefore I am," and, "For to be possessed of good mental powers is not sufficient; the principal matter is to apply them well." The French set up a trading post at the mouth of the Senegal River.

1639-1651:
Wars of the Three Kingdoms include the civil war in England (1642-47) and fighting in Scotland and Ireland. In England, Cavaliers, loyalist supporters of Charles I, oppose Roundheads (Parliamentary forces). Puritan Oliver Cromwell sides with the Parliamentarians and compares himself to Moses. The execution of Charles I sets the stage for Parliamentary influence over the monarchy. Included in the Wars are the Irish Confederate Wars between Irish Catholics and English Protestant colonizers. Smallpox halves the Huron population in Canada.

1640:
The Portuguese Restoration war, in which Portugal revolts successfully against Spanish Hapsburg rule.

1642:
Abel Tasman of the United East India Company spots New Zealand.

1644:
The Quing (Manchu) Dynasty takes over in China as the Ming Dynasty ends. John Stearne and Matthew Hopkins hunts witches in England for lucrative fees.

1647:
Cromwell, now Lord Protector, approves the seizure of Charles I from Parliament and has him beheaded. George Fox founds the Society of Friends; he tells his listeners to quake at the Word of the

Lord, so his followers are called Quakers.

1648:
The Treaty of Westphalia ends the Thirty Years War, the last large war to be fought for explicitly stated religious reasons, marks the decline of the Spanish and Holy Roman Empires, and clears the way for the rise of true nation states by emphasizing their sovereignty. Dutch independence from Spain.

1648-53:
The Fronde ("sling") civil wars in France: the peasants versus Cardinal Mazarin.

1651:
Thomas Hobbes writes *Leviathan* to offer job security to the ruling classes and the clergy by arguing that the innate wildness and badness of people requires strict governance. Gian Lorenzo Bernini sculpts *The Ecstasy of St. Teresa*.

1655:
The English take over the formerly Spanish island of Santiago and rename it Jamaica.

1660:
As with settlements in Latin America and the Caribbean, the Virginians begin to regard Africans as slaves rather than as indentured servants. The Monarchy is restored in England as Charles II returns from France and agrees to respect the Magna Carta and Petition of Rights. Mawlay-al-Rashid restores the sultanate of Morocco. The Royal Society is founded in England. The British establish Fort James on an island just upstream of Gambia.

1664:
Molière's *Tartuffe*. "It's as if you think you'd never find / Reason and the Sacred intertwined."

1665:
Robert Hooke identifies cells. A plague in London, with a great fire next. Portugal defeats the Kongo Kingdom (Battle of Mbwila). Jan Vermeer paints *Girl with a Pearl Earring*.

1666:
The Alaouite Dynasty comes to power in Morocco and rules it into the twenty-first century.

1667:
The Deluge wars and uprisings devastate the Polish-Lithuanian Commonwealth, and incoming Swedish forces loot it, marking growing Swedish influence in Europe. In the War of Devolution, France under Louis XIV invades the Netherlands but must surrender these possessions under pressure by the Triple Alliance of the Dutch, Swedish, and English (Treaty of Aix-la-Chapelle, 1668). The Holy League of Austria, the Polish-Lithuanian Commonwealth, and (eventually) Vienna and Russia stop the Ottomans from pushing into Europe. Rembrandt paints *The Jewish Bride*. Milton writes *Paradise Lost*: "The mind is its own place, and in itself can make a heaven of hell, a hell of heaven..."

1670:
Blaise Pascal's *Pensées*, wherein he introduces Pascal's Wager, evidently to appeal to gamblers: if disbelief in God risks infinite loss, and belief in God (whether correct or incorrect) means merely a paltry loss of some pleasures, then one should, logically, believe in God. Also: "A man does not show his greatness by being at one extremity, but rather by touching both at once."

1672:
Rampjaar ("Disaster Year") and the Franco-Dutch War in the Netherlands, attacked simultaneously by the English, French, and two German states but held off by William III of Orange when he rallies the troops and opens the dikes to flood out his opponents. Beginning of William's ascendency in Europe on behalf of Protestantism fighting back against "popery."

1674:
Shivaji Bhosale founds the Maratha Empire in much of India, with Marathas from Decca using guerrilla tactics to defeat the Ahmadnagar Sultanate and Mughal Empire. The Maratha government stands until the British win the Third Anglo-Maratha War in 1818 and seize India.

1675:
King Philip's War, named after "King Philip," head of the Wampanoags, starts after years of their being forced to sell land to New England colonists and become dependent on colonial goods. Two other tribes and all of New England get involved; in the end, most of the tribes are wiped out (clearing the way for white settlement) and the fur trade declines. "King Philip" is drawn and quartered and his head stuck on a pole.

1676:
Bacon's Rebellion, in which indentured servants and African slaves organize an attempt against oppressive US aristocrats, inspiring colonists to invent the term "white" to stave off further revolts. Anton von Leeuwenhoeck looks through a microscope and sees microorganisms.

1678:
The Treaties of Peace of Nijmegen end various wars between France, Spain, Sweden, Prussia, the Dutch Republic, Denmark, and the Holy Roman Empire. France acquires its modern border. Bunyan's *Pilgrim's Progress*.

1680s:
The Pueblo boot the Spanish out of New Mexico. Rise of Asante kingdom in West Africa. As statue-building ends on Easter Island, resources and then population decline, leading to internal war. The Butua kingdom expands across the Zimbabwe plains.

1681-82:
French explorer Robert Cavalier de La Salle traces the Mississippi

river from source to mouth, founds Louisiana, and claims the lot for France.

1685:
Baroque-era composer Johann Sebastian Bach (1685-1750) born in Germany; English composer George Frederic Handel (1685-1759) born. Idealist philosopher George Berkeley born (1685-1753).

1687:
Alchemist, mathematician, and physicist Sir Isaac Newton publishes his *Philosophiae Naturalis Principia Mathematica* to show how his principle of universal gravitation explains falling bodies on the earth as well as the motions of tides, falling objects, planets, comets, and other bodies in the heavens. He also elaborates three laws of motion: inertia, force, and equal reaction. He continues his alchemical studies, however, to search for the "vegetative principle" that he believes animates all matter. (Alchemy and Hermentic philosophy had inspired his idea of forces acting at a distance.) Elizabeth Cellier proposes a corporation of midwives because male doctors trained in clinics have decided they know more about delivering babies.

1688:
A bloodless "Glorious Revolution" in England against Catholic James II, who flees to Ireland, brings William III of Orange and Mary II Stuart to the throne by invitation of Parliament. The Siamese Revolution of 1688 overthrows a foreign king and frees Thailand.

1689:
A Bill of Rights is passed in England. James II leads a rebellion in Ireland and is defeated by William of Orange at the Battle of the Boyne. War of the Grand Alliance, a coalition of European powers organized by William against France; in North America this appears as King William's War between the British and the French. John Locke writes "A Letter Concerning Toleration."

1690:
John Locke publishes *Two Treatises on Government* and *An Essay*

Concerning Human Understanding, with the latter claiming that all knowledge comes from experience (empiricism). The *Two Treatises* make a large impact on the founders of the American Republic. "Being all equal and independent, no one ought to harm another in his life, health, liberty, or possessions."

1691:
The Manchus conquer Mongolia. Mongolia is a Chinese province from 1691 and 1911 and from 1919 to 1921.

1692:
The Salem witch trials prompted by a couple of frantic, accusatory teens who manage to frighten an entire community. Twenty people are hanged for crimes which Judge Sewall and the jury later believe had not been committed. A severe famine in France.

1696:
When Ivan V of Russia dies, Peter the Great takes over and modernizes Russia's navy and army, reorganizes the Russian Orthodox Church, adopts the Julian calendar, and makes his ministers wear modern garb. Leibniz admires Francis Bacon's willingness to "put Nature on the rack and torture her for her secrets," a sentiment never uttered by Bacon. A famine wipes out a third of Finland.

1700s:
The Enlightenment introduces revolutionary ideas—reason and science over religious tradition, individual rights, scientific inquiry, Progress ever upward—in Europe and replaces cynicism and skepticism with faith in human achievement armed with the wonder-working power of technology. The North American colonies begin to prosper. Buganda expands in Africa. First contact between Tahitians and Europeans, who meet in the Opunohu Valley on Moorea Island. In the Great Northern War (1700–21), Russia steps forward as an empire as it whittles down Sweden's. Bartolomeo Cristofori of Italy invents the piano.

1701:
Frederick I organizes the Kingdom of Prussia. Osei Kofi Tutu I and Okomfo Anokye raise up the Ashanti Empire in West Africa. Osei Tutu creates the free Asante nation in West Africa. "By crawling, a child learns to stand" - West African proverb.

1701-13:
Much of Europe gets caught in the War of Spanish Succession as the dying Charles II of Spain picks French Philip, Duke of Anjou to take the Spanish throne, making France a leading world power and diverting Spanish trade from England and Holland to France.

1702:
Queen Anne's War (1702-1713) between the British and the French in North America begins, a parallel to the War of Spanish Succession. The Camisard Rebellion in central France as French Huguenots fight back against Catholic persecution.

1704:
Newton's *Opticks*.

1706: Benjamin Franklin (1706-1790); his achievements will include The Kite, the Franklin stove, fire departments, modern libraries and colleges, street-cleaning services, the glass harmonica used by composers like Mozart and Beethoven, replacement of globular English street lamps with a more effective four-paned model, work on the US Constitution, and *Poor Richard Saunders' Almanac*.

1707:
The Act of Union welds England, Wales, and Scotland into Great Britain.

1709:
Mir Wais Hotak leads a revolt against the Persians and sets up the Hotaki Empire (1709-1738) in Afghanistan, Iran, and northern Pakistan.

1710:
George Berkeley publishes his *a Treatise Concerning the Principles of Human Knowledge*: "Upon the whole, I am inclined to think that the far greater part, if not all, of those difficulties which have hitherto amused philosophers, and blocked up the way to knowledge, are entirely owing to ourselves—that we have first raised a dust and then complain we cannot see." He also argues that the outside world as we perceive it is built solely of ideas, a popular notion in the Californian city named after him.

1711:
A treaty largely made possible by Catherine, Peter the Great's mistress, gives the powerful Ottomans back some territory and prevents Peter's captivity.

1712:
In England, Thomas Newcomen invents a workable steam pump for use in mines. Alexander Pope writes *The Rape of the Lock*.

1714:
George, German Elector of Hanover, becomes King George I of Britain, and his style of ruling in theory while leaving most of the work to the Prime Minister (Walpole) sets a precedent for future English politics. The Treaty of Utrecht ends the War of the Spanish Succession (Queen Anne's War); with the British taking Newfoundland, Acadia, and Hudson's Bay Territory from France, and Gibraltar and Minorca from Spain, Britain is on the way toward becoming a worldwide empire. Austria gets the Netherlands, and France, almost broke, finally faces that England is going to be ruled by Protestant kings. Gabriel Daniel Fahrenheit creates the first mercury thermometer. Leibniz writes the *Monadology*.

1716:
When sociopath John Law promises to inflate depressed France with paper money and shares of stock in worthless New Orleans swampland, he pumps up what will be known as the Mississippi Bubble, the first stock market bubble and bust in history. It wrecks the French

economy and paves the way for the French Revolution. The Sikh Confederacy fights against Mughal and Hindu potentates on what will become the border between India and Pakistan.

1721:
Transgender person Catherina Margaretha Linck is executed for sodomy in Prussia. The Treaty of Nystad establishes a string of new nations in Eastern Europe and peace between Russia and Sweden. Bach's *Brandenburg Concertos*. Montesquieu's *Persian Letters*.

1723:
Vivaldi's *The Four Seasons*.

1724:
The Treaty of Constantinople divides Persia between Russia and the Ottoman Empire.

1724-34:
King Agaja of Dahomey in West Africa temporarily disrupts the slave trade, but it will be reintroduced in the 1740s.

1725:
Catherine I of Russia takes the throne at her husband's death. Chinese Emperor Yongzheng commissions the *Gujin Tushu Jicheng*, the largest encyclopedia ever printed, at ten thousand volumes. Vico's *New Science*.

1726:
Jonathan Swift publishes *Gulliver's Travels*. Mother Clap's London molly house raided by police.

1729:
Charles and John Wesley start the Methodist movement in England.

1732:
Classical composer Franz Joseph Haydn (1732-1809) born. George Washington (1732-1799) born. Benjamin Franklin begins publishing

Poor Richard's Almanac.

1733:
John Kay invents the flying shuttle loom in England and switches on the Industrial Revolution.

1734:
Pope's *Essay on Man.* Voltaire's *Lettres Philosophiques.*

1735:
Linnaeus's *Systerna Naturae* is the first book to make consistent use of binomial nomenclature for taxonomy.

1736:
The first Russo-Turkish War erupts as Russia pushes for a Black Sea outlet.

1739:
The Russo-Turkish war ends (temporarily). The War of Jenkins' Ear starts when Spanish troops board an English ship and slice the ear from a sailor; the conflict blends into the War of the Austrian Succession. That war explodes when Maria Theresa's claim to the Hapsburg throne comes into dispute because she is a woman, whereupon Prussia, France, and Spain use the event as an opportunity to challenge Austrian power in Europe.

1740:
Inspired by the increasingly prevalent view of the cosmos as a Big Machine, Frederick II "the Great" invents the Prussian military drill and hugely expands his nation's territorial claims.

1741:
Vitus Bering finds Alaska.

1742:
Handel finishes *The Messiah*. Franklin invents the Franklin stove. Cotton mills open in England.

1744:
King George's War, the North American parallel to the War of the Austrian Succession, ignites when the French try to take Port Royal (Annapolis). When Iroquois elders meet American colonial governors in Lancaster, Pennsylvania, the Iroquois recommend that the colonists stop fighting each other and form a union. Muhammad ibn Saud founds the first Saudi State (Emirate of Diriyah) of three in eastern Arabia.

1745:
Charles Edward Stuart (Bonnie Prince Charlie) comes to Scotland to set off a Jacobite uprising among the Highlanders on behalf of his father James III. Moving to England, he fails (at the Battle of Culloden) to restore the exiled Stuart dynasty to British throne.

1746:
In Leyden, Dutch physicist Peter van Musschenbroek learns how to store electricity in a water-filled, metal-lined glass container (the Leyden jar). The first of three Carnatic Wars (offshoots of the War of Austrian Succession) as the British East India Company and the French East India Company vie for control of India.

1747:
La Mettrie's *Man A Machine*.

1748:
Montesquieu's *Spirit of Laws*. Hume's *Enquiry Concerning Human Understanding*: "And shall we esteem it worthy the labour of a philosopher to give us a true system of the planets, and adjust the position and order of those remote bodies; while we affect to overlook those, who, with so much success, delineate the parts of the mind, in which we are so intimately concerned?"

1752:
Ben Franklin invents the lightning rod, and women in Paris wear newly fashionable lightning rod hats.

1754:
The Albany Plan of Union, a forerunner of the US Constitution; it is heavily influenced by the Great Binding Law of the Iroquois Confederacy. Forty-two members of the Iroquois Grand Council are present to serve as advisors.

1754-63:
The Seven Years' War in which the British, Spanish, French, Prussians, and Austrians fight for territory, some of it colonial. George Washington fights in the first French and Indian War battle against the French. During this war he sees Native Americans using their surroundings for cover.

1755:
The great Lisbon earthquake in Portugal kills thousands. German scientist Kaspar Friedrich Wolff founds embryology by discovering that eggs and sperm are composed of a material that develops into specialized structures.

1757:
Robert Clive defeats Siraj Ud Daula, Nawab of Bengal, at the Battle of Plassy, which regains Calcutta for the British and Bengal for the British East India Company. English poet-mystic William Blake (1757-1827) born.

1758:
Mystic Emmanuel Swedenborg publishes *Heaven and Hell*.

1759:
Birth of poet, philosopher, and historian Friedrich Schiller (1759-1805). General James Wolfe defeats the French at the Battle of Quebec, leaving the British in charge of Canada. Sterne's *Tristram Shandy*. Voltaire's *Candide*: "Why did God create the world?" "To drive us mad." Franz Josef Haydn's first symphony.

1761:
The Battle of Panipat beats back the Marathas, who lose Punjab and

Delhi to the Afghan king.

1762:
Rousseau writes *Emile* and *The Social Contract*, arguing in the latter that governments must reflect the will of the people.

1763:
In the Pontiac Conspiracy, Native Americans rise against the British in North America. British officers stationed at Fort Pitt hand Native people blankets infected with smallpox. George III and John, Earl of Bute, sign the first Treaty of Paris, leaving England with a huge war debt—to be paid through America, where a standing army is also in need of funding. Ending also of the Third Carnatic War. The Peace of Paris gives Spain Louisiana, including New Orleans and all the land between the Mississippi and the Rocky Mountains. The trans-Allegheny West opens to settlement.

1764:
Treasury Lord George Grenville makes the first of several serious mistakes by pushing the Sugar Act through Parliament to enforce the duty on molasses imported from non-West Indies countries and used to make rum in the American colonies. The colonists protest because they weren't consulted. Further, Grenville proposes a Stamp Act that requires official and commercial American documents to bear an official English stamp (not a postage stamp). The angered colonists see this as taxation without representation because they have no actual representatives in Parliament. Scottish engineer James Watt invents the condenser, a steam cooler that makes steam engines run more efficiently.

1765:
Behind colonial rioting against the Stamp Act stands a group of middle-class tradesmen known as the Loyal Nine and later called the Sons of Liberty. The Act is repealed, but Grenville also pushes through the Quartering or Mutiny Act of 1765.

1767:
Failing to learn from Grenville's mistakes, Charles Townsend introduces the New York Restraining Act to invalidate New York assembly decisions until the Quartering Act is obeyed, a Revenue Act to impose new duties and writs for collection, an American Board of Customs Commissioner at Boston to enforce these, and other duties. He also uses the proceeds to pay colonial governors and other British officials. Philadelphian lawyer John Dickinson's "Letters from a Farmer in Pennsylvania" appear in the *Pennsylvania Gazette* and become the handbook of pre-independence patriotism.

1768:
England sends two regiments of soldiers to Boston, where rioting erupts with the customs seizure of John Hancock's sloop *Liberty* for smuggling Madeira.

1769:
Planter Thomas Jefferson joins the Virginia House of Burgesses. His first bill, to allow owners to free slaves, is unsuccessful. James Watt invents a new kind of steam engine and coins the term "horsepower." Sir William Arkwright patents the spinning machine. The first Spanish mission in California is established at San Diego near a Native village, and an armed fort called the Presidio is erected nearby. Captain James Cook sails to Australia and New Zealand.

1770:
Prime Minister Lord North repeals the retaliatory Townsend duties, but too late: on the same day, when an English sentry is pelted with snowballs, a crowd gathers, someone fires, and five colonists are killed. Though the soldiers are acquitted of murder, unsuccessful tax collector Samuel Adams, who wrote the circular letter that brought together the angry colonists, bills this far and wide as "the Boston Massacre." First killed in the Revolutionary War is black working man named Crispus Attucks. Poet William Wordsworth (1770-1850) born. Thomas Gainsborough paints *The Blue Boy*. James Hargreaves patents the spinning jenny.

1771:
Entrepreneur Richard Arkwright and associates build a water mill at Cromford. *Encyclopedia Brittanica published.*

1771:
Russia, Prussia, and Austria carve up the Polish-Lithuanian Commonwealth.

1773:
Lord North's Tea Act grants the failing East India Company a tea monopoly. To protest this, group of colonists disguised as Indians board three ships and throw three hundred and forty-two chests of tea into Boston Harbor. New York follows suit. Dr. Benjamin Rush of Philadelphia, a physician who later signs the Declaration of Independence, attacks "Slave Keeping." Pugachev's Rebellion of peasants in Russia. The East India Company begins to smuggle opium into China.

1774:
As Samuel Adams predicted, the British close Boston Harbor until the tea is paid for. Governor Hutchinson is replaced by General Gage, who lands at Boston. Colonists interpret this as a plan to induce slavery (the white kind, presumably) and begin pinning the blame on King George III. The Virginia House of Burgesses, dissolved in May because it appealed for public support of beleaguered Boston, meets at the Raleigh Tavern in Williamsburg and invites delegates from all the colonies to convene in a general congress to discuss the crisis.

1775:
General Gage marches reluctantly and, he hopes, secretly, for American arms collected at Concorde, but Paul Revere's cry of alarm musters the militia, and suddenly seven hundred British infantry face seventy-five American volunteers. After a shot rings out, by which side is unknown, the British drive the Minute Men from the field, killing eight and wounding ten. The British march on to Concord, but the stores have been moved. The Second

Continental Congress meets in Philadelphia. The British East India Company effectively controls Bangladesh. Arkwright invents a carding machine. Anton Mesmer invokes "animal magnetism" (hypnotism) in his patients.

1776:
Virginia instructs delegates in Congress to propose seceding from Great Britain. Sentences condemning slavery are struck out of the proposal to appease South Carolina and Georgia. The Declaration of Independence (Thomas Paine's idea) drafted by Jefferson receives approval on July 4th: "When in the course of human events, it becomes necessary for one people to dissolve the political bands which have connected them with another, and to assume among the powers of the earth, the separate and equal station to which the Laws of Nature and of Nature's God entitle them, a decent respect to the opinions of mankind requires that they should declare the causes which impel them to the separation." Adam Smith comes out for laissez faire capitalism in his *Wealth of Nations*, where he argues that the will to capital is inherent in human nature. Ueda Akinari publishes the *Ugetsu Monogatari*.

1776-79:
On Captain Cook's third and last voyage he lands in Hawaii and is clubbed or stabbed to death by the islanders. French navigator Comte la Pérouse leads an expedition to the Pacific and northwestern America. Stopping briefly in California, he is horrified by the abuse of Native Californians confined to the Missions.

1777:
Sidi Mohammed, ruler of Morocco (1757-90), abolishes Christian slavery. General Burgoyne surrenders to General Horatio Gates at Saratoga. This convinces France that Great Britain really can be beaten, and a year later it enters the American Revolutionary War, followed shortly by Spain, her ally. But the war further wrecks French finances.

1778:
The Tây Sơn brothers lead peasant revolts in Vietnam.

1779:
The Xhosa Wars between the Xhosa and British colonizers in South Africa; Gcalekaland becomes a British territory. Jan Ingenhouse discovers photosynthesis.

1780:
Rebellion of Túpac Amaru II in Peru, where he lead peasants and indigenous people against the Bourbon Spaniards. He is executed and the rebellion quashed.

1781:
Dug in at Yorktown and sealed off by French Admiral De Grasse's fleet in Chesapeake Bay, British General Cornwallis is trapped by Washington and Rochambeau as they march south. He asks for terms and surrenders two days later, ending the American Revolution. Kant writes his *Critique of Pure Reason* to argue that experience-ordering categories like causality and time already exist in the mind, and that naked reality is unknowable. William Herschel discovers Uranus, planet of revolution.

1782-1809:
Rama I reigns in Thailand and founds the Chakri dynasty.

1783:
The Treaty of Paris formally ends the Revolutionary War. Britain recognizes US independence and gives up huge Trans-Appalachian territories. The Russian government under Catherine annexes the Crimea as she seeks to drive the Ottoman Empire out of Europe. Joseph Michel and Jacques Étienne Montgolfier invent a hot-air balloon and become the first to fly. Marquis Claude de Jouffroy d'Abbans applies steam to navigation when his vessel *Pyroscaphe* runs against the current of the Saone River for fifteen minutes.

1785:
Sheikh Mansur leads the Chechens to resist Russia's expansion into the Caucasus. Little Turtle's War: Native American tribes of the Northwest Territory against the invading United States. Edmund Cartwright's power loom. James Hutton's *Theory of the Earth* starts the science of geology and puts the Earth's age at far older than traditional Christian estimates.

1786:
Andrew Meikle invents the threshing machine.

1787:
French physicist Jacques Charles writes Charles Law to express the relationship between the volume and temperature of a gas. The Qajar dynasty that rules Persia makes Tehran their capital, and they rule until the 1920s. King Andrianampoinimerina unites Madagascar. Tuaregs, who are nomads in Sahara, abolish the Moroccan pashalik of Timbuktu. Antoine Lavoisier modernizes chemical nomenclature, and by doing so effectively separates chemistry from alchemy. Mozart debuts his operas *The Marriage of Figaro* and *Don Giovanni*. A convention meets at Philadelphia to draw up the US Constitution: "We the People of the United States, in order to form a more perfect Union..." When a woman asks Benjamin Franklin after the Constitution Convention whether they had created a monarchy or a republic, he replies, "A republic, Madam, if you can keep it."

1788:
The first British convicts shipped to Botany Bay, Australia, where they found the first permanent European colony. King George, who suffered from severe porphyria, begins to lose his mind; the illness, which first struck him in 1765, may have impaired his ability to compromise with the American colonies. United States Constitution ratified. The Inconfidência Mineira revolt against the Portuguese in Brazil. Goethe's *Egmont*. Laplace's *Laws of the Planetary System*. Madison, Hamilton, and Jay publish *The Federalist*. "The accumulation of all powers, legislative, executive, and judiciary, in the same

hands, whether of one, a few, or many, and whether hereditary, self-appointed, or elective, may justly be pronounced the very definition of tyranny."

1789:
At a meeting of the French Estates General (because of the seating arrangements, the terms "leftist"—bourgeoisie—and "rightist"—clergy and nobility—are coined), the Third Estate, dissatisfied, declares itself the National Assembly, and the other Estates later join. At the instigation of journalist Camille Desmoulins and a rumor that the king plans to disband the Estates General, rioters storm the Bastille in Paris and start the French Revolution. Six thousand bread-demanding women force King Louis XVI to submit to their demands in Versailles and to move his court to Paris. While voyaging to the Pacific to find breadfruit plants, Lieutenant William Bligh in the *Bounty* is put to sea with eighteen men by a mutinous crew led by Fletcher Christian; they eventually settle on Pitcairn Island. Washington is inaugurated US President. Philadelphia is the temporary US capital as Congress votes to establish the new one in a swamp near the Potomac. The US population is about 3,929,000, including 698,000 slaves. Jerry Bentham starts utilitarian philosophy with his *Introduction to the Principles of Morals and Legislation* ("the greatest happiness of the greatest number"). He also calls for women's rights, abolition of slavery, an end to the death penalty, and an end to punishment for homosexuality. Alexander Radishchev publishes *Journey from St. Petersburg to Moscow*. Gibbon's *The History of the Decline and Fall of the Roman Empire*. William Blake's *Songs of Innocence*.

1790:
Goethe's *Metamorphosis of Plants*. Studying them, he comes to see plants and other living things as gestures moving in accord with their living archetype, and by doing this he founds an early version of phenomenology.

1791:
France declares war on Austria. Queen Marie Antoinette gives away

war secrets in the hope that Austria will win and rid France of revolutionaries, but her subjects find out, imprison her, and search for the king as well. As a consequence of the French Revolution, black slaves and mulattos on Haiti revolt against French whites. US Bill of Rights adopted. Luigi Galvani shows that electrically charged muscles twitch. George Vancouver circles the world. Boswell's *Life of Johnson*. In a rainy shack outside the public theater, Mozart, though ill, composes *The Magic Flute* and premiers it in Vienna.

1792:
War of the First Coalition: first of three wars by Austria, France, Spain, and other powers frightened by the revolution in France. New York Stock Exchange founded. Mary Wollstonecraft's *A Vindication of the Rights of Woman* published: "If then women are not a swarm of ephemeron triflers, why should they be kept in ignorance under the specious name of innocence? Men complain, and with reason, of the follies and caprices of our sex, when they do not keenly satirize our headstrong passions and grovelling vices. Behold, I should answer, the natural effect of ignorance! The mind will ever be unstable that has only prejudices to rest on, and the current will run with destructive fury when there are no barriers to break its force."

1793:
Louis XVI and Marie Antoinette are executed. Horrified, Britain kicks out the French ambassador, whereupon France declares war on Britain, Spain, and the Netherlands. During the fighting Colonel Napoleon Bonaparte is promoted to Brigadier-General and poses as a liberator of the people. Eli Whitney patents the cotton gin (short for "engine"). Philippe Pinel introduces humane treatments into insane asylums. Christian Sprengel writes *The Secret of Nature Discovered*, with his descriptions of interactions between plants and insects ignored by almost everyone...except Charles Darwin. William Blake's *Marriage of Heaven and Hell*. "Energy is Eternal Delight."

1794:
The White Lotus Rebellion in China by a religious secret society

protesting high taxes is put down but weakens the Qing government. William Blake's *Songs of Experience*.

1795:
F. Blumenbach writes *The Human Species* and founds anthropology. Paul Barras promotes Napoleon and gives him a mistress (Josephine), then forms a five-man Directory to lead France. Hoping for French help, the Irish rebel.

1796:
Edward Jenner of England finds and tests the first smallpox vaccination.

1798:
Napoleon invades Egypt and beats the Mamluk army, but his fleet is defeated by Admiral Nelson at the Battle of the Nile. A French officer discovers the Rosetta Stone in Egypt. The British take Ceylon from the Dutch. The British crush the Irish rebellion at the Battle of Vinegar Hill. Coleridge's Captain Cook-inspired *The Rime of the Ancient Mariner* published. The Dutch East India Company goes bankrupt and is dissolved. Thomas Robert Malthus publishes his *Essay on Population*, where he argues that famine, disease, and warfare lower the population. Haydn's *The Creation*.

1799:
Napoleon becomes dictator of France although, in theory, he is one of three consuls. Ranjit Singh founds a Sikh kingdom in Punjab, India. Civil war in Tonga.

1800:
Italian scientist Alessandro Volta invents the electric cell. In accord with the secret treaty of San Ildefonso, Spain gives France rights over the mouth of the Mississippi, the port of New Orleans, and Louisiana. The US capital moves to Washington, DC. Robert Owen pushes factory reform in England. William Herschel discovers infrared frequencies. Marie Francois Savier Bichat founds the science of histology. Fichte's *The Vocation of Man*. Schelling's *System*

of Transcendental Idealism.

1801:
Napoleon negotiates a Concordat with the Pope: Catholicism becomes France's favored religion, with clergy to be paid and selected by the state. First Barbary War between the US and the Ottoman Barbary States (Algiers and Tripoli) of Northwest Africa after their corsairs disrupt American commerce.

1802:
Ludwig van Beethoven performs the *Moonlight Sonata*.

1802-20:
Emperor Gia-Long unites Vietnam.

1803:
Fearing the renewal of war with Great Britain, Napoleon offers to sell, for $15 million, the port of New Orleans and the land from the Mississippi to the Rockies (the Louisiana Purchase); Jefferson buys it and US territory doubles. Following Democritus, English scientist John Dalton reintroduces the atomic theory of matter. William Symington of Scotland invents a steamboat.

1804-06:
Guided by the Shoshone woman Sacajawea, Lewis and Clark explore beyond the Mississippi.

1804:
French inventor Aimé Argand designs an oil lamp in England. Haiti wins independence from France, the first black nation to break free of European influence. Napoleon crowns himself Emperor, prompting an enraged Beethoven to rename the *Third Symphony*. Aaron Burr kills Alexander Hamilton in a duel. Francis I founds the Austrian Empire. The population of the world hits one billion.

1805:
Admiral Horatio Nelson defeats a numerically superior French fleet

off Cape Trafalgar near Spain without losing a single English vessel. He dies soon after of a sniper wound sustained on the deck of his flagship *Victory*. Napoleon takes Austerlitz, and Austria sues for peace. Muhammad Ali modernizes Egypt. Noah Webster publishes the first US dictionary. William Herschel shows that the Sun is moving relative to the rest of the universe.

1806:
Philosopher Georg Wilhelm Friedrich Hegel finishes his first book, the *Phenomenology of Mind*, in Jena on the night before a battle. Sweden organizes under a constitutional monarchy (until 1975).

1807:
The US bans the importation of slaves. The British ban the slave trade. Robert Fulton begins steamboat service on the Hudson River and builds the *Clermont*, not the first steamship but the first to be successful in the US. Wordsworth's "Ode: Intimations of Immortality."

1808:
Spain rises in rebellion (hence the word *guerilla*, or "little war") in a move that will drain Napoleon's resources. The conflict starts when Portugal refuses to comply with Napoleon's Continental System of economic warfare against Britain. Movements for independence from Spain stir in Cuba and Puerto Rico. In the Finnish War, the Grand Duchy of Finland is removed from Swedish control and established within Russia. Beethoven's *Fifth* and *Sixth Symphonies* performed. Goethe publishes the first part of *Faust*. "All theory is gray, my friend. But forever green is the tree of life."

1809:
Russia annexes Finland. Jean Baptiste de Lamarck proposes the evolutionary mechanism of inheriting acquired characteristics, foreshadowing Darwinian evolutionary theory and, later, epigenetics.

1810:
Antonio Nariño leads an independence movement in Bogotá,

Colombia, for the next nine years.

1811:
In Britain, Luddites riot and wreck machinery. Following Prussia and preceding other nations, Indonesia and the Netherlands decriminalize homosexuality. Paraguay and Uruguay win independence from Spain.

1812:
The US goes to war with Britain over shipping rights, a suspected British arming of Native Americans, and a desire by hawkish US politicians to obtain Canada from the British and western Florida from Britain's ally Spain. Napoleon's Grande Armee reaches Moscow but is forced to retreat to France with six hundred thousand men lost. Geroges Leopold Cuvier founds the science of paleontology. Lord Byron publishes the first parts of *Childe Harold*.

1814:
Defeated, Napoleon is replaced by Bourbon monarch Louis XVIII and sent to Elba. The British fleet surrenders to the US on Lake Champlain (the Battle of Plattsburg). A British expeditionary force burns the US Capitol but is stopped at Ft. McHenry, where Francis Scott Key is inspired to write "The Star-Spangled Banner." By the Treaty of Kiel, Denmark cedes Helgoland to England and Norway to Sweden but keeps possession of Greenland, Iceland, and the Faeroe Islands. George Stephenson builds the first practical steam locomotive. Franz Schubert creates the German lieder (art song).

1815:
Napoleon escapes from Elba. At the Battle of Waterloo, Wellington and von Blucher inflict a final defeat on Napoleon, and he is exiled to St. Helena. The Treaty of Ghent ends the War of 1812. Switzerland gains independence from France. At the Congress of Vienna following up the defeat of Napoleon, the winners redraw the map of Europe but cannot stop the movements of independence breaking out all over the world. Jakob Grimm completes *Grimm's Fairy Tales*.

1816:
Simón Bolívar defeats the Spanish in Venezuela, with Argentine independence following in 1821. He will prove pivotal in liberating much of South America from Spain. Theophile Rene Hyacinthe Laennec invents the stethoscope. Rossini stages *The Barber of Seville*.

1816-28:
Zulu ruler Shaka takes charge in South Africa.

1817:
Bernardo O'Higgins is first president of Chile after he helps free it from the Spanish. David Ricardo discusses labor value and the tendency of wages to stabilize around subsistence level (The Iron Law of Wages) in *On the Principles of Political Economy and Taxation*, a book that will influence Karl Marx. Muhammad Bello organizes a state at Sokotu in northern Nigeria that stands until the British arrive in 1900. Civil wars in the Oyo Empire of the Yoruba. Karl von Drais invents an early bicycle.

1818:
Chile achieves independence. Mary Wollstonecraft Shelly writes *Frankenstein*, a Faustian tale of idealism and technology gone wrong. As the doctor observes in retrospect, "If the study to which you apply yourself has a tendency to weaken your affections, and to destroy your taste for those simple pleasures in which no alloy can possibly mix, then that study is certainly unlawful, that is to say, not befitting the human mind." Karl Marx (1818-1883).

1819:
Eleven people protesting unemployment and high prices are shot in Manchester ("The Peterloo Massacre"). American poet Walt Whitman (1819-1892) born. Bolívar liberates New Granada (now Colombia, Venezuela, and Ecuador) as Spain loses its hold on South American countries, and he is named president of Colombia. Washington Irving's *The Sketchbook* published. Walter Scott writes *Ivanhoe*. Théodore Géricault displays his painting *The Raft of the*

Medusa. Schopenhauer's *The World as Will and Idea.* "At the age of five years to enter a spinning-cotton or other factory, and from that time forth to sit there daily, first ten, then twelve, and ultimately fourteen hours, performing the same mechanical labour, is to purchase dearly the satisfaction of drawing breath. But this is the fate of millions, and that of millions more is analogous to it."

1820:
The Missouri Compromise allows slavery in Missouri but bars it north of that state. Activist and suffragist Susan B. Anthony (1820-1906). The Fulani Emirate is founded in Adamawa, West Africa. Abolitionist Harriet Tubman (1820-1913). Hans Christian Oersted shows the relationship between magnetism and electricity. John Keats publishes "Ode on a Grecian Urn" ("Beauty is truth, truth beauty"). Percy Shelley's *Prometheus Unbound.*

1821-29:
The Greek War of Independence against the Turks, who invade when Greece declares independence. Peru wins independence. Rejecting British-style colonialism, President Adams says this about the US in his inaugural address: "She goes not abroad, in search of monsters to destroy. She is the well-wisher to the freedom and independence of all... She well knows that by once enlisting under other banners than her own, were they even the banners of foreign independence, she would involve herself beyond the power of extrication, in all the wars of interest and intrigue, of individual avarice, envy, and ambition, which assume the colors and usurp the standard of freedom. The fundamental maxims of her policy would insensibly change from liberty to force...."

1822:
Liberia founded in West Africa as a home for liberated slaves. Augustinian friar Gregor Mendel discovers the laws of heredity. Following the example left by Bolívar, Brazil kicks out the Portuguese and declares independence, with many other Latin American nations to follow. Jean Francois Champollion deciphers the Rosetta Stone and makes it possible to read ancient Egyptian

writing. Schubert composes the *Eighth* ("Unfinished") *Symphony*.

1823:
Devised by John Quincy Adams, the Monroe Doctrine named after the president gives the US permission to prevent European interference in the Western Hemisphere; this Doctrine will later be the basis of other Doctrines that justify widespread military intervention around the world. In Mexico, a rebellion lead by Antonio de Santa Anna forces the dictator Itubide out of power, and Mexico becomes a republic. Clement Clarke Moore introduces Santa Claus to Americans with his poem "A Visit from St. Nicholas." William Sturgeon designs the first electromagnet. Janos Bolyai formulates a non-Euclidean geometry (published in 1831).

1824:
Bolívar liberates Peru and becomes its president. Beethoven premiers his *Ninth Symphony*, which he never hears because of his deafness. James Neilson patents a method for burning coal efficiently.

1825:
European soldiers and settlers approach Brisbane. Birth of French neurologist and hypnotist Jean-Martin Charcot (1825-1893). George Stephenson lays down iron rails and puts an engine on them named Locomotion. Bolívar founds the new state of Bolivia. Prompted by a dream, Michael Faraday discovers the compound benzene. Robert Owen, who like Rousseau believes that people are inherently good if left to their own devices, sets up his New Harmony community in Indiana. It works for a while, then dissolves when its leaders argue with each other. The Erie Canal opens in New York.

1826:
Joseph-Nicéphore Niepce takes the world's first photograph. Ottoman sultan Mahmud II orders his loyalists to massacre the janissaries in their barracks; they had operated as an elite fighting force under Murad I, who recruited war captives and Christian youths and brainwashed them into converting to Islam. Felix Mendelssohn

writes *The Midsummer Night's Dream*. James Fenimore Cooper publishes *The Last of the Mohicans*.

1827:
The Battle of Navarino Bay, where British, French, and Russian navies destroy the Turkish fleet as part of the Greek War of Independence. Edgar Allen Poe publishes *Tamerlane and Other Poems*. Georg Ohm demonstrates Ohm's Law.

1828:
Russo-Turkish wars (again) during which Russia finally gains control of the eastern coast of the Black Sea. British colonists initiate the extermination of the Tasmanians. Indian Hindu Raja Ram Mohan Roy founds the reformist Brahmo Samaj movement that leads to a Bengal Renaissance that blends Western education with Indian traditions while seeking to end untouchability, suttee (widow-burning), polygamy, and infanticide. Uruguay wins independence.

1829:
The Greeks win independence from the Ottoman Empire. John Lambton, the Earl of Durham, recommends that Canadian rebels be allowed representative government. The English settle Perth in Australia.

1830:
In retaliation for a slap, French ships blockade Algiers and troops take over the country. Belgium wins independence. Malietoa Vaiinupo of Savai'i takes charge as king of Samoa. French Impressionist painter Camille Pissarro (1830–1903) born. Marie-Henri "Stendhal" Beyle publishes *The Red and the Black*.

1831:
Nat Turner leads an unsuccessful slave rebellion in the US and is hanged and skinned, and organized abolition halts temporarily in the South. The Indian Removal Act signed by President Andrew Jackson forces sixty thousand Native Americans of the Five Civilized Tribes to relocate to lands west of the Mississippi. A tenth

of the Choctaw tribe dies on their forced trek to Oklahoma during the coldest winter since 1776, and other tribes suffer great losses and misery as well. Charles Darwin goes voyaging aboard the *Beagle*. Cholera epidemics ravage Europe. Alexander Pushkin publishes *Boris Godunov* but state censors won't permit it to be shown.

1832:
The Reform Bill of 1832 bloodlessly reorganizes the British Parliament. Pope Gregory XVI uses Austrian troops to suppress an uprising in the Papal States and writes an encyclical against freedom of religion and speech and against all political dissent. Alfred, Lord Tennyson publishes "The Lady of Shalott." Goethe publishes *Faust II*.

1833:
Assisted by a slave named Jo Anderson, Cyrus McCormick patents the reaper that will industrialize the cotton economy of the South. Charles Lyell publishes *Principles of Geology*.

1834:
French painter and sculptor Edgar Degas (1834-1917). Michael Faraday formulates Faraday's Law of electrolysis. The first electric generator is invented in London. Henry Blair patents a seed-planter. Tocqueville writes *Democracy in America*. "It is indeed difficult to imagine how men who have entirely renounced the habit of managing their own affairs could be successful in choosing those who ought to lead them. It is impossible to believe that a liberal, energetic, and wise government can ever emerge from the ballots of a nation of servants."

1835:
The first multi-family tenement building since Rome goes up in New York, and it is confined, airless, and unsanitary. Hans Christian Anderson starts writing children's stories. European squatters settle Melbourne and Adelaide.

1836:
A confederation between Peru and Bolivia forms and then falls apart. Responding to Texan forces driving out Mexicans, general Santa Anna attacks the Alamo, and all armed defenders, including Davy Crockett and James Bowie, are wiped out. Texans respond by attacking and beating the Mexican Army at San Jacinto. Samuel Houston leads Texans to declare independence from Mexico. Heinrich Hössli publishes *Eros Die Männerliebe der Griechen*, a survey of same-sex love in Greece. Samuel Colt patents the revolver. John Ericsson invents the screw propeller. Emerson's "Nature" starts the Transcendentalism movement. "Nature never became a toy to a wise spirit. The flowers, the animals, the mountains, reflected the wisdom of his best hour, as much as they had delighted the simplicity of his childhood."

1836-37:
The Great Trek of Boers (Dutch/French farmers descended from Huguenots; also called Afrikaners) away from the British in South Africa. The Boers found the Republic of Natal in 1838 and the Orange Free State in 1854.

1837:
Victoria becomes Queen of Great Britain. Revolts for fair government in Canada. Samuel Morse invents the telegraph. Louis Braille designs his alphabet for the blind. Louis Daguerre invents the art of portrait photography named after him. Charles Dickens publishes *Oliver Twist*.

1838:
Although persecuted by Buddhists, Nakayama Miki founds the faith-healing Tenrikyo religion in Japan. By now railroads run through every eastern state of the US but Vermont. Costa Rica gains independence. Dickens publishes *Nicholas Nickleby*. Birth of naturalist John Muir (1838-1914).

1839:
Christian Schwann discovers ozone. The First Opium War begins in

China when Chinese authorities destroy a large opium supply delivered by the British, who benefit economically from Chinese drug use. British gunboats counter until the Chinese are forced to sign the Treaty of Nanking. Darwin publishes *A Naturalist's Voyage on the Beagle*. By accident, Charles Goodyear learns how to vulcanize rubber (heat it with sulfur).

1839-42:
First Afghan War with the British, who invade to keep Afghanistan from Russia. The British lose, heavily.

1840:
Kamehameha III sets up a constitutional monarchy in Hawaii, where its first written constitution evolves as Europe and the US recognize Hawaiian independence. New Zealand Maoris sign a treaty that brings them under the British Crown. Imam Sayyid Said, ruler of Oman (1806-56), makes Zanzibar, a small island off the East African coast, his capital. Emerson publishes his *Essays*. British and Maoris in New Zealand sign the Treaty of Waitangi.

1842:
Chinese ports open to foreign trade. Daniel Webster negotiates the Webster Ashburton Treaty that ends the long Canada/America boundary dispute.

1843:
William Miller picks 1843 as the Day of Judgment, and although the world does not end, his convictions inspire the Seventh-Day Adventists and the Jehovah's Witnesses. Daniel Emmett initiates the "Negro minstrel" show in which white men paint their faces black and stereotype African-American behavior; the tune "Dixie" was written for such shows. A modern ocean liner, the *Great Britain*, stretches three hundred and twenty-two feet in length. Kierkegaard publishes *Either/Or* and *Fear and Trembling* under a pen name. Poe publishes the first modern mystery: *The Gold Bug*. Dickens publishes *A Christmas Carol*.

1844:
Joseph Smith is murdered in Illinois, so Brigham Young takes over the Mormons. Alexandre Dumas publishes *The Three Musketeers* and *The Count of Monte Cristo*. German philosopher and philologist Friedrich Nietzsche (1844-1900) born; he will accurately boast, "I am no man, I am dynamite." Captain Robert Field Stockton of the *Princeton* takes President Tylor and assorted dignitaries on a Potomac cruise aboard the most advanced ship in the Navy, but the Peacemaker cannon blows up during a firing exercise and kills Secretaries Upshur and Gilmer and four others. The telegraph hurls its first demonstration message between Baltimore and Washington D.C.: "What hath God wrought?" Kierkegaard writes *The Concept of Anxiety:* "If a person could have a part just once, could lead the waltz of the moment just once—then he has lived, then he becomes the envy of the less fortunate, those who are not born but rush headlong into life, and headlong continue to rush forward, never reaching it...If I have ventured wrongly, well, then life helps me by punishing me. But if I have not ventured at all, who helps me then?"

1845:
A potato famine in Ireland, forced long ago by the British to depend on this single crop; a third of the population perishes. Edgar Allen Poe writes "The Raven." Christian Schonbein refines guncotton. Lawyer and editor John Lous O'Sullivan writes about "Manifest Destiny" in *The United States Magazine and Democratic Review* to argue in favor of annexing Texas. Margaret Fuller's *Woman in the Nineteenth Century*. "There is no wholly masculine man, no purely feminine woman."

1845-49:
The Sikh Wars with Britain, which annexes the Punjab, then Kashmir.

1846:
The Mexican War breaks out when the ambitious President Polk sends John Slidell to Mexico to tell them: sell California and New Mexico or we'll take them by force. Zachary Taylor's invading

troops are fired at and Polk declares war. The Smithsonian Institute is founded in Washington. Brigham Young leads the Mormons toward the Great Salt Lake, which they reach in 1847. Dred Scott sues his former master's widow for freedom for himself and his family on the grounds that living in a free state and territory had ended his slavery status. He wins before a lower court in St. Louis, but the Missouri Supreme Court reverses the decision. Elias Howe patents the sewing machine. Frederick Douglass launches the abolitionist newspaper *The North Star*. Hanging from a rope, Henry Rawlinson copies and later deciphers a cliffside inscription in Old Persian, Assyrian, and Elamitic, and the history of Babylon becomes legible.

1847:
The Caste War of Yucatán, in which native Mayans rise up against Yucatecos at the top of the colonial caste system. Hermann von Helmholtz formulates the conservation of energy law (the First Law of Thermodynamics). Hungarian doctor Ignaz Semmelweiss orders the doctors at his hospital to sterilize their hands before touching women giving birth, but the doctors get rid of him and go back to their prior habits, once again raising the death rate for childhood fever. Brontë sisters Charlotte and Emily publish *Jane Eyre* and *Wuthering Heights*.

1847-48:
A civil war in which Swiss Protestant cantons beat the Catholic leaves Switzerland a federal state.

1848:
Accession of Nasir ud-din of Persia's Kajar dynasty. Revolutions in France as Louis Philippe ignores the nation's economic woes and Louis Napoleon becomes president. Revolutions in the Austrian Empire, Italy, and Germany. Marx publishes *The Communist Manifesto*. The US acquires Texas. Gold is discovered in California, whose state motto will become "Eureka!" At the Treaty of Guadalupe Hidalgo, America gains California and New Mexico via the Mexican War denounced by Lincoln and sets the border between the two nations. A convention in Seneca Falls, New York calls for

equal rights for women and produces the Declaration of Sentiments patterned after the Declaration of Independence. August Comte publishes *A General View of Positivism* to argue for a new social science (sociology) and to elevate scientific understanding as the only adequate way to know things.

1849:
A new constitution curbs the power of the Danish monarchy. The California Gold Rush. Elizabeth Blackwell becomes the first American woman to receive a medical degree. Armand Fizeau and Jean Foucault measure the speed of light in a laboratory. Dickens publishes *David Copperfield*. On the way to New York to marry Sarah Royster Shelton, Edgar Allen Poe falls ill after a drinking debauch and croaks out his last words: "It's all over now...write: 'Eddy is no more.'"

1850:
End of the Little Ice Age. Led by Hong Xiuquan, a visionary from Guangdong who evolves a political creed influenced by elements of Christianity, Chinese peasants demand land and rights from the Manchus of the Qing Dynasty. With some outside help the rulers crush this Taiping Rebellion in which twenty million lose their lives. The Ali Muhammad "the Bab" ("the Gate") is murdered in Persia, and his mix of religious doctinres is taken up by Mirza Hosayn Ali Nuri, who calls himself Baha'-u-llah ("Glory of God") and begins the Bahai faith. German émigré Levi Strauss invents jeans. The four main Australian colonies achieve self-government. Emmanual Clausius demonstrates the Second Law of Thermodynamics (the operation of entropy). Europeans run all over Africa setting up mines and farms except in the Rift Valley held mostly by the Masai.

1851:
Gold found in Victoria and New South Wales, Australia, brings miners and settlers, and Sydney and Melbourne prosper and grow. The Great Exhibition of the Works of Industry of all Nations opens at the Crystal Palace in Hyde Park, London. It is the first international exhibition of manufactured products, and it will influence art and

design education, international trade, and tourism. Melville's *Moby Dick* ("If, then, to meanest mariners, and renegades and castaways, I shall hereafter ascribe high qualities, though dark; weave round them tragic graces; if even the most mournful, perchance the most abased, among them all, shall at times lift himself to the exalted mounts; if I shall touch that workman's arm with some ethereal light; if I shall spread a rainbow over his disastrous set of sun; then against all mortal critics bear me out in it, thou just Spirit of Equality, which hast spread one royal mantle of humanity over all my kind!") Nathaniel Hawthorne hits back at religious self-righteousness in *The Scarlet Letter* ("No man, for any considerable period, can wear one face to himself and another to the multitude, without finally getting bewildered as to which may be the true."). Jean Foucault shows that the Earth rotates on its axis. Lord Kelvin (William Thomson) calculates an absolute zero temperature scale. Sojourner Truth's electrifying "Ain't I A Woman" speech at a women's rights convention in Ohio: "Then that little man in black there, he says women can't have as much rights as men, 'cause Christ wasn't a woman! Where did your Christ come from? Where did your Christ come from? From God and a woman! Man had nothing to do with Him."

1851-68:
King Rama IV rules Thailand; he opens it to foreign trade.

1852:
Verdi's *Il Trovatore*. Britain recognizes Transvaal's independence. Russian forces under Nicholas invades Ottoman territories Moldavia and Walachia, ostensibly to guard their Eastern Orthodox institutions, and this flames into the Crimean War, with Russia against Turkey, Britain, France, and Sardinia. Florence Nightingale works as a nurse during this war. Harriet Beecher Stowe writes *Uncle Tom's Cabin*. "There are in this world blessed souls, whose sorrows all spring up into joys for others; whose earthly hopes, laid in the grave with many tears, are the seed from which spring healing flowers and balm for the desolate and the distressed."

1853:
Japanese trade isolation ends with Commodore Perry's expedition to Tokyo, where he threatens to land with his cannons unless the officials speak to him, which they do. Antoinette-Louisa Brown is ordained as the first woman minister in the US. The Gadsden Purchase gives the US some southern land and finalizes its continental boundaries. Verdi's *La Traviata*. George Cayley constructs a glider and makes his coach driver test it. Antoine Chabot and Edward Matteson invent hydaulic mining.

1853-78:
King Mindon Min reigns ably in Burma.

1854:
George Boole creates Boolean algebra, a tool of the coming digital revolution. Coal tar derivatives are discovered, laying the basis for fossil fuel consumption, the petrochemical industry, and the textile industry. In London Italians Eugenio Barsanti and Felice Matteucci patent the first working internal combustion engine. Walt Whitman writes *Leaves of Grass*. Lord Tennyson's *Charge of the Light Brigade*. Henry David Thoreau's *Walden*: "I went to the woods because I wished to live deliberately, to front only the essential facts of life, and see if I could not learn what it had to teach, and not, when I came to die, discover that I had not lived."

1855-68:
Reign of Emperor Theodore of Ethiopia.

1856:
Louis Pasteur discovers that microorganisms cause fermentation. The first Neanderthal remains resurface in the Neander Valley in Germany. The Congress of Paris ends the Crimean War with Russia no longer a dominant power in southeastern Europe. The Second Opium War in China. The Royal Niger Company enjoys a trade monopoly on the Niger River. Gustave Flaubert writes *Madame Bovary*. Henry Bessemer refines iron into steel industrially. In Staten Island Antonio Meucci invents and tests the telephone.

1857:
The US Supreme Court decides in *Scott v. Sandford* that Congress can't prohibit slavery in the territories, which means the Missouri Compromise is unconstitutional. This sad verdict further inflames the growing conflict between North and South. Britain takes over control of India from the East India Company. Baudelaire's *Les Fleurs du Mal*. Herman Melville visits the war-ravaged Holy Land and writes in his journal, "Is the desolation of the land the result of the fatal embrace of the Deity? Hapless are the favorites of heaven."

1858:
In Springfield, Illinois, Lincoln speaks out against slavery. A new constitution for Colombia. Cyrus Field lays the Transatlantic Cable, prompting Henry David Thoreau to wonder whether it would transmit anything but trivia.

1859:
Birth of Pierre Janet (1858-1947), pioneer of depth psychology. John Brown's attempt to start a slave revolt alarms Southern whites, who hang him. Marx writes *Das Kapital*. In northwestern Pennsylvania Edwin Drake drills the first successful commercial oil well. Edward Fitzgerald translates *The Rubaiyat of Omar Khayyam* into English ("One thing is certain and the rest is Lies;/The Flower that once has blown forever dies"). Charles Darwin publishes *On the Origin of Species* to lay out his version of the theory of evolution based on natural selection ("It is not the strongest of the species that survives, nor the most intelligent, but the one most responsive to change"). Alfred Russell Wallace comes up with a Creationist version of the theory. John Stuart Mill's *On Liberty*. Thoreau publishes *On Civil Disobedience*, a work that will impress Gandhi and Martin Luther King Jr. "If the machine of government is of such a nature that it requires you to be the agent of injustice to another, then, I say, break the law."

1860:
The throne of Rwabugiri oversees much of what is now Rwanda and

Burundi. Bishop Samuel Wilberforce and Thomas Huxley disagree about evolutionary theory at Oxford; when the bishop asks Huxley whether he had descended from an ape on his grandmother's side or his grandfather's, Huxley replies that he wouldn't mind being descended from an ape but would mind being connected to a man who obscured the truth. It is doubtful that Wilberforce had even read *The Origin of Species*; the theory actually maintains that humans and apes descended from a common ancestor.

1861:
Tsar Alexander II abolishes serfdom in Russia. Moldavia and Walachia unite into the strife-torn Kingdom of Romania. After South Carolina secedes because of Lincoln's election to the presidency, the Confederate States of America are organized in Montgomery, Alabama with Jefferson Davis as President and Alexander Stephens as Vice President. Both men affirm in public speeches that the war is about preserving the institution of slavery. Outgoing President James Buchanan does nothing about any of this. Attacked by Confederate forces, Fort Sumter surrenders, and the Civil War is on in the US Indian poet Rabindranath Tagore (1861-1941). George Eliot (Mary Ann Evans) writes *Silas Marner*. Bachofen's *Mother Right*.

1862:
The Port Royal Experiment of returning land to freed black slaves starts up in the US, where land is also given to European immigrants. The French begin colonizing Southeast Asia. The Muslim Hui people rise up in China near the Yellow River (the Dungan Revolt) and many end up emigrating to Russia and Eastern Europe. Richard Gatling tests a rapid-fire gun that pumps out two hundred shots a minute and that will kill many thousands of people. Victor Hugo publishes *Les Miserables*. Ivan Sergeyevich Turgenev publishes *Fathers and Sons*. The ironclad *Virginia* (formerly a Union ship called *Merrimack*) sinks Union ships preparing to blockade the Confederacy; the Union responds with the ironclad *Monitor*, and the two fight to a draw. Pacifist and feminist Julia Ward Howe writes "The Battle Hymn of the Republic."

1863:
France takes over Cambodia. Lincoln issues the Emancipation Proclamation on New Year's Day. Stonewall Jackson is accidentally shot by his own sentries and dies. The Battle of Gettysburg, where Colonel Chamberlain's bayonet charge on Little Round Top saves the Union army and where Pickett's charge uphill is cut to pieces. The Gettysburg Address, which Lincoln thought a failure. Jules Verne gets popular with his book *Five Weeks in a Balloon*. William Huggins shows with spectroscopy that the elements on Earth also blaze in the stars above.

1864:
Running for reelection, Lincoln goes with incompetent racist Andrew Johnson of Tennessee, partly to convince the world that the Union isn't just a Northern power. General Sherman's march to the sea cuts and burns brutally through Georgia, the state from which the Cherokee had previously been expelled. Pius IX writes an encyclical demanding that the Church hold sole control over education and the last word on nationalism and science, but no secular authority pays him any attention. Dostoevsky publishes *Notes From Underground*. William James opens the first psychological lab in the world at Harvard. Through President Lincoln's effort the Thirteenth Amendment to the US Constitution passes: "Proposed and Adopted: An Amendment to the Constitution of the United States, Section 1: Neither slavery nor involuntary servitude, except as a punishment for crime whereof the party shall have been duly convicted, shall exist within the United States, or any place subject to their jurisdiction...."

1865:
Lewis Carroll (Charles Dodgson) writes *Alice's Adventures in Wonderland*. The Thirteenth Amendment to the US Constitution outlaws slavery, in theory. General Lee surrenders to tenacious General Grant at Appomattox and ends the Civil War. Lincoln is heard reciting, "Out, out brief candle! Life's but a walking shadow..." and tells his wife and an aide, Ward Hill Lamon, that in a dream he saw himself dead in the Capitol's East Room. Following eerie misprints

announcing Lincoln's death, Lincoln is shot at Ford's Theater by John Wilkes Booth, and his body is laid out in the East Room. Tolstoy publishes *War and Peace*: "If everyone fought for their own convictions there would be no war."

1866:
Mendel publishes a paper on the rules of heredity. Otto von Bismarck of Prussia allies with Italy and uses a dispute over Holstein to go to war with ex-ally Austria, which he defeats with modern weaponry like needle-guns, railroads, and telegraph lines: this is the Seven Weeks War or Austro-Prussian War. Severe famine in Finland. Writer and futurist H.G. Wells (1866-1946). Alfred Nobel invents dynamite. Dostoevsky writes *Crime and Punishment*. Mary Baker Eddy founds Christian Science.

1867:
Diamonds found near Kimberley in South Africa will instigate a European rush to industrialize the entire region. The last Japanese shogun, Hitotsubashi, resigns, and the Emperor regains his position as head of government. Kazakhstan absorbed into Russian Turkestan. The British Government recognizes the Dominion of Canada. Karl Heinrich Ulrichs comes out as a homosexual and campaigns for gay rights in Munich. Strauss's *Beautiful Blue Danube*. Henrik Kibsen's *Peer Gynt*.

1868:
A revolution in Spain deposes Queen Isabella, so she flees to France. Louisa May Alcott writes *Little Women*. Cro-Magnon remains are found by accident in Cro-Magnon Valley, Lez Eyzies, southwestern France. Christopher Sholes patents the typewriter. Brahms composes his famous lullaby.

1868-1910:
Reign of Rama V, the founder of modern Thailand.

1868-1912:
Meiji Restoration period of modernization in Japan: great leaps in

industrialization while the imperial capital moves back to Edo (renamed Tokyo). In 1875-88 a civil legal code is drawn up.

1869:
The National Woman Suffrage Association and American Woman Suffrage Association organize in the US. The Fifteenth Amendment gives African-Americans the vote, in theory. John Stuart Mill publishes *The Subjection of Women*. Journalist Karl-Maria Kertbeny coins the words "homosexual" and "heterosexual" and insists that both orientations are inborn. The Suez Canal connects the Red Sea with the Mediterranean. The American transcontinental rail line completed. Johann Miescher discovers nucleic acids. Edward von Hartmann describes the unconscious in his book *Philosophy of the Unconscious*. Verdi's *Aida* airs. Birth of Mohandas K. Gandhi (1869-1948): "Strength does not come from physical capacity. It comes from an indomitable will...The pledge of nonviolence does not require us to cooperate in our humiliation. It, therefore, does not require us to crawl on our bellies or to draw lines with our noses or to walk to salute the Union Jack or to do anything degrading at the dictation of officials. On the contrary our creed requires us to refuse to do any of these things even though we should be shot."

1870:
Pale and shadowy John D. Rockefeller founds the nefarious Standard Oil Company and tells his competitors privately that resisting his buy-outs is futile. Provoked by German chancellor Bismarck, Emperor Napoleon III declares war on Germany, but he French lose the Franco-Prussian War to the modernized, rail-equipped, and intelligence-informed Prussians. The Vatican Council I establishes the doctrine of papal infallibility, but it backfires by causing widespread resentment and disbelief. Franz Bretano resigns his Catholic priesthood and turns to psychology and philosophy. Bayard Taylor publishes *Joseph and His Friend*, the first gay novel in the US Jules Verne publishes *Twenty Thousand Leagues Under the Sea*. Ernst Haeckel coins the term *oekologie* (ecology).

1870s:
The independence movement in India starts to grow.

1871:
Severe famine lingers in Persia. Prussian king William I becomes emperor of a unified Germany that has recently gained Alsace-Lorraine. In Japan, an imperial decree abolishes all fiefs, and a ministry is set up to promote universal education. Italy is unified, with Rome as its capital. Feudalism abolished in Japan. Cakobau establishes a national monarchy in Fiji. The reporter Sir Henry Stanley meets explorer Dr. David Livingstone in Africa, where Livingstone seeks to trace the Nile's source and to end slavery, but Stanley's dramatic reports of pygmies, Amazons, cannibals, and exotic animals unleashes a rush of European explorers, tourists, and colonizers. Zambia remains relatively unplumbed by Europeans until the Livingstone expedition. Anthropologist Edward Tylor writes that "primitives" who believe in a soul separate from the body think nature has a soul as well ("animism"). Darwin applies the principles of evolution to human beings in his *The Descent of Man*. P. T. Barnum opens "The Greatest Show on Earth."

1872:
Birth of Indian liberation activist, poet, and guru Aurobindo Ghose (1872-1950). In increasingly warlike Germany, Catholics are suppressed and Jesuits expelled (the Kulturkampf). Susan B. Anthony leads women to the polls and is arrested, but she refuses to pay the subsequent fine, and the Supreme Court overturns her conviction. Lewis Carroll's *Through the Looking Glass*. Jules Verne's *Around the World in 80 Days*. Ferdinand Cohn founds the science of bacteriology. James Whistler paints "Whistler's Mother." George Smith deciphers the cuneiform tablets on which *Gilgamesh* is written.

1873:
The people of Aceh are among the last in Indonesia to keep fighting against Dutch rule, and they lose the fight in 1903. Color photographs develop. James Clerk Maxwell publishes his equations on electromagnetism in *A Treatise on Electricity and Magnetism*. He

also works on color, heat, dynamics, and a kinetic theory of gasses. Brahms composes his first string quartet.

1874:
Impressionists stage their first showing in Paris. Spain gets its first republic. Ghana becomes a British Crown colony.

1875:
A lethal famine in India. British prime minister Benjamin Disraeli buys almost half the shares of the Suez Canal to allow Britain into Egypt and to secure a quicker route to India. Georges Bizet composes *Carmen*.

1876:
Just before George Armstrong Custer makes a last stand against the Sioux under Crazy Horse, he is heard to shout, "Hurrah, boys, we've got them!" Severe famine ravages northern China. Japanese pressure forces Korea to open its ports to trade. Wilhelm Kuhne describes enzymes. Mark Twain (Samuel Clemens) publishes *The Adventures of Tom Sawyer*. Alexander Graham Bell patents the telephone, and Clemens later wishes he'd funded Graham's work when he had the chance. Wagner finishes his *Ring of the Nibelungen* operas. Brahms composes his first symphony.

1876-78:
In a terrible famine in the Deccan, southern India, over five million die. As with many famines, causes include monocropping soils to exhaustion, leaving them and their crops vulnerable to heat waves. Villages and regions forced to grow cash crops are often hit hardest.

1877:
Takamori Saigo leads the Satsuma clansmen in an unsuccessful samurai rebellion against the imperial government after it outlawed the samurai class. German writer Hermann Hesse (1877-1961). Russo-Turkish wars reignite (1877-1978). Thomas Edison, the Ford of electrical engineering, patents the phonograph. The Great Railroad Strike in the US for a livable wage and safer work. The Nez

Perce leader Chief Joseph is forced to surrender. He is known to have said, "Do not misunderstand me, but understand me fully, and my affection for the land. I never said the land was mine to do with as I chose. The one who has the right to dispose of it is the one who has created it. I claim a right to live on my land, and accord you the privilege to live on yours." He and the members of other Native American tribes have no way of knowing they deal with the still-traumatized ancestors of people who were displaced and murdered by Huns and Romans long ago, just as the Huns were mistreated by the Han, the Romans by the Etruscans, and on and on back to the once-Fertile Crescent where all empire arose. Crazy Horse too is forced to surrender.

1876-1911:
The rule of President Porfirio in Mexico ushers in a period of expansion and, for the US, lucrative access to Mexican railroads, minerals, and petroleum.

1878:
The Congress of Berlin and Treaty of San Stefano end the Russo-Turkish War, give Serbia, Romania, and Montenegro independence, and mark the end of Turkey's power in Europe. The first commercial telephone exchange switches on in New Haven, Connecticut. Thomas Hardy writes *The Return of the Native*.

1879:
Bismarck negotiates a military alliance between Germany and Austria-Hungary. Wilhelm Wundt establishes a psychological laboratory at the University of Leipzig in Germany. The Anglo-Zulu War involves the British, who want to federate Africa and who lose at Isandlwana but win at Ulundi. Edison invents a workable incandescent light. Dostoevsky publishes *The Brothers Karamazov*, with its famous Grand Inquisitor passage. Ibsen's *A Doll's House*.

1879-84:
The War of the Pacific between Chile, Peru, and Bolivia over Peruvian mineral deposits.

1880:
Australia's bushranger Ned Kelly wears makeshift armor to fight police in Victoria, is captured, is hanged, and becomes a folk hero. Famine burns East Africa. Auguste Rodin sculpts *The Thinker*. European powers continue their scramble for Africa. The First Boer War, after diamonds are found near the Vaal River in 1867, between Dutch-speaking settlers and the British. General Lewis Wallace writes *Ben Hur*. Rockefeller's Standard Oil controls 90% of the oil business in the US and around the world and is the first modern transnational corporation.

1881:
Britain loses the First Anglo-Boer War, in which Transvaal and its Boer (Dutch) citizenry fight for independence. Clara Barton founds the American Red Cross. The Mahdist War in which Sudanese fight the Egyptians and British, who administrate until 1956. Sitting Bull of the Lakota surrenders and is shot to death. Gunfight at the OK Corral in aptly named Tombstone, Arizona. Artist Pablo Picasso (1841-1973). Ex-slave Booker T. Washington founds the educational Tuskegee Institute (later: University) in Alabama on a former plantation.

1882:
The US Congress approves the Chinese Exclusion Act to ban immigration of Chinese laborers—widely blamed for depressed post-Gold Rush wages—for ten years. Nietzsche publishes *The Gay Science:* "God is dead. God remains dead. And we have killed him. Yet his shadow still looms....who will wipe this blood off us? What water is there for us to clean ourselves? What festivals of atonement, what sacred games shall we have to invent? Is not the greatness of this deed too great for us? Must we ourselves not become gods simply to appear worthy of it?"

1883:
Krakatoa explodes, destroying most of the island and causing damage for hundreds of miles. Hiram Maxim invents the machine gun; it fires over six hundred rounds a minute and does not need crank-

ing. It will slay millions in the coming World Wars. Mark Twain's *The Adventures of Huckleberry Finn*. Nietzsche bellows *Thus Spake Zarathustra* ("Become who you are!"). Robert Louis Stevenson's **Treasure Island**. Dilthey's *Introduction to Human Sciences*.

1884:
A Berlin West Africa Conference meets to discuss how to carve up Africa; Germany takes Kamerun (Cameroon) and some of its neighbors. Prompted by Bismarck, Germany, Austria-Hungary, and Russia sign a secret "Three Emperors' League" to preserve the balance of power in Europe. France takes over North Vietnam from China. The world's first skyscraper goes up in Chicago. Charles Parsons tinkers together the first practical steam turbine. Young Albert Einstein receives a compass as a gift, and this triggers his lifelong passion for science. Sigmund Freud discovers the medicinal properties of cocaine and is outraged when the credit goes to a colleague, although he calms down when cocaine turns out to be highly addictive. Mark Twain publishes *Huckleberry Finn*.

1885:
The Indian National Congress is organized to achieve India's independence from Britain. Under Leopold II, who calls for humanitarian interventions to get at African resources, Belgium sets up the Congo Free State. German warships arrive at Zanzibar just before the French and British to carve up Kenya. The Canadian Pacific railway opens. Auguste Bartholdi gives "Liberty Enlightening the World" (the Statue of Liberty) to the US. German Karl Benz sells the first cars to be powered by internal combustion. Pasteur's vaccinations against anthrax also work against rabies.

1886:
A bombing at Haymarket Square, Chicago, kills seven police and injures many others; of the eight alleged anarchists accused of the bombing, three are imprisoned, one commits suicide, and four are hanged. Samuel Gompers founds the American Federation of Labor. The Supreme Court rules by implication in *Santa Clara County v. Southern Pacific Railroad Company* that corporations enjoy the

rights of individuals. Apache Indian chief Geronimo finally surrenders. A pharmacist creates a headache tonic called Coca-Cola. Colombia is a republic. Psychiatrist Richard von Krafft-Ebing publishes *Sexual Psychopathy: A Clinical-Forensic Study* that popularizes terms like bisexual, homosexual, sadism, and masochism, all of which he considers abnormal. Robert Louis Stevenson (1850-1894) publishes *The Strange Case of Dr. Jekyl and Mr. Hyde*. Gold is found in Transvaal.

1887:
The US Government passes the Dawes Act to break up reservations by treating Native American land owners as individuals instead of as tribe members. The Allotment Act costs Native Americans eighty-six million acres. Arthur Conan Doyle publishes *A Study In Scarlet*, his first Sherlock Holmes story. Polish physician Ludwig Zamenhof invents Esperanto ("One Who Hopes"), an international language he hopes will increase people's understanding of one another. Gottleib Daimler designs the first four-wheeled automobile.

1888:
Cecil Rhodes acquires mineral rights in northern and southern Rhodesia (Zambia and Zimbabwe), and the British East Africa Company takes over Kenya. "Jack the Ripper" murders at least five women in the Whitechapel district of London and disappears into the fog while Scotland Yard makes a hash of the case. J. B. Dunlop invents the pneumatic tire. Heinrich Hertz detects radio waves. George Eastman produces the hand-held Kodak camera. (Like "Exxon," "Kodak" is a contrived word that didn't mean anything.) Edward Bellamy publishes the immensely popular utopian novel *Looking Backward*.

1889:
In Washington DC the first Pan-American Conference is held to promote trade. Herman Hollerith patents the first data processing computer. Alexander G. Eiffel designs the Eiffel Tower. Pedro II is deposed by an army revolt, and Brazil becomes a republic. Emperor Menelik II of Ethiopia (ruling from 1889 to 1913) fends off Western

attempts to take over the country. Nietzsche loses his mind, perhaps as a result of a syphilitic infection. He is given into the custody of his sister, who will sell his remaining papers piecemeal. Vincent van Gogh paints *Starry Night*.

1890:
The impetuous William II becomes Kaiser of Germany and forces Bismarck to resign. Congress passes the Sherman Antitrust Act to break up monopolies like Standard Oil but enforces it irregularly. Sioux Chief Sitting Bull is arrested and murdered by police at the Pine Ridge reservation; two weeks later, troops shoot hundreds of Sioux men, women, and children at Wounded Knee, a definitive slaughter at the end of the Indian Wars. Germany and Britain sign a treaty to give what will become Uganda, Zanzibar, and South Sudan to Britain in exchange for Heligoland. Alfred Mahan's book *The Influence of Sea Power Upon History* convinces the Americans and the Germans to beef up their navies. During this decade European nations will control 90% of Africa, with most of that owned by Britain, France, Belgium, and Germany. Luxembourg achieves independence. William James's *Principles of Psychology* before his disgust with materialist reductionism transfers his interest to philosophy. Frazer's *The Golden Bough*.

1891:
Lydia Liliuokalani becomes Queen of Hawaii. George Stoney names the basic unit of electricity an electron. Thomas Hardy publishes *Tess of the D'Ubervilles*. German aeronaut Otto Lilienthal devises the first practical glider. He will die in a glider crash in 1896, however.

1892:
Tchaikovsky performs his least favorite work, the *Nutcracker*. Susan B. Anthony is President of the National American Woman Suffrage Association she helped found. Women's rights supporter James Hardie gains a seat in the British Parliament and will found the Independent Labour Party. Poet Edna St. Vincent Millay (1892-1950).

1893:
Women get voting rights in New Zealand. Queen Liliuokalani of Hawaii is deposed when she tries to replace the settler-devised constitution with a Hawaiian one. Sanford Dole, the cousin of pineapple capitalist James Dole, demands protection, as do sugar plantation owners from abroad, and armed men land, after which Dole sets up a Republic of Hawaii with himself as president. Marie Dubois discovers a skull cap and other bones of Java Man. The Parliament of the World's Religions, the first world forum for bringing together many faiths, opens in Chicago. Anton Dvorak composes *From the New World*. Edvard Munch paints *The Scream*. Katherine Lee Bates composes "America the Beautiful." Kinetoscopes debut in New York City as forerunners of motion pictures.

1894:
Jacob S. Coxey of Ohio leads "Coxey's Army" of unemployed men on Washington. Eugene V. Debs calls a general strike of rail workers to support Pullman Company strikers, whose wages have been cut but whose rents (also paid to Pullman) have not. With the strike broken, Debs is jailed for six months and embraces socialism. In Hawaii, Sun Yat-Sen begins to organize against the Manchu dynasty in China. Rudyard Kipling writes *The Jungle Book*. The first gramophone plays a vinyl record. Hertz's *Principles of Mechanics*.

1894-95:
The Sino-Japanese War erupts between Japan and China when Japan puts troops into rioting Seoul, supposedly to restore order. The Japanese win (Treaty of Shimonoseki) and occupy Korea. China's obvious lack of preparedness will fuel the coming revolution.

1895:
Oscar Wilde receives two years of hard labor for "gross indecency" (for being gay). H.G. Wells publishes *The Time Machine* and turns into a full-time writer. Appropriating ideas developed by Nikola Tesla, George Westinghouse designs a generating system and wins a contract to build a power station at Niagara Falls. Guglielmo Marconi gets credit for inventing wireless telegraphy already patent-

ed by Tesla. Wilhelm Röentgen discovers X rays. Six French colonies dot Senegal and gather as French West Africa. In France, the Lumire brothers invent the film projector. Freud and Joseph Breuer publish *Studies in Hysteria*. Stephen Crane writes *The Red Badge of Courage*. Wilde's *The Importance of Being Earnest*. Durkheim's *Rules of Sociological Method*.

1896:
Forces under Menelik beat an Italian army at Adowa and Ethiopia wins independence from Italy. After efforts to quell guerrilla activity fail, Spanish military commander Valeriano Weyler y Nicolau sets up the *reconcentrado,* or concentration camp, system, in Cuba, whose rural population is confined to centrally located garrison towns where thousands die from disease, starvation, and exposure. French troops topple the monarchy of Madagascar. Ethiopia stops Italy from invading at the Battle of Adwa, the first-ever victory of an African power over a colonial one. The US Supreme Court's *Plessy v. Ferguson* decision on behalf of "separate but equal" allows railway (and other) segregation of whites from blacks. Hungarian-born Theodor Herzl publishes his pamphlet *The Jewish State* and names his push for a Jewish homeland Zionism after the hill where Solomon built his temple. Checkhov's *The Seagull*.

1897:
The Germans grab Rwanda and Burundi. The Scientific-Humanitarian Committee is founded in Berlin to campaign for LGBTQ rights. New Zealand introduces the eight-hour work day. Bram Stoker publishes *Dracula*. Karl Braun invents the oscilloscope. Edmond Rostand stages *Cyrano de Bergerac*.

1898:
The battleship *Maine* is sunk in Havana Harbor. Spain gets the blame, though unproven, so, under pressure from expansionists, President McKinley blockades Spanish ports, and Spain declares war (Spanish-American War), which the US wins (Treaty of Paris). American troops overrun Cuba and run the government for the next four years. American forces also take Puerto Rico, Guam, and the

Philippines, where US troops kill thousands of civilians. An Anti-Imperialist League of influential US citizens like Jane Addams, Mark Twain, and William James protests to stop this wave of imperialism. A British army under Horatio Kitchener proves the worth of the machine gun by cutting apart the Egyptian Mahdists with it. Wells writes *The War of the Worlds*. Paul Cézanne paints his Mont Sainte-Victoire series.

1899:
The Second Boer War breaks out after gold shows up in 1886 at Witwatersrand just south of Praetoria; the British win this time but with heavy losses. The Hague Conference establishes the Permanent Court of International Justice. France proclaims a protectorate in Laos, Southeast Asia. In England, economist Alfred Marshall suggests a national fresh air tax to pay for permanent green belts and playgrounds between towns, but he is ignored. The United Fruit Company founded; it will exert its influence among "banana republics" throughout Central and South America. In 1984 it will form part of Chiquita. Jorge Luis Borges born (1899-1986).

1900:
Two-thirds of the Masai in the Rift Valley die of smallpox brought by Europeans, who accelerate their takings of ivory, loads of it carried to the coast by Africans enslaved by Arab traders. Uganda is a constitutional monarchy. Encouraged by Tsu Hsi, the Society of the Righteous Harmonious Fists briefly combats foreigners and Chinese Christians (Boxer Rebellion). William II tells the German part of the punishment force unleashed on the Boxers to act so harshly that the Chinese will fear the Germans as Europeans once did the Huns. Ferdinand von Zeppelin builds the first successful dirigible airship. Between 1900 and 1914, Germany's tripled spending on warships makes it the world's second strongest naval power. Russia doubles its spending on its army. Venezuela and the Dominican Republic default on loans from Britain, Germany, and Italy, and when the European countries retaliate, President Roosevelt invokes the Monroe Doctrine to hold them at bay. The first Hague Peace Conference includes ceremonies and handshakes but no plans for

addressing the underlying impulsions, paranoid and colonial, toward a war nobody believes could happen but that nations arm themselves to fight. Russia annexes Manchuria. The British win big in Africa and create Boer concentration camps in which a sixth of their inmates die of disease and maltreatment. Although Max Planck works out the math in which atoms absorb and emit energy only in discrete bundles (quanta), he sees quantization as purely abstract rather than a real event that will break through the limiting mechanist paradigm in physics into quantum theory. Marconi patents the radio. Hugo De Vries, who has discovered genetic mutation, rediscovers Mendel's laws of inheritance. Henry Matisse initiates the Fauvist movement in painting. Husserl's *Logical Investigations*. Thomas Mann becomes famous with *Buddenbrooks*. Freud publishes *The Interpretation of Dreams*, which dethrones Reason in favor of Instinct and which inaugurates psychoanalysis. "Properly speaking, the unconscious is the real psychic; its inner nature is just as unknown to us as the reality of the external world, and it is just as imperfectly reported to us through the data of consciousness as is the external world through the indications of our sensory organs."

1901:
The Russian Social Revolutionary party (Bolsheviks) founded. Australia gains nationhood and a constitution. Troubled by massacres committed by US troops in the Philippines, anarchist Leon Czolgosz shoots and kills William McKinley during the President's visit to the World's Fair in Buffalo. Theodore Roosevelt is sworn in. The US withdraws troops from Cuba but pushes through the Platt amendment and its host of conditions to make Cuba a de facto US protectorate. William James delivers a series of lectures published as *Varieties of Religious Experience*: "The potentialities of development in human souls are unfathomable. So many who seemed irretrievably hardened have in point of fact been softened, converted, regenerated, in ways that amazed the subjects even more than they surprised the spectators, that we never can be sure in advance of any man that his salvation by the way of love is hopeless."

1902:
Highly conservative tribal leader Ibn Saud takes Riyadh from the rival Rashidi. A British expedition under Francis Younghusband enters the Tibetan capital of Lhasa and forces a treaty that imposes trade relations. The Treaty of Verceniging ends the Second Boer War in South Africa but embitters the defeated Boers.

1903:
Desiring two-ocean access for its fleets, the US supports an uprising in Panama in the hope that the new government will permit construction of the Canal, which it does. Henry Ford founds the Ford Motor Company. Marie Curie wins the Nobel Prize for Physics for co-discovering radioactivity with her husband, an achievement by which she refuses to profit commercially. A women's meeting in the Manchester home of Emmeline Pankhurst evolves into the Women's Social and Political Union. The Wright brothers make their first flight at Kitty Hawk, for twelve seconds, then go up again for a full minute. Willem Einthoven invents the electrocardiogram. *The Great Train Robbery* is the first modern movie to tell a story. Russian physicist Konstantin Tsiolkovsky writes lucidly about the possibility of rocketry. Shaw's *Man and Superman*. W.E.B. DuBois publishes *The Souls of Black Folk*. Anticipating later theories of internalized oppression: "It is a peculiar sensation, this double-consciousness, this sense of always looking at one's self through the eyes of others, of measuring one's soul by the tape of a world that looks on in amused contempt and pity."

1904:
The Herero and Namaqua Genocide in modern-day Namibia when the Herero and Nama people revolt against German colonial rule and are forced into the desert by Lothar von Trotha; over a hundred thousand die in the first genocide of the twentieth century. The British raise tensions among native Kenyans by inviting South Africans and Indian railroad workers to settle there. Peasants revolt in Romania. Persia gets a parliament. Russo-Japanese War (1904-1905). Roosevelt adds the Roosevelt Corollary to the Monroe Doctrine to self-appoint the US a hemispheric police power with authority to go

debt-collecting among Latin American countries that owe money to the rest of the world: exactly the reverse of how the Monroe worked previously. Emile Berliner creates the flat phonograph record. Puccini composes *Madame Butterfly*.

1905:
The Maji Maji rebellion to German colonial oppression in Tanzania (German East Africa), where farmers required to grow cotton for export. The revolts fail in the short term but do prompt long-term reform. Arthur Griffith founds the Sinn Fein political movement to push for Irish independence. Norway breaks away from Sweden and selects King Haakon VII. The British divide Bangladesh into East Bengal and West Bengal (until 1911). Japan presses Korea to sign a treaty whereby Japan "protects" Korea. Einstein submits his paper "On the Electrodynamics of Moving Bodies" to the leading German physics journal and explores the idea of energy quanta to revolutionize physics. He also traces Browning motion to atomic movements, writes his famous mass-energy equation $E=MC^2$, and publishes Special Relativity to reconcile Maxwell's equations for electricity and magnetism with the laws of mechanics. Hermann Nernst comes up with the Third Law of Thermodynamics: it's impossible to reach a state of absolute zero temperature without drawing heat from somewhere. The first movie theater sells ten-minute shorts for a nickel in Philadelphia: hence "nickelodeon." Max Weber's *The Protestant Ethic and the Spirit of Capitalism*. "Man is dominated by the making of money, by acquisition as the ultimate purpose of his life. Economic acquisition is no longer subordinated to man as the means for the satisfaction of his material needs. This reversal of what we should call the natural relationship, so irrational from a naïve point of view, is evidently as definitely a leading principle of capitalism as it is foreign to all peoples not under capitalistic influence. At the same time it expresses a type of feeling which is closely connected with certain religious ideas."

1906:
The British put to sea the *Dreadnought*, the first modern large-gunned ship of steel, and, predictably, the Germans respond by

building dreadnoughts of their own. The British also conquer Niger and divide it in two. Ivan Pavlov publishes his famous study of dogs he trains to salivate when a bell is rung (classical conditioning). The Triple Entente (France/Britain/Russia) forms to counterbalance the Triple Alliance (Germany/Austria-Hungary/Italy). The Muslim League is organized in India to preserve Muslim rights in the midst of a Hindu majority. A treaty between China and Japan that "recognizes" China's right to rule Tibet forces the Dalai Lama to flee to India. Democratic reform sweeps Finland. Muckraking journalist Upton Sinclair writes *The Jungle* to expose abuses in the meatpacking industry. Edward Irenaeus Prime-Stevenson publishes *Imre: A Memorandum*. Shortly after a new statue in San Francisco is dedicated to Enyo, destroyer of cities, an earthquake and fire kill more than twenty-five hundred residents. Building on landfill continues anyway.

1907:
In Rome Maria Montessori (1870-1952) opens her school of holistic child-centered education. The second Hague Peace Conference officially adopts ten paper conventions of war but in actuality gets nowhere as nations go on arming. Alfred Adler coins the term "inferiority complex." The Eulenburg affair unfolds as a series of trials and court-martials involving a circle of gay government officials working for Kaiser Wilhelm II. Picasso's *Les Demoiselles d'Avignon* introduces cubism. In a speech Woodrow Wilson of Virginia exclaims with rare candor, "Concessions obtained by financiers must be safeguarded by ministers of state, even if the sovereignty of unwilling nations be outraged in the process." Henri Bergson's *Creative Evolution*. William James's *Pragmatism*. Picasso's *Les Demoiselles d'Avignon*. D.T. Suzuki's *Outline of Mahayana Buddhism*.

1908:
The Young Turk revolution forces the restoration of the Ottoman-suppressed parliament in Turkey. Franz Joseph, Hapsburg Emperor of Austria-Hungary, uses the authority received from the Berlin Conference to annex Bosnia and Herzegovina, thereby infuriating

the Serbs. Two days later, the Black Hand secret society bands together in Serbia to regain this territory. Oil is discovered in southwestern Persia at Masjed Soleyman by William Knox D'Arcy. Bulgaria achieves independence. Henry Ford develops the Model T and the assembly line method of producing automobiles. A meteorite levels forests near Tunguska.

1909:
Swedish writer Selma Lagerlöf is the first woman to receive the Nobel Prize for literature. Women finally force their way into the English House of Commons and are imprisoned, with some starting hunger strikes. The same House debates the wartime possibility of terrorizing enemy civilians by dropping bombs on them. A Union of South Africa is established in which Boers and British, but not blacks, are equal citizens. The Ottomans continue to massacre Armenians in Turkey. The North Pole is reached by American explorers Robert E. Peary and black colleague Matthew Henson, who reaches it first in a final dash. The National Association for the Advancement of Colored People is founded in New York. Fritz Haber and Carl Bosch invent the atmospheric nitrogen-fixing process named after them, at once providing explosives for weapons (depopulation) and fertilizer for farms (overpopulation). James rescues Gustav Fechner's nature writing from obscurity and publishes excerpts in *A Pluralistic Universe*: "On a certain spring morning I went out to walk. The fields were green, the birds sang, the dew glistened, the smoke was rising, here and there a man appeared; a light as of transfiguration lay on all things. It was only a little bit of earth; it was only one moment of her existence; and yet as my look embraced her more and more it seemed to me not only so beautiful an idea, but so true and clear a fact, that she is an angel, an angel so rich and fresh and flower-like, and yet going her round in the skies so firmly and so at one with herself, turning her whole living face to Heaven, and carrying me along with her into that Heaven, that I asked myself how the opinions of men could ever have so spun themselves away from life so far as to deem the earth only a dry clod, and to seek for angels above it or about it in the emptiness of the sky—only to find them nowhere...."

1910:
The Mexican Revolution, when idealistic liberal leader Francisco I. Madero stages an armed revolt against President Díaz for breaking his word not to seek reelection in 1910. Madero is quickly successful. A Portuguese revolution ends the monarchy as Manuel II flees, and Joaquim Braga is elected President. Japan annexes Korea. Psychiatrist Eugen Bleuler coins "depth psychology" (*Tiefenpsychologie*) to describe psychoanalytic models for which the mind is an arena of balanced interacting forces. Birth of Jacques Cousteau (1910-1997). Emma Goldman speaks publicly on behalf of gay rights.

1911:
Aircraft are first employed as a weapon in the Turkish-Italian (or Tripolitan) War in which ambitious Italy defeats the Turks and annexes Tripoli and Libya. In Hamburg, William II says of Germany, "No one can dispute with us the place in the sun that is our due." In New York, a fire at the Triangle Shirtwaist factory kills a hundred and forty-six people, mostly young immigrant women, and sweatshop reforms are called for despite the usual complaints by industrialists about government interference. The Ch'ing Dynasty moves to nationalize the Chinese railroad and sets off insurrections that draw Sun Yat-sen to China. Mongolia wins independence from China. Roald Amundsen reaches the South Pole. Ernest Rutherford describes an atom as a nucleus surrounded by particles. Marie Curie is awarded a second Nobel Prize, this time in chemistry for her discovery and isolation of pure radium. William Carrier assembles the first modern air-conditioner. Edith Wharton writes *Ethan Fromm*. John Muir writes *My First Summer in the Sierra*.

1911-12:
The Manchus fall and the Republic of China is established, with Sun Yat-sen as president, but two months later he resigns in favor of Yuan Shih-kai, who kicks him out of China. Grigori Rasputin gains behind-the-throne influence over the Romanov royal family in Russia; for this he will be poisoned, shot, clubbed, and drowned. The Supreme Court forces Rockefeller's Standard Oil Company into

several companies that are the forerunners of Mobil, Exxon, Chevron, BP, Amoco, and ARCO.

1912:
The African National Congress founded. During the Nicaraguan civil war US forces ensure that conservative candidate Adolfo Diaz is elected, and by doing this initiate a century of self-serving and often violent interference in foreign elections, especially those held in South America. Montenegro, then Serbia, Bulgaria, and Greece fight over what's left of the Ottoman Empire in the First Balkan War, resulting in Turkey's partitioning and, at the insistence of Austrio-Hungary, Albania's founding on the coast, to the fury of landlocked Serbia. An exercise in hubris called the *Titanic* sinks in an odd replay of the Greek myth about the end of the Titans. Her sister ship *Olympia* comes to no harm. Airplanes carry the mail. George Bernard Shaw writes *Pyglamion*. After C.G. Jung publishes *Symbols and Transformations of the Libido* he sends Freud a copy, which Freud returns with the inscription "Resistance to the father," meaning himself. Jung responds by cutting off their correspondence.

1913:
Having never heard of General Custer, the South African government passes laws to reserve 87% of available land for whites. France colonizes Chad. Francisco Madero and his vice president are assassinated by General Huerta, who sets up a regime in Mexico. Serbia and Greece and then Romania attack Bulgaria (whose strength they fear) in a second Balkan War and win. Suffragettes demonstrate in London. Striking garment workers in New York and Boston get pay raises and shorter work hours. Indian poet Rabindranath Tagore is awarded the Nobel Prize for Literature. Niels Bohr postulates that electrons move around the nucleus of the atom in restricted orbits and explains how the atom absorbs and emits energy. Rudolf Steiner founds anthroposophy. Henry Brearly refines stainless steel. D.H. Lawrence writes *Sons and Lovers*. Stravinsky's *Rite of Spring*. Proust's *Remembrance of Things Past*. Unamuno's *The Tragic Sense of Life*: "I cannot, no, cannot stand the purity of it all: pure concept, pure cognition, pure will, pure reason, all that purity leaves me

breathless...And I want to descend to the lowest depths, where the air is heavy and I can clutch at the earth covered with the flowers of passion, illusion, lucky deceits, consulting superstitions (yes, even superstitions), old lullabies from infancy...No, no, no! I will not resign myself to reason." Jung starts writing down his dreams and visions in what will become his *Red Book*; as war clouds gather, he observes that the collective failure to deal with one's hero complex makes bloodshed in battle inevitable.

1914:
European nations and former colonies like the US control 84% of the planet surface. The Panama Canal is completed. The Canadian Pacific steamer *Empress of Ireland* and the Norwegian ship *Storstad* collide in the Gulf of St. Lawrence, killing more than a thousand. The Archduke Francis Ferdinand, heir to the Austria-Hungary throne, is assassinated by Gavrilo Princip, a member of the Black Hand. Franz Joseph responds by serving Serbia (whose government did not support the assassination) an ultimatum: give up national sovereignty or else. Despite a placating reply from Serbia, Franz Joseph declares war and begins shelling Belgrade. Everyone mobilizes, and World War I breaks out in Europe. Britain passes the India Home Rule Bill but suspends it because of the war. Freud and Jung and most other psychoanalysts of the time interpret the war as a predictable outbreak of repressed hostility smoothed over but left unmanaged by the mask of the Enlightenment. The passenger pigeon goes extinct. W.C. Handy comes out with the "St. Louis Blues." Kafka's *The Trial*.

1915:
Alfred Wegener predicts plate tectonics in his book *The Origin of Continents and Oceans*. Throughout the war, armies in Europe, particularly the Allies, try old-fashioned charges, only to be slaughtered wholesale by machine guns. The Germans use poison gas (chlorine) at the Second Battle of Ypres, and soon the Allies do the same. The Germans warn the US not to let citizens travel on the supposedly unsinkable British liner *Lusitania* because its cargo of guns and ammunition make it fair game, but the warning goes unheeded, and

U-boats sink the ship. The Turks slaughter 1.5 million Armenians. German zeppelins under Captain Peter "the cause is holy" Strasser, head of the Naval Airship Division, drop bombs on London, inflicting on civilians what was previously military bloodshed. William Somerset Maugham publishes *Of Human Bondage*. Freud writes: "We had expected the great world-dominating nations of white race upon whom the leadership of the human species has fallen, who were known to have world-wide interests as their concern, to whose creative powers were due not only our technical advances towards the control of nature but the artistic and scientific standards of civilization—we had expected these people to succeed in discovering another way of settling misunderstandings and conflicts of interest....Then the war in which we had refused to believe broke out, and it brought—disillusionment. Not only is it more bloody and more destructive than any war of other days, because of the enormously increased perfection of weapons of attack and defence; it is at least as cruel, as embittered, as implacable as any that has preceded it."

1916:
Military factions of warlords divide China. To counter the machine gun, the British develop the tank ("tank" was a code word for these secret devices) and drive it into the Battle of the Somme. Margaret Sanger opens the first birth control clinic and is widely reviled. Jeannette Rankin of Montana is the first woman elected to Congress and will be the only House member to vote against US entry into the war. Einstein completes his paper on General Relativity. James Joyce writes *Portrait of the Artist as a Young Man*. Charles Birdseye invents a method for quick-freezing food. Spanish writer Vicente Ibanez publishes the antiwar novel *The Four Horsemen of the Apocalypse*.

1917:
The Mexican Revolution ends with a new constitution establishing an eight-hour work day, a minimum wage, and the right of peasants to own land. Colombia settles a border dispute with Ecuador. Provoked by a gala performance at the Alexander Theater in Petroglad, where wealthy patrons in furs gather while peasants and

soldiers shiver in the cold, a crowd storms the Winter Palace. Nicholas II abdicates, and a provisional government takes control until the revolutionary Lenin (Vladimir Ulyanov) returns from Germany to send the Bolshevik party into action. On the night of Novrmber 6th, the Bolsheviks stage a coup engineered by Leon Trotsky (Lev Davidovich Bronstein). The Council of People's Commissars is set up with Lenin as chair. The French munitions vessel *Mont Blanc* goes up in Halifax Harbour, and 1,600 lose their lives. The British Balfour Declaration looks favorably upon a Palestine homeland for Jews. British troops capture Baghdad and Jerusalem. The US declares war on Germany to "make the world safe for democracy," in President Wilson's words. Poland and Finland independence. T. S. Eliot publishes *Prufrock and Other Observations*.

1918:
An armistice ends World War I after nine million deaths and thirty-seven million casualties. Kurt Vonnegut, who was born on this day, will write that soldiers on the battlefields perceived the sudden silence as the voice of God, whereas Hemingway writes, "I did come very close to the big adventure." As a result of various treaties, Austria and Hungary separate, Czechoslovakia is carved out of northern Austria-Hungary, Polish regions merge with an independent Poland, other regions join Romania, and Slavic regions and Serbia combine to form Yugoslavia. Bolshevik forces crush a gathering of indigenous Uzbeks in Kokand. A flu pandemic kills five hundred million in Europe. Hungarian feminist and pacifist Rosika Schwimmer travels to Switzerland as ambassador. Iceland gains independence from Denmark. US President Wilson puts forward the Fourteen Points for settling WWI and forming a League of Nations. Emir Faisal proclaims the state of Syria and becomes king of it in 1920. With the Treaty of Sèvres in France, the Ottoman Empire formally comes to an end. Civil war between the Bolsheviks (Reds) and the anti-Bolsheviks and anti-Communists (Whites) tears Russia apart until the Reds win in 1920. Gustav Holst composes *The Planets*.

1919:
The Treaty of Versailles, fruit of the Paris Peace Conference and one of five that ended WWI, is signed, appropriately, in the Hall of Mirrors. Georges Clemenceau of France pushes for harsh conditions against the Germans, who aren't asked for any input while the treaty is drafted. Not wanting a League of Nations, the US Senate never ratifies it. Estonia and Finland win independence. An eclipse that demonstrates Einstein's prediction that gravity can bend light makes him famous. The Mongolian People's Republic is formed. Dictator Federico Tinoco Granados deposed and exiled from Costa Rica. Britain and France partition Cameroon. The African National Congress demonstrates against pass laws in Transvaal. Adding fuel to the fire for Indian independence, British troops under Reginald Dyer massacre over three hundred Indian civilians at Amritsar. The Eighteenth Amendment to the US Constitution outlawing the sale of alcohol ("Prohibition") guarantees that it sells illegally for huge profits, and the gangs that peddle it gain power and influence. In Italy, Benito Mussolini, who likes the concept of the citizen soldier, organizes the *fascio de combattimento* ("fighting band") to stamp out post-war reforms. Germans starve and their middle class begins to die as the Allied blockade remains in place eight months after the treaty. Taking advantage of all this, Hitler joins the National Socialist Workers Party (because the word "national" in German is pronounced "nah-tsee-oh-nal," the name Nazi sticks). Leon Trotsky puts together the Red Army. Psychologist John Watson starts the school of Behaviorism and will eventually transition from academia to advertising. Ernest Rutherford splits the atom by bombarding various elements with helium nuclei (alpha rays), and a student named Enrico Fermi reads his work. Institute of Sex Research founded in Berlin. The film *Different From The Others* debuts in Germany.

1920:
With the Nineteenth Amendment to the US Constitution, women get the vote. Palestine now a British mandate. Agatha Christie publishes *The Mysterious Affair At Styles*. Isaac Asimov (1920-1992) and Ray Bradbury (1920-2012) born. Pittsburgh's KDKA transmits the first live radio broadcast: the results of the US presidential race.

Edith Wharton publishes *The Age of Innocence* and wins a Pulitzer for it. Yeats's "The Second Coming." Freud's *Beyond the Pleasure Principle*. Claude Monet starts painting his Water Lilies series.

1921:
Great Britain imposes dominion status on Ireland and starts a civil war there. Russia annexes Georgia. Czech dramatist Karel Capek's play *"R.U.R."(Rossum's Universal Robots)* introduces the word *robot* (from a Czech term for "manual labor"). Henry Ford publishes *The International Jew*, a collection of anti-semitic writings that will greatly please the Nazis, the Hitler Youth in particular. Langston Hughes composes "The Negro Speaks of Rivers": "I bathed in the Euphrates when dawns were young...."

1921-25:
Progressive government of President Juan Bautista Saavedra established in Bolivia.

1921-26:
Abd al-Karim al-Khattabi leads Berbers and Arabs of the Rif in northern Morocco against French and Spanish colonizers of North Africa. They defeat him with chemical bombs and exile him to the isle of Reunion.

1922:
Egypt gains independence from Britain. Northern Ireland secedes from the Irish Free State and joins the United Kingdom, and the Irish Civil War leaves the island divided for decades. In an attempt to end border disputes, Sir Percy Cox, the British High Commissioner in Iraq, draws new borders between Iraq, Kuwait and Saudi Arabia. The US effectively controls the railroad, revenues, and national bank of Nicaragua. The International Court of Justice is established at the Hague; the US refuses to join. Russia reorganizes itself into the Union of Soviet Socialist Republics. Russian mathematician and meteorologist Alexander Friedmann conceives the Big Bang theory of the universe's origin. Mustafa Kemal Ataturk, army officer and founder of modern Turkey, overthrows its last sultan. James Joyce's

Ulysses. F. Scott Fitzgerald's *The Great Gatsby*. Frederick Banting and Charles Best isolate insulin. King Tut's tomb is opened. T.S. Eliot's "The Waste Land." "I sat upon the shore / Fishing, with the arid plain behind me / Shall I at least set my lands in order?"

1923:
An earthquake levels a third of Tokyo. With the approval of King Aolfonso XIII, Spanish general Miguel de Rivera suppresses a Catalan revolt and sets up a Fascist government. For attempting a putsch in Munich by starting a shootout at a beer hall, Hitler, who is inspired by Mussolini's march on Rome, is arrested, convicted of treason, and imprisoned for nine months in the fortress at Landsberg, where he writes *Mein Kampf* ("My Struggle"). Kemal as president modernizes Turkey but does little for the Armenian minority. Britain annexes Zimbabwe. The National Women's Party proposes an Equal Rights Amendment to Congress. Bessie Smith, "the Empress of the Blues," cuts her first record. William Butler Yeats wins the Nobel Prize for Literature. Edna St. Vincent Millay's *The Ballad of the Harp-Weaver* makes her the first woman to receive the Pulitzer Prize for poetry. Elsa Gidlow publishes *On a Grey Thread*. Rilke composes the *Duino Elegies*. Santayana's *Scepticism and Animal Faith*. Martin Buber's *I and Thou*. "I perceive something. I am sensible of something. I imagine something. I will something. I feel something. I think something. The life of human beings does not consist of all this and the like alone. This and the like together establish the realm of It. But the realm of Thou has a different basis. When Thou is spoken, the speaker has no thing for his object. For where there is a thing there is another thing. Every It is bounded by others; It exists only through being bounded by others. But when Thou is spoken, there is no thing. Thou has no bounds. When Thou is spoken, the speaker has no thing; he has indeed nothing. But he takes his stand in relation."

1924:
Sun Yat-Sen's Kuomintang party holds its first national congress. Death of Lenin, who is succeeded by Joseph Stalin. Interior Secretary Albert B. Fall and oilmen Harry Sinclair and Edward L.

Doheny are charged with conspiracy and bribery in the Teapot Dome scandal involving fraudulent leases of naval oil reserves; in 1931, Fall is sentenced to a year in prison, but Doheny and Sinclair are acquitted. Sun Yat-Sen forms the Republic of China's Whampoa Military Academy, with Chiang Kai-shek as its commandant. The Soviet Union dissolves Khorezm, Turkestan, and Bukhara and forms Uzbekistan and, within it, Tajikistan. Zambia is a British protectorate. Belgium occupies Ruanda-Urundi and the Congo a year later. Henry Gerber establishes the Society for Human Rights in Chicago to advocate for gay people. Rudolf Steiner's Silesian lectures on organic agriculture make a case for biodynamic farming. Using a Coke truck driver as a model, Swedish-American Artist Haddon Sundblom designs the rosy-cheeked Santa Claus used in Coca-Cola's Christmas advertisements. George Gershwin's *Rhapsody in Blue*. Thomas Mann's *The Magic Mountain*.

1924 - 1929:
Despite warnings from climatic scientists, fifteen million acres join those already under mechanized farming in the US The resulting destruction of plant cover worsens a severe drought in 1931.

1925:
In Tennessee, high school teacher John Thomas Scopes is tried and convicted for teaching the theory of evolution but gets off on a technicality. Wolfgang Pauli, who will later work closely with C.G. Jung on the concept of synchronicity, wins the Nobel Prize for demonstrating the Exclusion Principle governing how electrons and other fermions are arranged within atoms. Franz Kafka's *The Trial* is published a year after his death. Fitzgerald's *The Great Gatsby* published. John Dewey's *Experience and Nature*. English civilian naval intelligence specialist Hector Bywater publishes *Sea Power in the Pacific*, where he outlines a campaign that Admiral Yamamoto will find quite sensible, just as the German High Command will learn from Basil Liddell-Hart's writings about what the Nazis call blitzkrieg.

1926:
Dictatorships rise to power in Italy, Greece, Japan, Poland, and Portugal. Werner Heisenberg develops matrix mechanics, a form of quantum theory equivalent to Erwin Schrödinger's wave mechanics (also 1926). Robert Goddard creates and fires the world's first liquid-fuel rocket from his Aunt Effie's farm in Massachusetts and goes on to develop many rocketeering theories and inventions. Will Durant publishes his *Story of Philosophy*. Kafka's *The Castle*.

1927:
Chiang Kai-shek, ally of Sun Yat-sen, establishes his Kuomintang government at Nanking but is opposed by the Chinese Communist Party for courting conservative Chinese businessmen. Heisenberg develops the Uncertainty Principle: a subatomic particle's velocity and mass cannot be measured simultaneously. As Stalin rises in Italy, Trotsky is expelled from the Communist Party in Russia. Socialist begin a long-term period of power in Norway. Charles Lindbergh is the first pilot to fly solo across the Atlantic. Talkies debut on the big screen when Lithuania-born Al "You Ain't Heard Nothin' Yet" Jolson stars in *The Jazz Singer*. Under General Trenchard, the Royal Air Force launches a pilotless missile with a two-hundred-mile range, but the government doesn't follow up with more tests. Davidson Black finds a tooth in a cave near Beijing: it belongs to Peking Man, a member of Homo erectus. World population: two billion. Hesse's *Steppenwolf*. From the Author's Note: "Of course, I neither can nor intend to tell my readers how they ought to understand my tale. May everyone find in it what strikes a chord in him and is of some use to him! But I would be happy if many of them were to realize that the story of the Steppenwolf pictures a disease and crisis—but not one leading to death and destruction, on the contrary: to healing."

1928:
The Kellogg-Briand Pact (or Pact of Paris) is signed to condemn "recourse to war for the solution of international controversies." Japanese troops murder Chang Tso-lin, military ruler of Manchuria, but Chang's son Chang Hsueh-liang takes over and joins with

Chiang Kai-Shek. Women compete for the first time in Olympic field events. The French begin to build the Maginot Line to stop possible German advances over their border; it works as well as any wall previously erected by any government. *Steamboat Willie* introduces cartoons and Disney's Mickey Mouse. Twenty-six million cars motor through the US Scottish bacteriologist Sir Alexander Fleming proves that penicillin kills bacteria. Radclyffe Hall publishes *The Well of Loneliness*. Anthropologist Margaret Mead publishes *Coming of Age in Samoa*.

1929:
The Wall Street Stock Exchange crashes, and the Great Depression follows. Martin Luther King Jr. (1929-1968) born. Uprising of the Mau people of Samoa against the New Zealand government. Through the Lateran Treaties with Mussolini, Pius XI recognizes the Kingdom of Italy and in turn rules the tiny Vatican City. Edwin Hubble observes that all galaxies are moving away from each other, a fact that supports the Big Bang theory. As Prohibition continues in the US, gang members dressed as police lure seven of George "Bugs" Moran's mobsters into a garage on St. Valentine's Day, then shoot them. Erich Remarque publishes *All Quiet on the Western Front*. Jose Ortega y Gasset publishes *The Revolt of the Masses*. Whitehead's *Process and Reality*. Virginia Woolf's *A Room of One's Own*.

1930:
Wanting to promote space exploration, German scientist Wernher von Braun begins to experiment with liquid-fuel missiles, but the results buttress the German V-series of weapons. The scientists who invent that series will help the US create ICBMs. Germany conducts a national census to identify Jews and compiles the data on punchcards provided by IBM. Gandhi defies British law and makes salt, a symbolic attack on the British salt monopoly in India. Herbert Hoover signs into law the Smoot-Hawley Tariff Act that raises duties on raw materials, but the resulting retaliatory actions by other nations deepen the Depression. Ernest Lawrence develops the cyclotron that will refine weapons-grade uranium. Astronomer

Clyde Tombaugh discovers the planet Pluto—the Roman name for Hades, the invisible Greek god of the underworld—after it hid on previously taken photographic plates. Ortega y Gasset's *The Revolt of the Masses*. Freud's timely *Civilization and Its Discontents*.

1931:
Independence for South Africa. King Alfonso XIII abdicates, and Spain is a republic. The British Commonwealth of Nations comes into being. Canada achieves full independence from Britain. The Scottsboro trial resulting from nine black boys being framed for raping white girls and nearly lynched for it highlights lingering Southern racism. US- and United Fruit Company-backed dictator Jorge Ubico, who boasts that he is another Napoleon, takes over in Guatamala. Hitler claims Henry Ford as an inspiration. On a pretext (the Mukden Incident in which bombs probably set by the Japanese go off in Mukden), the Japanese claim to be attacked and seize Manchuria, taking a clear, firm goose step away from the optimitic-peace hopes of the Twenties. *The Star Spangled Banner* is the US national anthem. Salvador Dali paints *Persistence of Memory*. *Girls in Uniform* screens in Germany.

1932:
One out of four US families are on relief because of the Depression. The US Congress sets up the Reconstruction Finance Commission to help, but it only helps banks and railways, with nothing trickling down. As the Depression deepens around the world, fascist Salazar takes over in Portugal as premier, and fascist Gyula Gombros as Premier of Hungary. Military rule in Thailand as the long period of monarchy ends. Now in control of northern China, Japan leaves the League of Nations. Amelia Earhart is the first woman to pilot a plane across the Atlantic. Hattie Caraway is first woman elected to the US Senate. Aldous Huxley publishes *Brave New World*. Karl Jansky detects radio waves from outside the solar system. Edwin Land invents Polaroid.

1932-35:
The discovery of oil in a narrow strip of the barren section of the

Chaco Boreal, at the foot of the Bolivian Andes, precipitates the Chaco War between Bolivia and Paraguay.

1933:
During his inaugural address, FDR calls for stricter banking regulation and an end to speculation with other people's money, but the Emergency Banking Act he will sign was written mostly by bankers. Hitler comes to power as Chancellor in Germany. When the Reichstag burns down, he blames communists, trade unionists, and liberal intellectuals, whereupon President Hindenburg agrees to suspend civil liberties in service to state security. Nazi stormtroopers take over, and the Third Reich begins (the First having been the Holy Roman Empire and the second Bismarck's German Empire). The head of the SS, Heinrich Himmler, opens the first permanent concentration camp at Dachau. The Vatican signs a Concordat with the Nazis to gain equal footing with Protestants in Germany. As the Twenty-First Amendment to the US constitution repeals Prohibition, Eliot Ness, who sent bootlegger Al Capone to jail for tax evasion, remarks that he's overdue for a drink. New Deal laws like the National Industry Recovery Act help revive the US economy. Hungarian physicist Leo Szilard, recently fled from Nazi Germany to London, entertains an odd thought: what if an unstable element could be concentrated in sufficient quantity to cause a nuclear chain reaction?

1934:
Nazis assassinate Chancellor Dollfuss of Austria. Mussolini meets Hitler. Mao Zedong and Zhu De lead a hundred thousand communists on a Long March demonstration through China. Stalin's chief aid Sergey Kirov is assassinated, precipitating Stalin's latent paranoia. A British oil pipeline runs from Kirkuk (the Mosul oil fields in Iraq) to Tripoli (Syria). The US passes the Indian Reorganization Act to install "modern democratic" governments among American Indians who have not traditionally been subject to hierarchical power systems. German racial hygiene law is drafted from a compulsory eugenics bill written by Harry H. Laughlin. Fulgencio Batista, the head of the Cuban army, rules through a series of puppet

presidents as the US supplies training for Cuban officers. Jung's *The Archetypes and the Collective Unconscious*. "My thesis, then, is as follows: In addition to our immediate consciousness, which is of a thoroughly personal nature and which we believe to be the only empirical psyche (even if we tack on the personal unconscious as an appendix), there exists a second psychic system of a collective, universal, and impersonal nature which is identical in all individuals."

1935:
The rearmament of Germany looks to the Allies like a good thing at first because it provides a European bulwark against Russian communism. US companies like United Aircraft and Pratt & Whitney sell war planes to Germany. Poland's new constitution gets rid of parliamentary government, and fascist Edward Rydz-Smigly takes over. Mussolini invades Ethiopia, so the League of Nations imposes sanctions; he also grabs Abyssinia. Pressured by Gandhi, the Government of India Act grants autonomy to provinces of British India as of 1937. The US Social Security Act takes a step toward welfare, unemployment compensation begins, and Republicans bitterly oppose both. Hitler introduces the Nuremberg Laws to rescind the rights of German Jews he intends to round up. Marine Major General Smedley Butler admits in *War Is a Racket* that he had soldiered for decades as "a high class muscle-man for Big Business, for Wall Street and for the Bankers.... I helped make Mexico, especially Tampico, safe for American oil interests in 1914. I helped make Haiti and Cuba a decent place for the National City Bank boys to collect revenues in. I helped in the raping of half a dozen Central American republics for the benefits of Wall Street.... I helped purify Nicaragua for the international banking house of Brown Brothers in 1909–1912. I brought light to the Dominican Republic for American sugar interests in 1916. In China I helped to see to it that Standard Oil went its way unmolested." Persia's name changes to Iran. Robert Watson-Watt devises "radio detection and ranging," or radar. Ortega y Gasset writes *History as a System:* "Man is a substantial emigrant on a pilgrimage of being, and it is accordingly meaningless to set limits to what he is capable of being."

1936:
Mussolini briefly annexes Ethiopia. The League of Nations proposes an oil embargo against Italy, but the US, which sells half the oil in the world, will not comply. Germany and Japan are greatly emboldened by Italy's territory-seizing example. Hitler denounces the Treaty of Versailles and then invades the Rhineland, admitting later that effective opposition to this move would have discouraged him from it. Agreeing with Hitler on how to treat Austria—namely, conquer it—Mussolini brags that Rome and Berlin will form a new axis for the world (hence the term "Axis Powers"). Heinrich Himmler organizes a special Gestapo section to eradicate abortion and homosexuality; gay men in prison camps are made to wear a pink triangle badge. The oddly named Representation of Natives Act denies political equality to black South Africans. The investigative Nye Committee in the US Senate concludes that US bankers, automobile industries (e.g., Ford, Firestone, and General Motors), and arms factories had made huge profits in both World Wars, and that Woodrow Wilson had known of secret agreements between the Allies of WW I to reorganize Europe in their own image, yet a US bill to take the profits out of war goes nowhere. Stalin has Sergei Kirov killed as part of an initial purge and then executes millions for supposed disloyalty. The Spanish civil war begins as the elected reformist Popular Front composed of liberals, socialists, and communists are taken on by the reactionary General Francisco Franco, who leads an army in Morocco while far-right groups rebel in Spain. Pope Pius XI roots for the Fascists. After a general strike in Syria, the French agree to home rule. Dust storms that dry out a hundred and thirty-five million acres in the farmed-out Midwest force hundreds of thousands of farmers to flee west in search of land that most of them will not find. Margaret Mitchell publishes her sole novel *Gone With the Wind*. Mona's 440 Club opens in San Francisco. Maynard Keynes's *General Theory of Employment, Interest and Money*.

1937:
US National Labor Relations Act. The Golden Gate Bridge opens in San Francisco. The Rape of Nanking as occupying Japanese soldiers

attack thousands of Chinese civilians. German bombers hit Guernica, a Spanish a town of no military worth, and kill hundreds of civilians. An encyclical by Pius XI bans providing aid to communists attacked by Hitler. Roosevelt heeds conservative calls to cut spending and focus on balancing the budget, and stocks and corporate profits drop sharply and unemployment rises. He also ignores recommendations by the Committee of Physicians for the Improvement of Medical Care to organize a workable national healthcare system. Amelia Earhart disappears on a round-the-world flight attempt. Theodore Seuss Geisel begins to write for children. Isak Dinesen (Karen Blixen) writes *Out of Africa*. *Snow White* plays as the first feature-length cartoon. J. R. R. Tolkien publishes *The Hobbit*. "Saruman believes it is only great power that can hold evil in check, but that is not what I have found. I've found it is the small everyday deeds of ordinary folk that keep the darkness at bay... small acts of kindness, and love."

1938:
When American, Dutch, and British oil companies refuse to raise wages for Mexican employees, Mexico nationalizes the oil fields. Hitler compels Austria to ally with Germany (the "Anschluss"). The Munich Pact: Italy, France, and Britain agree to stand by while Germany partitions Czechoslovakia, prompting Prime Minister Chamberlain to wrongly claim they had bought "peace in our time." The Nazis decorate Henry Ford and James Mooney of General Motors for the helpful transport provided by their companies. Bolivia and Paraguay sign the treaty that ends the Chaco War. German scientists Otto Hahn and Fritz Strassman carry forward Enrico Fermi's nuclear fission work. In a late-night rampage called *Kristallnacht* for the shattered glass in the streets, Nazis assault Jews and wreck their property. A year before Germany invades the rest of Europe, Orson Welles frightens thousands of Americans with his "War of the Worlds" broadcast, convincing them that Martians have invaded the US Thornton Wilder publishes *Our Town*. The ballpoint pen is invented. Vladimir Zworykin invents the first practical TV camera. In the film *Bringing Up Baby*, Cary Grant uses the word "gay" in its contemporary sense.

1939:
The League of Nations performs its last significant act by expelling Russia for attacking Finland. Snubbed by the West, Stalin signs a non-aggression pact with Hitler and agrees to divide Poland between them, and two weeks later World War II begins when Germany invades Poland. The Spanish Civil War ends, won by the fascist Franco with financial support from US oil company Texaco, which will also ship oil to Hitler. Television is first broadcast publicly from the Empire State Building by the National Broadcasting Company. Einstein writes to Roosevelt about the possibility of developing an atomic bomb but comes to regret doing so. Paperback books bring reading to a wider public. John Steinbeck publishes *The Grapes of Wrath* to describe the plight of farmers driven from their lands by the banks; for this he is branded a communist, widely reviled, and secretly investigated by the FBI. Robert May, a Montgomery Ward advertiser, invents Rudolph the Red-Nosed Reindeer for the company's Christmas coloring book. Frances V. Rummell publishes *Diana: A Strange Autobiography*.

1940:
In the Battle of Britain, the outnumbered Royal Air Force pummels the Germans over London in the first major German failure of the war. The British hurl the Italians out of Egypt and Libya, then destroy the Italian fleet at Taranto and Cape Matapan. Trotsky is assassinated in Mexico. The Muslim League under Muhammad Ali Jinnah demands a Muslim country: Pakistan, which means "Land of the Pure." The first US freeway opens in Pasadena. The Japanese take Indochina. France surrenders to Germany but continues underground resistance. The Rodale Organic Gardening Experimental Farm established in Lynn Township, Pennsylvania.

1941:
Jet aircraft developed in England and Germany. Ethiopian and British soldiers free Ethiopia from the Italians and enforce its independence. Hoping for a hostile incident, Roosevelt provokes the Axis by providing the British with military intelligence and by supplying British troops in North Africa. Reacting to President

Roosevelt's blockage of oil flowing from Indonesia to Japan, the Japanese attack the US Pacific Fleet by air at Pearl Harbor, Hawaii, destroying fourteen combat ships (including eight battleships) while the real prize, the aircraft carriers, are away on maneuvers. The US enters World War II. The Japanese occupy islands whose inhabitants offer little resistance because (as FDR admits) they are tired of European colonialism. The US Congress passes the Lend-Lease Act to loan billions in military hardware to the Allies, but aid promised to the Russians never arrives, angering them. US forces engage the Japanese in the Battle of the Coral Sea, the first sea action fought by airplanes, and block Japanese access to Australia.

1942:
Instead of keeping their promise to war-weary Russia to open a second front in Europe, American and British forces focus on North Africa with the long-range goal of securing access to Middle Eastern oil. Eager for a win after losing the Battle of Britain, Germany invades Russia, catching Stalin off guard (he distrusted British predictions based on broken codes). The chief code-breaker, Alan Turing, commits suicide after the war after being hounded about his homosexuality. Heading for oil fields in the Caucasus, the Nazis are stopped by forces under Marshall Georgi Zhukov at Stalingrad, where Hitler refused to let his men retreat despite huge casualties and bad weather. In a flagrant violation of citizens' rights, the US Government moves thousands of Japanese to "relocation centers" and incarcerates them there. The Union Banking Corporation is seized for trading with the enemy because the Nazis hold accounts managed by Prescott Bush. Chase and Morgan also collaborate. Calling for an end to empires, colonial imperialism, and international exploitation, Vice President Henry Wallace gives a speech in which he seeks to replace the so-called American Century with that of the Common Man. At the University of Chicago, Leo Szilard and Enrico Fermi ignite the world's first sustained nuclear chain reaction. Edith Hamilton's *Mythology*. Albert Camus, a veteran of the French resistance, writes *The Stranger* and *The Myth of Sisyphus*.

1943:
German troops crush the Warsaw Ghetto Uprising of Jews struggling to avoid deportation to the Treblinka concentration camp. Lebanon gains independence from France. Despite undersupplied Erwin Rommel's best efforts, German and Italian troops are driven from North Africa. After Italian defeats in Africa and Sicily, the Grand Council of Fascism bypasses Mussolini's authority and signs a secret armistice with the Allies. Churchill and Roosevelt meet at the Casablanca Conference. The US gives lend-lease aid to Saudi Arabia and in a year will receive permission to build an air base at Dharan. Arturo Rosenblueth, Norbert Wiener, and Julian Bigelow coin the word "cybernetics" in a technical paper. The Allies ignite the first artificial firestorm by dropping masses of incendiary bombs on Hamburg. The Green Revolution brings agriculture, chemical fertilizers from nitrates left from WW I, quickly mass-produced food—and massive booms in world population. Hesse publishes *The Glass Bead Game*, a novel that wins him the Nobel Prize for Literature (1946).

1944:
Under General Dwight Eisenhower, the Allies initiate Operation Overlord, invade France (D-Day) at Normandy and not Calais, as Hitler had predicted over the objections of Rommel and Runstedt, and start to reconquer Europe. This prompts Hitler to launch his V-series rockets into Britain and Belgium. At a meeting German war hero Clause von Stauffenberg leaves a briefcase bomb near Hitler, but an aid moves it before it goes off. The conspirators are hanged except for Rommel, who is ordered to commit suicide in exchange for his family being spared. Soviet forces in combination with the Partisans of Tito reenter Belgrade and install Josip Broz as leader of Yugoslavia. Syria gains independence from France. In a last gamble, the Germans counterattack at the Battle of the Bulge in the Ardennes, where they seek to punch a hole in invading Allied forces. The International Bank for Reconstruction and Development (later the World Bank) and the International Monetary Fund (IMF) are planned at an international conference at Bretton Woods, New Hampshire, to shape the postwar economic world order. Democrat

party bosses stage the "Pauley's coup" to arrange the Vice Presidential nomination for Harry Truman of Missouri and effectively kill Wallace's vision of postwar cooperation feared by Wall Street bankers and southern segregationists alike. George Orwell (Eric Blair) publishes *Animal Farm*. Dr. Raphael Lemkin coins the word "genocide." C.G. Jung publishes *Psychology and Alchemy* to reintroduce the ancient art-science-mystery tradition as both coded map of the psyche and underground compensation for centuries of Christian ascensionism away from matter and embodiment.

1945:
Churchill, FDR, and Stalin meet at the Yalta Conference to discuss the end of the war; Stalin proposes to send in Soviet troops in ninety days if Japan is still fighting. The US having been effectively if quietly run by Eleanor Roosevelt, FDR finally dies. Secretary of State and former US Steel chairman Edward Stettinius convinces President Truman, who is ignorant of international affairs, that Soviet bids for peaceful collaboration cannot be trusted. Churchill agrees, as does adviser James Byrnes of South Carolina. Truman's hard line stuns Soviet diplomat Vyacheslav Molotov and Stalin, whose war-shattered country is in no position to spread communism around the world. The secret Manhattan Project builds a fission bomb while Norwegian sabotage prevents the Germans from experimenting with heavy water as a prelude to their own nuclear device. When the first fission bomb explodes successfully near Alamogordo, New Mexico (an effort code-named Trinity), Enrico Fermi gets so upset that his wife must drive him home. Project director and Coordinator of Rapid Rupture J. Robert Oppenheimer, a graduate of the Ethical Culture School in New York, recalls these words from the *Bhagavad-Gita:* "I am become Death, the shatterer of worlds." Hitler commits suicide with Eva Braun. Mussolini is shot, then hung. Truman, Churchill, and Stalin meet at Potsdam to discuss how to divide up Germany. An incendiary air attack on Tokyo kills upward of a hundred thousand. Although many advisers try to talk him out of it, and in spite of decoded Japanese cables showing the Japanese ready for a peaceful end to war, Truman, supported by Byrnes, sticks to his demand that Japan surrender uncon-

ditionally. Generals MacArthur, LeMay, Spaatz, and Eisenhower, and Admirals Nimitz, King, and Halsey think the bombs unnecessary. Authorized by President Truman, who wants to make it plain that the US has no need of Stalin's help, the B-29 bomber *Enola Gay*, commanded by Colonel Paul Tibbets and named after his mother, drops a uranium bomb nicknamed Little Boy on Hiroshima on August 6th, the day before the Soviet ninety-day deadline to advance on Manchuria. Three days later, when weather prohibits a strike at the primary target city of Kokura, a second bomb, a plutonium device called Fat Man, falls from the B-29 *Bockscar* on Nagasaki and explodes over the largest Catholic cathedral in Asia. After these two blasts at least two hundred thousand civilians die within two months, with more sick and dying in the months and years to follow. (In mythology Plutonium is the gateway to the Underworld.) Japan surrenders to avoid an imminent Soviet invasion. With Japan defeated, Colonel Dean Rusk "temporarily" divides Korea into northern (communist) and southern halves. The United Nations is launched in San Francisco. The Veterans Benevolent Association for LGBTQ vets formed in New York. In a letter to a British magazine, science fiction writer Arthur C. Clarke proposes the concept of an artificial satellite in Earth orbit. Representative John Rankin secures adoption of a resolution setting up the House Committee on Un-American Activities (HUAC) to stage show trials of Americans suspected of communist sympathies. Walt Disney and Ronald Reagan will support this crusading. Merleau-Ponty's *The Phenomenology of Perception*. "As I contemplate the blue of the sky I am not set over against it as an acosmic subject; I do not possess it in thought, or spread out towards it some idea of blue such as might reveal the secret of it, I abandon myself to it and plunge into this mystery, it 'thinks itself within me,' I am the sky itself as it is drawn together and unified, and as it begins to exist for itself."

1946:
The US fires its first V-series rocket, then tests an atomic bomb at Bikini Atoll in Marshall Islands, after which ongoing US and French nuclear testing on Pacific islands causes widespread fallout, fear,

and resentment. The US passes the Indian Claims Act supposedly to settle claims about stolen lands but actually to offer quit-claims to keep those lands. Ahmad Qavan, prime minister of Iran, signs an agreement allowing the Russians to develop the oil fields. Russian troops leave Iran, and the Azerbaijan and Kurdistan republics collapse, allowing Iran to gain control of them again. Jordan wins independence. The Dead Sea Scrolls—60% of them copies of Jewish religious texts not included in the Bible—are discovered at the West Bank in Palestine. A powerful quake strikes Vancouver Island. At Nuremberg, where SS officer Adolf Eichmann defends himself by saying he was merely following orders, twelve Nazis are sentenced to hang, and Hermann Goering commits suicide. Bloodshed and rioting as Muslims and Hindus are separated into two countries. The GATT (General Agreement on Tariffs and Trade) is signed to lower tariffs and introduce the World Trade Organization. The first of a series of short-lived constitutions in Nigeria offers limited native representation in local legislatures. In Fulton, Winston Churchill justifies continuing British colonial rule by warning of an "iron curtain" dividing Europe. Republican Senator Owen Brewster replies, "We cannot assume the heritage of colonial policy represented by the British foreign and colonial office. Nine-tenths of the world is not Anglo-Saxon. We must consider how we are going to gain the confidence of the world that is not Slav or Anglo-Saxon." Truman threatens the Soviets with the atomic bomb if they do not withdraw from Iran immediately. They do. Truman rejects a Soviet plan to end the production and use of atomic weapons. The French war on the Viet Minh resistance in Indochina. Harvard developers introduce the ENIAC (Electronic Numerical Integrator And Computer), which can perform forty-five hundred calculations per second. COC Nederland formed; it is the oldest continuing LGBTQ organization. Viktor Frankl publishes *Man's Search for Meaning.* "The gas chambers of Auschwitz were the ultimate consequence of the theory that man is nothing but the product of heredity and environment—or, as the Nazi liked to say, of 'Blood and Soil.' I am absolutely convinced that the gas chambers of Auschwitz, Treblinka, and Maidanck were ultimately prepared not in some Ministry or other in Berlin, but rather at the desks and in the lecture halls of nihilistic scientists and philosophers."

1947:
India and Pakistan declare independence and then fight each other. Postwar manufacturing brings industry and housing to Australia. The Truman Doctrine: the US government will aid any country that resists communism, especially Greece (ruled by Nazi-sympathizing aristocrats) and Turkey, where US troops resort to mass executions, torture, and concentration camps. This edict, written by religious zealot Dean Acheson, deepens the Cold War and sets up an interventionist policy that leads to fighting in Korea and Vietnam. Wallace predicts that the US will become the most hated nation in the world. The Marshall Plan is proposed to help rebuild Western Europe at a grand total of $13 billion. The US National Security Act creates the Departments of Defense, Army, Navy, and Air Force, the National Security Council, the Central Intelligence Agency (authorized by Truman to conduct a wide range of covert operations of plausible deniability), and the National Security Resources Board. US test pilot Chuck Yaeger breaks the sound barrier, and Jackie Robinson the color barrier as the first black baseball player in the major leagues. Anne Frank's diary is published. Lisa Ben publishes *Vice Versa*.

1948:
The Universal Declaration of Human Rights: *Whereas recognition of the inherent dignity and of the equal and inalienable rights of all members of the human family is the foundation of freedom, justice and peace in the world....* Mohandas K. Gandhi is shot and killed by a Brahmin Hindu who fears Gandhi's tolerance of Muslims. Peaceful populist liberal Jorge Eliécer Gaitán's assassination—possibly by the CIA—precipitates Colombia into a period of extreme violence until 1958. Burma and Ceylon win independence from Britain. The Costa Rican Civil War when the government of Teodoro Michalski annuls the election of Otilio Ulate Blanco as president; the army deposes Michalski. The Afrikaner National Party comes to power in South Africa and declares apartheid. With CIA backing, the

Christian Democrats win a general election in Italy. The World Council of Churches is formed. The Jewish State of Israel declares its independence, and Arab forces invade it temporarily (the Arab-Israeli War, which the Israelis win with Czech and Soviet aid). In reaction to the Marshall Plan and to US efforts to build up Germany again, plans that include US-backed currency reform, the Soviets cut off Berlin, so the US airlifts supplies to the city and uses the crisis as leverage to found the North Atlantic Treaty Organization. Having described the Soviet Union as "inherently expansionist," US diplomat George Kennan writes in a secret memorandum that "we have about 50 percent of the world's wealth, but only 6.3 percent of its population... Our real task in the coming period is to devise a pattern of relationships which will permit us to maintain this position of disparity... We should cease to talk about vague and...unreal objectives such as human rights, the raising of the living standards, and democratization." Bell Telephone Laboratories introduces the transistor, leading to miniaturization of circuits in computers, radios, and many other devices. Alfred Kinsey founds the field of sexology by studies of male (1948) and female (1953) sexuality. Tennessee Williams' *A Streetcar Named Desire* wins the Pulitzer Prize. Thomas Merton's *The Seven Storey Mountain*. Wiener's *Cybernetics*.

1949:
The Soviets test-detonate their first nuclear bomb. The US and various West European allies charter the North Atlantic Treaty Organization (NATO). Britain recognizes the independence of Ireland, in theory. Indonesia wins independence. A new constitution for Costa Rica. Chiang Kai-shek reassumes control of the Kuomintang and opposes militant Chinese Communists. A US State Department memo says the Third World's major function is to serve as a resource for raw materials and marketing opportunities. Believing Truman is about to dismiss him, James Forrestal, Secretary of Defense, jumps out a window sixteen stories up. He had been copying out Sophocles' "The Chorus from Ajax" and jumped when he reached the word "nightingale." George Orwell publishes *1984*. Simone de Beauvoir publishes *The Second Sex*. George Orwell publishes *Nineteen Eighty-Four*. Aldo Leopold's *San County*

Almanac: "A thing is right when it tends to preserve the integrity, stability, and beauty of the biotic community. It is wrong when it tends otherwise." Joseph Campbell's *Hero with a Thousand Faces*: "Myth is the secret opening through which the inexhaustible energies of the cosmos pour into human cultural manifestation. Religions, philosophies, arts, the social forms of primitive and historic man, prime discoveries in science and technology, the very dreams that blister sleep, boil up from the basic, magic ring of myth. The latest incarnation of Oedipus, the continued romance of Beauty and the Beast, stand this afternoon on the corner of 42nd Street and Fifth Avenue, waiting for the traffic light to change."

1950:
Truman orders development of the hydrogen bomb, a device vastly more powerful than the previous fission bombs. Einstein and Leo Szilard appear in public to protest this decision. Senator Joseph McCarthy charges without proof that the State Department is overrun by communists. The Lavender Scare, in which homosexuals are purged from political office in the US Chiang Kai-shek's forces are pushed off the continent and onto Taiwan, and Chairman Mao Zedong proclaims the People's Republic of China. Turkey holds its first free election. The Chinese occupy Tibet. Taking advantage of the unpopularity of the corrupt US-backed president of South Korea, North Korea invades, with China assisting, while UN troops, half sent from the US without authorization by Congress, aid the South. MacArthur and Acheson are certain China will not intervene directly even though MacArthur has ordered bombing near the Chinese border. Guatemalans elect Jacobo Árbenz Guzmán as their president, but when he promotes reform, support for the poor, and nationalization of land owned by the United Fruit Company, the CIA engineers a coup to overthrow him in favor of Carlos Castillo (1954). The coup leaves a lasting impression on young Che Guevara. John Hops of Winnipeg invents the pacemaker. Isaac Asimov defines the Three Laws of Robotics in *I, Robot*. After Sir Fred Hoyle makes fun of the "Big Bang" theory the criticism fades but the nickname sticks. At Wheeling, West Virginia, Joe McCarthy gives his famously divisive speech about a supposed communist infiltration of the US

Government. In *The Authoritarian Personality*, Theodor W. Adorno, Else Frenkel-Brunswik, Daniel Levinson, and Nevitt Sanford publish research findings linking racism and reactionary politics with a traditionalist mindset and fear of change. "Intolerance of ambiguity is the mark of an authoritarian personality."

1951:
Having suffered a disastrous reverse in Korea because of an unexpected Chinese counterattack, General MacArthur cables Washington to request permission to nuke northern Asia to intimidate the communists; later that year, Truman relieves him of command. US jets drop napalm bombs widely on North Korea. Julius and Ethel Rosenberg receive a death sentence for passing atomic secrets to the Russians. Libya gains independence, and Nigeria a new constitution. Iran nationalizes its oil industry, after which Britain and the US impose sanctions on Iran. Color television in the US. J. D. Salinger's *Catcher in the Rye*. Bonhoeffer's *Letters and Papers from Prison* published after his death. "If we look more closely, we see that any violent display of power, whether political or religious, produces an outburst of folly in a large part of mankind; indeed, this seems actually to be a psychological and sociological law: the power of some needs the folly of others."

1952:
The Mau-Mau Uprising under Dedan Kimathi against the British in Kenya. They suppress it, but Kenya gains independence by 1963. Egypt is a republic. The short-lived Mau Mau revolt in Kenya. The US test-detonates an H-bomb at Enewetak. The Bolivian government (the Movimento Nacional Revolucionario) nationalizes a large number of mines owned by tin barons. Elections held in Puerto Rico. Buckminster Fuller designs a geodesic dome. Microbiologist Jonas Salk develops a vaccine for poliomyelitis. Ralph Ellison publishes *The Invisible Man*. Marijane Meaker publishes *Spring Fire*. Christine Jorgensen becomes the public face of sex reassignment surgery. Gerald Gardner of Britain introduces Wicca. Jung's *Answer to Job* and *Synchronicity*. Beckett's *Waiting for Godot*. Paul Tillich's *The Courage to Be:* "It takes tremendous courage to resist the lure

of appearances. The power of being which is manifest in such courage is so great that the gods tremble in fear of it."

1953:
Stalin dies of a stroke, and reformer Nikita Khrushchev takes over. The USSR test-detonates an H-bomb. To restart oil production the US and British Intelligence overthrow the democratically elected Mossadeq government in Iran, where a new consortium opens oil riches to the West. Northern and southern Rhodesia (Zambia and Zimbabwe) combine with Nyasaland (now Malawi) into the Federation of Rhodesia and Nyasaland.The French establish a garrison camp at Dien Bien Phu in Vietnam to preserve their influence and access. Cambodia and Morocco win independence. When gay rights group ONE, Inc. publishes *ONE Magazine*, the first US pro-gay publication, the US Post Office refuses to deliver it, so ONE, Inc. sues them to reverse this decision. New Zealander Edmund Hillary and Nepalese Sherpa Tenzing Norkay reach the summit of Mt. Everest. Watson, Crick, and Frank analyze the structure of DNA by leaning on the work of biologist Rosalind Franklin.

1954:
Firing from the Ladies' Gallery balcony in the House of Representatives, five Puerto Rican gunmen wound five US congressmen to protest US interference with Puerto Rican independence. The wounded survive, and President Carter will pardon the gunmen. The first nuclear submarine, the *Nautilus*, slips beneath the waves. The Bikini Atoll test explosion contaminates the Japanese tuna boat *Lucky Dragon 5* with radioactive fallout. As the US Strategic Air Command plots to exterminate 80% of the Soviet Union's population, nuclear missiles stand on European soil relatively close to Soviet borders. Iran's new US-backed government signs an oil agreement with companies from Britain, the US, France, and the Netherlands. Algeria fights France for independence and wins it in 1962. Hurricane Hazel washes streets and bridges away in Toronto. A Geneva Conference held to discuss Korea and Vietnam partitions the latter into north and south even though this never worked for Korea. A legitimate Guatemalan government is over-

thrown in a US-backed coup. *Brown v. the Board of Education of Topeka* draws on the work of psychologists Kenneth and Mamie Phipps Clark to ban racial segregation in schools. Psychologist Abraham Maslow publishes his famous Hierarchy of Needs (in *Motivation and Personality*). Huxley's *The Doors of Perception*. In *A Study of History*, Arnold Toynbee coins the term "post-modern." Bill Haley and the Comets sing "Rock Around the Clock."

1955:
In Montgomery, Alabama, African American Rosa Parks refuses to move to the back of a General Motors-owned bus, prompting Martin Luther King Jr. to lead a widely publicized black boycott of Montgomery buses. After West Germany joins NATO, eight European communist nations sign the Warsaw Pact defense agreement. The Western European Union comes into being. Indonesian President Sukarno organizes an Afro-Asian conference in Bandung, initiating the Non-Alliance Movement of Third World Nations unwilling to take sides in the Cold War. The Daughters of Bilitis founded in San Francisco to promote civil rights for lesbians. The AFL and CIO labor groups merge. Hideki Yukawa wins a Nobel Prize for postulating the strong interaction that holds the nucleus of atoms together. Psychoanalyst Erich Fromm argues in *The Sane Society* that the West is, in effect, mad. Marcuse's *Eros and Civilization*. Bo Diddley inspires generations of American rockers after appearing, if briefly, on the *Ed Sullivan Show*. Ginsberg's "Howl." Teilhard de Chardin's *The Phenomenon of Man*: "Having got so far, what are the minimum requirements to be fulfilled before we can say that the road ahead of us is open? There is only one, but it is everything. It is that we should be assured the space and the chances to fulfill ourselves, that is to say, to progress till we arrive (directly or indirectly, individually or collectively) at the utmost limits of ourselves." Maslow's *Toward a Psychology of Being* calls for more research on healthy and self-actualizing human beings.

1956:
Morocco, Tunisia, and Sudan gain independence. To the discomfort of Britain, France, and the US, Egypt nationalizes the Suez Canal;

Israel invades Egypt. Corrupt US-backed President Ngo Dinh Diem cancels the 1956 reunification elections in South Vietnam, Ho Chi Minh denounces this move, and Diem's government faces increasingly serious opposition from Viet Cong insurgents. The US Interstate Highway Act funds a road system modeled on Hitler's Autobahn. Woody Guthrie composes *This Land is Your Land*. John F. Kennedy publishes *Profiles in Courage:* "The courage of a life is often a less dramatic spectacle than the courage of a final moment; but it is no less a magnificent mixture of triumph and tragedy. A man does what he must—in spite of personal consequences, in spite of obstacles and dangers and pressures—and that is the basis of all human morality." M. King Hubbert predicts that U.S. oil supplies will peak between 1965 and 1970 before dropping. They do.

1957:
Ghana, the former Gold Coast, is the first independent country in sub-Saharan Africa. The Eisenhower Doctrine, formulated after Egypt accepts aid from the Soviets, self-authorizes the US to help Middle Eastern countries fight off communism. Eisenhower also speaks about his willingness to use nuclear bombs as he would conventional forces. The Eastern and Western regions of Nigeria become self-governing. Nine African American children try to enter Little Rock High School, are blocked by angry crowds, and are escorted in by federal troops dispatched by Eisenhower. The USSR launches Sputnik Zemlya ("fellow traveler"), the world's first artificial satellite, on the SS-6, a failed missile weapon. Dr. Harry Benjamin coins "transsexual."

1958:
China takes a Great Leap Forward from an agrarian nation to a mechanized and industrialized one. The European Economic Community (or European Common Market) founded. The Van Allen Radiation Belt discovered. Pro-Nasser Arabs start a revolution in Lebanon until the US intervenes. The US sponsors a rebellion against Sukarno, Indonesia's first elected president. Egypt and Syria join up as the United Arab Republic. Three thousand nuclear missiles posted by the US in Western Europe point at the Soviets. The

US Senate censures Joseph McCarthy for his outrageous rants about communists in the government, after which he fades in influence until he dies of hepatitis made worse by alcoholism. For a prank, Ray Wallace of Humboldt, California designs special snowshoes whose tracks are attributed to Bigfoot. The resulting frenzy convinces him to say nothing publicly until he is on his deathbed. Chinua Achebe publishes *Things Fall Apart*. The peace sign debuts in an anti-nuclear protest.

1958-60:
Independence for Zaire, Nigeria, Somalia, and twelve of France's former sub-Saharan colonies.

1959:
US companies control more than 80% of Cuba's cattle ranches, mines, refineries, and utilities and a large chunk of sugar industries and railroads until US-backed Cuban president Batista is booted out and Fidel Castro takes over. Hutu and Tutsi activists fight in Rwanda. Singapore and Cypress achieve independence. The Soviet spacecraft Luna 2 visits the Moon. Texas Instruments engineers invent the microchip to house an integrated circuit, setting the stage for microprocessing and personal computers. World population: three billion.

1960:
The European Free Trade Association welcomes nations unable to join the European Economic Community. A Soviet missile shoots down a CIA U-2 spy plane piloted by Francis Gary Powers; as a result, Krushchev cancels a Paris summit. Belgian Congo (Zaire) is granted independence, with Patrice Lumumba its first president, but five days later the Congolese army mutinies and CIA- and Belgian-backed secessionists take over the government and execute the president. (The atomic bombs dropped on Japan had carried uranium mined in the Congo.) Cameroon is a republic. Chad declares independence. A second civil war in south Sudan—the first was in 1955—claims two million lives until a treaty is signed in 2005. Nigeria wins independence from Britain and is admitted to the UN.

Togo and Somalia independent. Jane Goodall observes chimpanzees in Gombe, Tanzania. OPEC is formed by Iraq, Iran, Kuwait, Saudi Arabia, and Venezuela to oppose top-down policies imposed by Western oil giants like Exxon. Senegal, Madagascar, and Ghana gain independence. Gadamer's *Truth and Method.* Harper Lee's *To Kill a Mockingbird.* Elie Wiesel's harrowing *Night.*

1961:
Amnesty International is founded in London to monitor human rights and to protect those of political prisoners. US President Kennedy calls for landing a man on the moon. The CIA equips a bungled invasion of the Bay of Pigs in Cuba, with whom the US has broken off diplomatic relations; two of the invading ships belong to the United Fruit Company. João Goulart is elected president of Brazil and orders land redistribution and local reinvestment of multinational profits, but a CIA-backed coup ousts him in 1964, and fifteen years of brutal military dictatorship follow. Cosmonaut Yuri Gagarin is the first human to reach space. In response to President Kennedy's army expansion buildup the East German government begins construction on the Berlin Wall. Americans who can afford it buy fallout shelters and guns. The contraceptive pill hits the market. The US signs an agreement with South Vietnam and begins sending in "advisers" and other military assistance. Drag queen José Julio Sarria becomes the first openly gay candidate to run for office in the US. *The Rejected* broadcast in San Francisco. Carl Rogers's *On Becoming a Person.*

1961-67:
Independence for Tanzania, Uganda, Kenya, Sierra Leone, Rwanda, Burundi, Malawi, Zambia, Lesotho, Botswana, Gambia, and Swaziland.

1962:
India and China fight over their Himalayan border. Independence for Uganda, Rwanda, and Burundi. Movements in Mozambique fight the Portuguese for independence. John Glenn Jr. is the first US astronaut to orbit the Earth. France grants sovereignty to Algeria.

Escorted by federal marshals, African American James H. Meredith registers at the racially segregated University of Mississippi. Pope John XXIII opens the Second Vatican Council, which establishes Mary as the Mother of the Church, approves of liturgy not in traditional Latin, and invites Protestant and Eastern Orthodox observers to attend even though one of its edicts maintains that non-Catholics aware of the Church's mission cannot be "saved." The UN calls for sanctions against racist South Africa. The Cuban Missile Crisis begins with Khrushchev's installation of ballistic missiles in Cuba to deter a preemptive attack by the US, whose government has long given every indication it could make one. General LeMay wants to use the crisis as a chance to wipe out both Cuba and the Soviet Union, but the US blockades Cuba instead while Kennedy secretly agrees to withdraw Jupiter missiles from Turkey, and the Russians withdraw their own missiles, a decision that costs Khrushchev his job at home. As a US squadron drops depth charges (practice rounds) around the Soviet submarine *B-59* to signal her to surface while she heads for Cuba, Captain Valentin Savitsky believes that a war has started—the sub is too deep for radio contact—and decides to launch a nuclear torpedo at the *USS Randolph*, but he is overridden by Vasili Arkhipov, the political officer on board whose decision averts World War III. (Oddly enough, Arkhipov had been exposed to radiation in a prior reactor breach aboard another Soviet sub.) Leftists in Nicaragua assemble the Sandinist National Liberation Front (named after insurgent Augusto Sandino) to get rid of the US-supported Somoza dictatorship and its brutal National Guard. Canada phases out executions of criminals. Jamaica wins independence from Great Britain. Peter and Eileen Caddy and Dorothy Maclean establish the Findhorn Community—now the Findhorn Foundation to promote ecospirituality and sustainable living—on the northeast coast of Scotland. Michael Murphy and Dick Price found Esalen Institute at Big Sur, California. Jung's *Memories, Dreams, Reflections*: "My life is a story of the self-realization of the unconscious." Rachel Carson restarts the environmental movement in the US with *Silent Spring*. Psychedelic experiments with Timothy Leary and Richard Alpert at Harvard. Kuhn coins "paradigm" in *The*

Structure of Scientific Revolutions. Ken Kesey's *One Flew Over the Cuckoo's Nest.*

1963:
Kenya wins independence, and Malaysia forms a government. Backed by the British and the CIA, the Baath Party in Iraq overthrows Prime Minister Qasim, who had threatened oil profits, executes him, and seizes power. Canada, Britain, and the US block the Peruvian Congress from nationalizing oil fields pumped by Standard Oil while citizens starve. Russian cosmonaut Valentina Tereshkova is the first woman in space. Organization of African Unity founded. Martin Luther King Jr. gives his "I Have A Dream" speech. Having fired high-ranking CIA officials, Kennedy decides to call off the space race with the Soviets, push for greater cooperation with them, and pull out of Vietnam. He is shot in Dallas, Texas, and his identified killer, Lee Harvey Oswald, is shot by Dallas nightclub owner Jack Ruby before Oswald can be interrogated. Lyndon Johnson of Texas becomes President and escalates involvement in Vietnam to guard access to resources like tin, rice, manganese, ore, and rubber. He has nightmares of Robert Kennedy and a crowd of shouters accusing him of disloyalty and cowardice. Feminist Betty Friedan publishes *The Feminine Mystique*, a key text of second-wave feminism. The number of "advisers" in Vietnam reaches fifteen thousand. Students under Mario Savio rise at Berkeley in the Free Speech Movement protesting the bureaucratization of education: "There's a time when the operation of the machine becomes so odious, makes you so sick at heart, that you can't take part, you can't even passively take part. And you've got to put your bodies upon the gears and upon the wheels, upon the levers, upon all the apparatus, and you've got to make it stop. And you've got to indicate to the people who run it, to the people who own it, that unless you're free, the machine will be prevented from working at all!"

1964:
Independence for Malawi, Tanzania, and Malta. Zambia is a republic. South African activist Nelson Mandela is imprisoned. The US Civil Rights Act bans racial discrimination in federal funding and

employment. North Vietnamese torpedo boats in the Gulf of Tonkin are alleged to attack, without provocation, US destroyers conveying intelligence to South Vietnam, a lie echoed in many US newspapers. President Johnson and his advisers order retaliatory air attacks on North Vietnam and the FBI to find communist sympathies among war protesters (Operation Chaos). "We will find ourselves," predicts John McCone of the CIA, "mired down in combat in the jungle in a military effort that we cannot win, and from which we will have extreme difficulty in extracting ourselves." Hanoi makes secret contact to discuss peace, but Johnson and the Joint Chiefs show no interest. The CIA funnels $20 million dollars into Chile to get Eduardo Frei elected as President instead of the Marxist Allende. With US help, military leaders seize power in Brazil and the Dominican Republic. Malcolm X makes pilgrimage to Mecca, takes the name El-Hajj Malik El-Shabazz, and, risking his life, gives speeches about how blacks and whites can live together in peace. His house is set on fire. Arab leaders set up the Palestine Liberation Organization to unite Palestinian refugees. The Warren Report concludes that Oswald acted alone when he shot Kennedy. Alex Haley publishes *The Autobiography of Malcolm X*.

1965:
Martin Luther King Jr. and twenty-six hundred African Americans are arrested at a peaceful demonstration in Selma, Alabama. After being refused police protection, Malcolm X is shot to death at the Audubon Ballroom while preaching for racial tolerance; in his pocket police find a list of the presumed gunmen's names. Pakistan and India fight over their border again. Medicare goes into effect in the US. The Watts Riots rage for six days in Los Angeles, and although thirty-four people die, no significant efforts are made to address poverty, racism, or other underlying causes. In Indonesia, US-backed President Suharto organizes the mass murder of communists, killing half a million and making his family billionaires.

1966:
Military takeovers in northern Nigeria, where many Igbo are slaughtered. Cleve Backster experiments with plant consciousness. Betty

Friedan founds the National Organization for Women (NOW). Compton's Cafeteria Riot breaks out in San Francisco when the police show up to arrest transgender customers. Independence for Barbados, Lesotho, and Botswana. Shusaku Endo publishes *Silence*. *Star Trek* debuts with hopeful visions of the future.

1967:
The first successful human heart transplant, performed by Dr. Christiaan Barnard. Astronauts Grissom, White, and Chaffe burn to death in an Apollo 1 accident. The Six-Day War: Israeli forces cripple Arab air capability and capture Old Jerusalem and the Golan Heights. Aboriginal people gain limited government representation in Australia. China test-detonates an H-bomb. National Guardsmen fortify police after a night of rioting in Detroit as similar outbreaks inflame New York City's Spanish Harlem, Rochester, Birmingham, and New Britain. Inspired by Third World struggles for social justice, the Chicago Westside Group meets and comes up with the term "women's liberation." P.R.I.D.E. (Personal Rights in Defense and Education) organizes protests in Los Angeles against police raids like those carried out at the Black Cat Tavern. The Oscar Wilde Bookshop opens in New York. A hundred thousand turn out for the Summer of Love in San Francisco's Haight-Ashbury. R.D. Laing's *The Politics of Experience*. Pope Paul VI issues the *Popularum Progressio* to condemn imperialism, colonialism, and poverty caused by runaway capitalism.

Information Age:
Eradigm Earthrise

1968:

Warsaw Pact forces crush the Prague Spring democratization and reform movement in Czechoslovakia. Widespread war protests rock the US. Nixon privately tells Chief of Staff Bob Haldeman, "I call it the madman theory, Bob. I want the North Vietnamese to believe I've reached the point where I might do anything to stop the war. We'll just slip the word to them that, 'for God's sake, you know Nixon is obsessed about Communists. We can't restrain him when he's angry—and he has his hand on the nuclear button." The Viet Cong overrun American bases in Vietnam (the Tet Offensive). Soldiers under Lt. William Calley murder three hundred and forty-seven Vietnamese civilians at My Lai. Polish leader Wladyslaw Gomulka stirs up anti-Semitic feelings, and within the next two years most of Poland's thirty thousand Jews are forced to leave. The US, USSR, and Britain sign the Nuclear Non-Proliferation Treaty. After preaching against war, Martin Luther King Jr. is assassinated in Memphis by James Earl Ray. Robert Kennedy wins the California primary but is shot to death in Los Angeles by Sirhan Sirhan. Demonstrators protesting the Miss America beauty pageant in

Atlantic City trash bras, heels, curlers, and other such objects and are labeled "bra-burners." On the day before Christmas, Apollo 8 snaps a photograph of Earth hovering over the lunar horizon and beams "Earthrise" back home to enthrall millions. Arthur Clarke and Stanley Kubrick collaborate on the film *2001: A Space Odyssey*. Von Bertalanffy's *General Systems Theory*. In San Francisco Haridas Chaudhury founds the California Institute of Asian Studies (known later as the California Institute of Integral Studies).

1969:
The Woodstock Music & Art Fair takes off in the Catskills. Belaunde Terry, president of Peru, finds himself kicked out of office for failing to nationalize Standard Oil's International Petroleum Company. Nixon and Kissinger plan the secret intensive bombing of Cambodia (Nixon will later claim, "When the President does it, that means it is not illegal"). Muammar Gaddafi stages a coup in Libya. The Stonewall riots erupt in New York when plainclothes police raid the Stonewall Inn in Greenwich Village and inadvertently fuel the gay rights movement. The first gay pride parade is held in New York. The Department of Defense sets up four computer network nodes on university campuses and establishes ARPANET (Advanced Research Projects Agency Net). This network, built to test the feasibility of packet-switching links that survive a nuclear attack, will eventually expand into the Internet. Lovelock comes up with the Gaia Hypothesis that Earth self-adjusts its ecologicalsystems to support life. Neil Armstrong on the Moon: "That's one small step for a man, one giant leap for mankind." N. Scott Momaday wins a Pulitzer Prize for *House Made of Dawn*. Millett's *Sexual Politics*. Roszak's *The Making of a Counter Culture*. Jane Goodall's *My Friends the Wild Chimpanzees*.

1970:
Rhodesia cuts ties with Britain and declares itself a racially segregated republic. Civil war in Nigeria ends, but one breaks out in Cambodia: the communist Khmer Rouge versus the Khmer Republic that loses. Rise of powerful drug cartels in Colombia. A huge cyclone kills three hundred thousand coast-dwellers in

Bangladesh. Nixon announces on TV a withdrawal of troops from Vietnam, but instead, in response to a purported North Vietnamese buildup, he launches bombing raids on Cambodian "sanctuaries" that kill half a million people in a "defensive action for peace." The Khmer Rouge will use this catastrophe for recruitment. Four student protesters at Kent State, Ohio are shot by National Guardsmen. Tonga and Fiji gain independence from Britain. Iraq nationalizes its oil industry. Libya does the same and works toward health care and education. The Marxist leader Allende is elected President of copper-rich Chile despite CIA efforts prompted by ITT and Chase Manhattan Bank. Greenpeace is founded in Vancouver, Canada to protest nuclear testing in the Pacific. The first black hole candidate, Cygnus X-1, is discovered (Einstein's theories predicted them, but he didn't believe in them). A massive oil spill off the coast of Santa Barbara inspires the first Earth Day. The Boston Women's Health Book Collective publishes the immensely popular *Our Bodies, Ourselves*. Henri Ellenberger's *The Discovery of the Unconscious*. Robin Morgan edits *Sisterhood is Powerful*. Carl Wittman's *A Gay Manifesto*, and Paulo Freire *Pedagogy of the Oppressed:* "Education either functions as an instrument which is used to facilitate integration of the younger generation into the logic of the present system and bring about conformity or it becomes the practice of freedom, the means by which men and women deal critically and creatively with reality and discover how to participate in the transformation of their world."

1971:
The US Supreme Court decides that students can be bussed to schools to achieve racial desegregation. Daniel Ellsberg leaks the secret *Pentagon Papers*, a study revealing unreported military activity in Vietnam across four US administrations, to the *New York Times*. Europe-supported mass murderer Idi Amin stages a coup that brings him to power in Uganda. Nigeria joins OPEC. After a brief Indo-Pakistani war, East Pakistan is declared independent and calls itself Bangladesh. Gutierrez's *Theology of Liberation*. The Boston Women's Health Book Collective's *Our Bodies, Ourselves*.

1972:
Under the Australian Labor Party citizens acquire free college education and universal healthcare. The US Congress passes the Equal Opportunity Act in response to pressure from the Women's Movement. Britain takes over direct rule of Northern Ireland; "Bloody Sunday" in Londonderry, Northern Ireland, when troops fire on civil rights marchers. At the Munich Olympics, Israeli athletes are shot dead by the Arab "Black September" organization. Five of Nixon's Committee for the Re-Election of the President (CREEP) henchmen are caught breaking into the Democratic Party headquarters at the Watergate Hotel. (Nixon sends in the Watergate burglars for fear the Democrats might possess a file documenting his sabotage of Vietnam peace talks in 1968. He sabotaged them to win election.) The US and USSR sign the Strategic Arms Limitation Talks Agreement (SALT I), but no restraints are placed on MIRVs. Honeybees vanish mysteriously from their hives ("Disappearing Disease"). The first issue of *Ms. Magazine* appears. Sweden is the first country to legalize sex reassignment surgery. Nancy Wechsler is the first openly gay politician in the US. Gregory Bateson's *Steps to an Ecology of Mind*. "But the myth of power is, of course, a very powerful myth, and probably most people in this world more or less believe in it. It is a myth, which, if everybody believes in it, becomes to that extent self-validating. But it is still epistemological lunacy and leads inevitably to various sorts of disaster."

1973:
The US launches space station Skylab 4. The last US troops leave Vietnam after Henry Kissinger and Le Duc Tho sign a treaty in Paris; US spies and diplomats stay in Saigon but South Vietnamese forces crumble. Salvador Allende, president of Chile, is killed in a coup by US-backed General Pinochet, whose junta takes over and whose hit squad will be known as the Caravan of Death. Egypt and Syria fight Israel in the oxymoronically named Yom Kippur War in which the Arab coalition cuts the oil supplies of Israel's supporters, triggering an energy crisis, but Israel wins anyway. The Canadian House of Commons censures US bombing in North Vietnam. Spiro Agnew resigns as US vice president and pleads no contest to tax

evasion charges. Egypt and Israel sign a US-brokered cease-fire. Incredibly, Kissinger and North Vietnam's Le Duc Tho are awarded the Nobel Peace Prize, but only Le Duc Tho has the integrity to turn it down. Aleksandr Solzhenitsyn publishes *The Gulag Archipeligo* to describe Soviet political oppression. Homosexuality is no longer listed in a mental disorder in the *Diagnostic and Statistical Manual* used by psychiatrists and psychotherapists. The US Supreme Court rules in *Roe v. Wade* that abortion is legal in the first trimester of pregnancy. Astronaut Edgar Mitchell founds the Institute of Noetic Sciences to study heightened states of consciousness from a scientific perspective. E.F. Schumacher's *Small is Beautiful.* "Wisdom demands a new orientation of science and technology toward the organic, the gentle, the elegant and beautiful."

1974:
The Carnation Revolution overthrows the Estado Novo dictatorship in Portugal. Patricia Hearst is captured and brainwashed by young thugs calling themselves the Symbionese Liberation Army. US president Nixon states "I am not a crook" on national TV but resigns after the Watergate scandal. Gerald Ford is sworn in and pardons Nixon. South Africa is expelled from the UN. Nigeria becomes a leading oil producer. Bangladesh joins the UN. Australopithecus afarenis (nicknamed "Lucy") found in Ethiopia. Portuguese Guinea wins independence. Cheikh Anta Diop publishes *The African Origin of Civilization: Myth or Reality?* Ruether's *Religion and Sexism.* Gimbutas's *The Goddesses and Gods of Old Europe.* World population: four billion. At a conference ecologist and philosopher Arne Naess calls for a "deep ecology" that questions the assumptions of human superiority over the natural world. Françoise d'Eaubonne coins "ecofeminism" to describe a philosophy that pairs the mistreatment of women subjugated by patriarchy with mistreatment of the natural world.

1974-75:
The remaining Portuguese colonies finally gain independence.

1975:
Pol Pot, China-backed leader of the Khmer Rouge communist rebels, takes over Phnom Penh, Cambodia, evacuates the city, and enslaves or kills "class enemies." The Economic Community of West African States founded. Bill Gates and Paul Allen found Microsoft. Mozambique (formerly Portuguese East Africa) gains independence. Angola's independence will be contested by decades of civil war. A revival of Maori culture and language in New Zealand. Apollo and Soyuz meet in space on a Soviet-US friendship mission. US President Ford evades two assassination attempts. James Hillman publishes *Re-Visioning Psychology*. Fritjof Capra's *The Tao of Physics*.

1976:
African high school children rise up in Soweto in South Africa to protest having to read and speak in Africaans. Israeli commandos attack Uganda's Entebbe Airport and free a hundred and three hostages held by pro-Palestinian hijackers of an Air France plane, with one Israeli and several Ugandan soldiers killed. The Thammasat University Massacre in Thailand against students protesting military rule. In a quest for the independence of Aceh in Sumatra, the Free Aceh Movement battles with the Indonesian military until 2005. Steven Wozniak designs what will become the Apple I personal computer, and his friend Steven Jobs suggests that he sell it.

1977:
South African activist Stephen Biko dies in prison. Five rings are spotted circling Uranus. Elvis Presley dies on the toilet, probably of a heart attack brought on by drug use. Jimmy Carter takes office and fills his administration with Trilateral Commission neoliberals. Wangaari Mathai heads the Green Belt movement of tree-planting and ecological restoration in Kenya. The Free Aceh Movement in Sumatra fights back against Mobil Oil. Borrowing Joseph Campbell's schema of the Hero's Journey, George Lucas writes and produces *Star Wars*. Apple II makes a splash at computer trade shows; its user-friendly interface will have a wide influence on

future computer design. Scientists use bacteria to make insulin. Voyager 1 departs on its journey beyond the Solar System. Ken Wilber publishes *The Spectrum of Consciousness*. Leslie Marmon Silko publishes *Ceremony*. "I will tell you something about stories . . . They aren't just entertainment. Don't be fooled. They are all we have, you see, all we have to fight off illness and death." At SETI (Search for Extraterrestrial Life), scientist Jerry Ehrman detects a candidate signal seeming to emanate from outside the solar system, from the direction of Sagittarius the Archer, but the signal only lasts for just over a minute.

1978:
Rhodesia transfers power to black majority rule. Multi-party elections in Senegal. The US Senate agrees to turn the Canal over to Panama in 2000. Sweden is the first nation to cut aerosol sprays to stop destruction of the ozone layer. Louise Brown, the first test-tube baby, born in London. Muhammad Zia-ul-Haq becomes president of Pakistan and accepts money from President Carter to fight the Soviets despite an abysmal human rights record. Carter hosts the Camp David summit between Egypt (Sadat) and Israel (Begin). The US designs the launch system for the Tomahawk cruise missile, and soon nuclear cruise missiles are based in Europe. Mass murder-suicide in Jonestown, Guyana, as cult leader Jim Jones inspires his followers to drink poisoned Kool-Aid. San Francisco Supervisor Harvey Milk and Mayor George Moscone are shot to death by former supervisor Dan White, who is convicted of manslaughter rather than of murder. Gilbert Baker designs the rainbow pride flag. Edward Said publishes *Orientalism*. Bill Mollison and David Holmgren publish *Permaculture One* to lay out a system of food production that imitates growing patterns found in the natural world.

1979:
Vietnam invades Cambodia and forces out the Khmer Rouge and the Pol Pot regime. Ayatollah Khomeini takes over Iran from the deposed US-backed Shah and sets up an Islamic constitution. Coup-torn Peru writes a new constitution. In Nicaragua the Sandinista army forces US-backed dictator Anastasio Somoza Debayle to flee

to Miami. Jerry John Rawlings initiates a coup and takes over Ghana. Alhaji Shehu Shagari is elected President of Nigeria and works toward agricultural reform and less dependence on food imports. Zimbabwe achieves independence. Carter and Brezhnev sign the SALT II agreement, but the Soviets invade Afghanistan, so the US refuses to ratify. Angered by Carter allowing the deposed Shah into the US, students storm the US embassy in Iran and take a hundred people hostage. A nuclear reactor undergoes partial meltdown at Three Mile Island in Pennsylvania. Robert Bullard and Linda Keever Bullard start the Environmental Justice Movement by initiating a lawsuit, *Bean v. Southwestern Waste Mangement, Inc.*, to stop a garbage dump from landing in a black neighborhood in Houston. Bohm's *Wholeness and the Implicate Order*. Prigogine's *From Being to Becoming*. Carolyn Merchant's *The Death of Nature*.

1980:
Two years of civil war in El Salvador. President Carter announces his willingness to defend US assets in the Middle East: the Carter Doctrine that will ease the way for two coming Gulf Wars. A military accident for which Carter receives much blame prevents a hostage rescue attempt in Iran. Neocons Robert McFarlane and Paul Wolfowitz approach Yassir Arafat and ask him if he can do anything to keep the hostages in Iran until after Reagan's election, and they are freed on his first day in office. Reagan also has secret dealings with Khomeini. Lech Walesa puts together the independent trade union Solidarity in Poland. Mt. St. Helens erupts in Washington State. Samuel Doe stages a coup in Liberia, opens its ports to European and Asian trade ships, and turns his country into an international offshore tax haven. The inconclusive Iran-Iraq war starts when Iraq invades. Having begged President Carter not to fund the junta in charge of El Salvador, whose brutal leader Duarte is hailed as a moderate in US newspapers, Archbishop Oscar Romero is assassinated during Mass. Between 1980 and 1985 the US defense budget deficit rises 51%. The Democratic Party is the first in the US to endorse gay rights. David McReynolds is the first openly gay candidate for the US Presidency. John Lennon is shot and killed in New

York City: "You may say I'm a dreamer / But I'm not the only one...."

1981:
AIDS (Acquired Immune Deficiency Disorder, the acronym eerily reminiscent of AIDOS, the original name of Hades) is recognized as a lethal illness. President Reagan gives the CIA permission for paramilitary operations against the Sandinista government in Nicaragua to help the "freedom fighter" Contras, a reactionary, reconstituted version of ex-dictator Somoza's brutally sadistic National Guard. This maneuvering prompts comedian George Carlin to ask, "Well, if crime fighters fight crime and fire fighters fight fire, what do freedom fighters fight?" US-trained and armed Salvadoran troops slaughter the village of El Mozote. Palau achieves independence. Shortages of goods and food in Romania. The US Space Shuttle program debuts. Sandra Day O'Connor is the first woman to serve as a US Supreme Court Justice. John Hinkley Jr. shoots President Reagan, but Reagan survives. Pope John Paul II is wounded by a gunman but survives. The University of Waterloo, Ontario, invents the first local area network. Gloria Anzaldúa and Cherrie Moraga publish *This Bridge Called My Back: Writings by Radical Women of Color*.

1982:
Cynically named Operation Peace for Galilee launched by Israel to oust the Palestine Liberation Organization besieges southern Lebanon for eleven hard months. Syrian forces attack and massacre the Muslim Brotherhood in Hama. Argentina takes control of the Falkland Islands, and Britain sends in forces that take control back. Margaret Thatcher, first woman prime minister of the UK, embarks on a program of deregulation and privatization: in the words of economist Susan Strange, "casino capitalism." The US Equal Rights Amendment is not ratified because of heavy conservative opposition. Dictator-president Ahmadou Ahidjo steps down in Cameroon. Mexico's failure to repay foreign loans stirs an international financial crisis. Reagan tours Latin America and returns surprised, he tells reporters, that they are all individual countries. Carol Gilligan's *In a*

Different Voice. Julia Kristeva's *Powers of Horror: an Essay on Abjection.* Alice Walker's *The Color Purple:* "I think it pisses God off if you walk by the color purple in a field somewhere and don't notice it."

1983:
Sally K. Ride aboard the shuttle *Challenger* is the first US woman in space. The US Government admits shielding former Nazi Gestapo chief Klaus Barbie, the Butcher of Lyon, for use as a CIA agent in South America. Over 1.5 million people die in another Sudanese civil war. A South Korean Boeing 747 jetliner bound for Seoul enters Soviet airspace and is shot down by a SU-15 fighter. African countries adopt IMF (International Monetary Fund) plans for reforming their economies and going into debt. Reagan orders an invasion of Grenada, ostensibly to rescue endangered American medical students. He also calls the Soviet Union an "evil empire" and makes jokes about bombing it. Gerry Studds is the first openly gay member of the US Congress. Cellular phone networks go online in the US. Ex-CIA agent and drug trafficker Manuel Noriega takes over in Panama. Independence for Brunei. Scientists reveal the ozone layer shrinkage over the South Pole. During the Lebanese Civil War, in which Islamic forces fight the French colonial government, a Hezbollah truck bomb explodes at US Marine base in Beirut, killing two hundred and ninety-nine American and French troops. Reagan prompts widespread international anxiety by backing "Star Wars," an anti-missile laser system, which the Soviets believe is designed to guard against a Soviet nuclear response following an American first strike. The US deploys Pershing missiles in Europe near the Soviet Union. In his journal Reagan writes of his surprise that the Soviets are afraid of the US. Feminist Gloria Steinem writes *Outrageous Acts and Everyday Rebellions.* The ancient Gospel of Judas resurfaces; in it Judas's betrayal is ordered by Jesus himself so he can die in fulfillment of his mission.

1984:
Widespread famine in Ethiopia. A strike by UK coal miners levers the Conservatives back into power. In the UK, Chris Smith is the

first openly gay member of Parliament. The US Congress rebukes Reagan on his use of federal funds to mine Nicaraguan harbors. US-backed mass murderer Jose Napoleon Duarte becomes president of El Salvador. Three hundred die as the Indian Army occupies the Sikh Golden Temple in Amritsar; Indira Gandhi is assassinated by her Sikh guards. Geraldine Ferraro becomes the first woman vice presidential nominee in the US. The Pentagon's classified master plan for 1984–1988 ranks defense of the Middle East second only to the defense of North America and Western Europe: "Our principal objectives are to assure continued access to Persian Gulf oil and to prevent the Soviets from acquiring political-military control of the oil directly or through proxies." Lyotard's *The Postmodern Condition*.

1985:
Between 1985 and 1988 the US national deficit triples. Although the US enacts a budget-balancing bill, Reagan raises defense spending by 51% over 1980 expenditures while cutting federal support for domestic programs like food stamps for the poor, school lunch funding, Medicaid, housing and energy programs, and Aid to Families with Dependent Children as federal funds for cities are halved and the highest-bracket income tax drops from 70% to 28%. Konstantin Chernenko dies, and Mikhail Gorbachev takes over in the Soviet Union. Pro-nuclear French Intelligence agents sink Greenpeace's vessel *Rainbow Warrior*. Terrorists seize an Egyptian Boeing 737 airliner after it takes off from Athens, and fifty-nine passengers die when Egyptian forces storm the plane on Malta. Gorbachev decides to end the war in Afghanistan and reduce a Soviet defense budget that takes up a full 40% of government spending. The The Live Aid concert plays to thousands in London and Philadelphia to aid famine sufferers in Ethiopia. Jorge Luis Borges publishes *The Conspirators*.

1986:
Astronauts aboard Space Shuttle *Challenger* die when it explodes shortly after liftoff. US-backed Haiti president Jean-Claude Duvalier flees to France. US-backed president/dictator Ferdinand Marcos

deposed in the Philippines. A nuclear accident at Chernobyl releases massive and lingering radioactive pollution. The Treaty of Rarotonga sets up a South Pacific Nuclear-Free Zone. Reagan denies trading arms for hostages in Iran. In the spirit of *glasnost* ("openness"), Gorbachev writes to Reagan to suggest ending nuclear weapons and all nuclear testing; instead, Reagan orders more testing and increased support for Afghan mujahideen fighters raiding the Soviets. About their meeting in Iceland Gorbachev writes, "Reagan reacted by consulting or reading his notes written on cards. I tried to discuss with him the points I had just outlined, but all my attempts failed. I decided to try specific questions, but still did not get any response..... The cards got mixed up and some of them fell to the floor. He started shuffling them, looking for the right answer to my arguments, but he could not find it." The Soviet offer is to cut nuclear arms in half, freeze their development, stop testing, confine SDI (Star Wars) experimentation to laboratories for ten years, and allow on-site inspections of missile sites, with a final goal of eliminating nuclear weapons entirely everywhere. Foreign Minister Shevardnadze adds that future generations would never forgive any of them for missing such an opportunity to disarm. Heeding his neo-conservative advisers, Reagan refuses to budge on SDI, so the opportunity passes.

1987:
Aretha Franklin is the first woman inducted into the Rock and Roll Hall of Fame. The Philippines gets a new constitution. Reagan accepts ultimate responsibility for the Iran-Contra affair but claims he can't recall the details. Officials convicted of crimes within his "Law and Order" administration include the National Security Advisor, his successor, the Assistant Secretary of State, and Lieutenant Colonel Oliver North. Vice President George H. Bush and Deputy CIA Director Robert Gates avoid prosecution, Defense Secretary Casper Weinberger is indicted but pardoned, and CIA Director William Casey dies of a brain tumor during the hearings. An Iraqi jet fires two Exocet missiles and cripples the *USS Stark* as it patrols the Persian Gulf, an act that kills thirty-seven and for which Saddam Hussein apologizes. Muslim-Hindu riots in Meerut.

The Spectacle of Ourselves | 219

The New Zealand Nuclear Free Zone, Disarmament, and Arms Control Act. A Lyon court sentences Klaus Barbie to life in prison. The Brundtland Report from the UN World Commission on Environment and Development emphasizes the need for worldwide sustainability. Typhoon Nina brings thousands of deaths in the Philippines. North Korean operatives blow up Korean Air Flight 858. The First Intifada revolt against Israeli occupation of Palestine breaks out in a refugee camp and spreads rapidly. In the deadliest peacetime maritime disaster ever, the oil tanker *MT Vector* (license expired) collides with the ferry *MV Doña Paz* of the Philippines at Tablas Strait with a loss of forty-three hundred people, most killed by burning oil. Gloria Anzaldúa publishes *Borderlands: The New Mestiza*. World population: five billion.

1988:
US and Canada reach a free trade agreement, the Nicaraguan Contras and the Sandinista government a cease-fire agreement, the same with the Soviets and Afghans, and Iran and Iraq a peace treaty. PLO leader Yassir Arafat vows to give up terrorism. Benazir Bhutto is the first Islamic woman prime minister in Pakistan. Canadian astronomers Bruce Campbell, Stephenson Yang, and G. Walker locate the first planet outside our solar system. Gorbachev introduces *perestroika* (a "restructuring" program to repair Soviet society) and says the Cold War is over. Dick Cheney advises Reagan not to organize an early summit with Gorbachev, who dismisses Reagan's patently unfair offer to cut thirty thousand troops in Europe while demanding that the Soviets remove three hundred and twenty-five thousand as a precondition for taking tactical nukes out of Europe. Reagan also refuses to sign a co-statement with Gorbachev disallowing unwanted military interference in other nations. A military coup turns Burma into Myanmar. Libyan terrorists blow up Pan Am Flight 103 over Lockerbie, Scotland. A US Navy ship accidentally shoots down an Iranian airliner in the Persian Gulf. As Iraq uses both conventional and chemical weapons on the Kurds, US intelligence aid to Iraq increases, and the US government authorizes a sale to Iraq of $1.5 million in weaponizable insecticides manufactured by Dow Chemical, producer of the napalm dropped in

Vietnam. Arabs flooding into Pakistan to train to fight communists include a Saudi named Osama bin Laden and Ayman al-Zawahiri of Egypt. Terrorists receiving US-funded training murder most of the moderate and progressive leaders in Afghanistan, leaving a power vacuum for fanatical fundamentalists. As the Soviets prepare to leave Afghanistan, American officials ignore repeated warnings about the dangers of arming Islamic radicals. Vandana Shiva's book *Staying Alive* highlights the struggles of Third World women against economic injustice perpetrated by agricultural giants like Monsanto, a transnational that will seek to buy up and monopolize seed all over the world. Spirit Rock Meditation Center founded in Marin, California. Thomas Berry publishes *The Dream of the Earth:* "Of all the issues we are concerned with at present, the most basic issue, in my estimation, is that of human-earth relations." Kevin Kelly edits *The Home Planet*: "I think this sense of wonder at our universe and the strangeness of our lives within our tiny part of it is important to our sense of ourselves and perhaps to our very survival."

1989:
The tanker *Exxon Valdez* spills eleven million gallons of crude oil into Alaska's Prince William Sound. Mass demonstrations for democracy in Tiananmen Square, Beijing, China, end in the military's massacre of defenseless students. In El Salvador, priest-psychologist Ignacio Martín-Baró and his staff are murdered by a US-trained hit team; his last words are, "This is an injustice!" A gunman kills fourteen female engineering students at the University of Montréal. In Ethiopia, the Tigrayan People's Liberation Front joins with the Amhara and Oromo Liberation Fronts to form the Ethiopian Peoples' Revolutionary Democratic Front (EPRDF) that forces dictator Mengistu Haile Mariam to flee to Zimbabwe. The Berlin Wall is dismantled, and the US Government takes the credit for winning the Cold War. Romania and Czechoslovakia get rid of their communist governments, and Uzbekistan wins independence. US soldiers invade Panama and depose the drug-dealing General Noriega. Tenzin Gyatso, the 14th Dalai Lama, receives the Nobel Peace Prize for his work to liberate Tibet. A US delegation demands that Iraq privatize its oil industry, but Iraq refuses. Elections bring reform to

Zambia. Nicolae Ceausescu, Europe's last Stalinist, is deposed and executed four days after he orders his troops to fire on Romanian protesters. Iran's Ayatollah Khomeini declares Salman Rushdie's book *The Satanic Verses* offensive and sentences him to death, whereupon Rushdie goes into hiding.

1990:
Invented by Tim Berners-Lee, the World Wide Web goes online. Aung San Suu Kyi wins the popular election in Myanmar but the junta disallows it and places her under house arrest. South Africa frees Nelson Mandela after he has spent twenty-seven years in prison. After a long civil war, Mozambique gains a new constitution and works toward a multi-party democracy, with elections in 1994. The Hubble Space Telescope launches. Bush and Gorbachev agree to cut nuclear arms and chemical weapons. After US AmbassadorGlaspie assures Saddam Hussein that the President has "no opinion" in Iraq's border conflict with Kuwait, Iraqi troops invade Kuwait in the first Persian Gulf War. Stunned, Cheney, Powell, and General Normal Schwarzkopf show King Fahd false photographs of Iraqi troops and armor across his border to prompt him to allow the US to station troops in Saudi Arabia. This move prompts Osama bin Ladin to declare holy war against the US. The US and Saudi Arabia bribes several governments to vote for UN Security Council authorization to use force against Iraq in Kuwait. The Inuit receive land in Canada. Rescuing Gorbachev from hard-line conservative kidnappers opposed to his reforms, the alcoholic Boris Yeltsin is elected president of the Russian Federation and allows financiers and gangsters to pillage what's left of the Russian economy. Ukraine declares sovereignty. Democratic elections in Mongolia. Leaders of thirty-four nations in Europe and North America proclaim a united Europe. Haiti elects a leftist priest as president in its first democratic election. Namibia gets independence. Chile returns to democracy after seventeen years, and Augusto Pinochet is replaced by Patricio Awlyn Azocar. Mary Robinson is elected President of Ireland. AIDS activists take over the word "queer" and form Queer Nation in New York. The first assessment

report by the Intergovernmental Panel on Climate Change links carbon dioxide increases in the atmosphere to global warming.

1991:
The Sudanese government practices apartheid-like tactics on the non-Arabs of the Zaghawa in South Sudan. Operation Desert Storm defeats the Iraqi army in Kuwait. Communist rule of Albania ends. Jiang Qing, widow of Mao Zedong, commits suicide. Kazakhstan becomes a republic. The South African Parliament repeals the apartheid laws. Lithuania, Estonia, Latvia, and Tajikistan win independence. A new constitution goes into effect in Colombia. Haitian troops seize the president, and the US suspends assistance to Haiti. Anita Hill accuses Judge Clarence Thomas of sexual harassment, but the US Senate confirms his Supreme Court appointment anyway. Gorbachev resigns, the USSR comes to an end, and its former republics form a Commonwealth of Independent States. Civil wars in Algiers, Sierra Leone, and Somali. Richard Tarnas publishes *The Passion of the Western Mind.*

1992:
Six republics of Yugoslavia, including Slovenia and Croatia, declare themselves independent. When four LAPD police officers are acquitted in the videotaped beating of Rodney King, rioting erupts in South-Central Los Angeles. The acquitted officers are indicted on federal civil rights charges. The US Senate and the Russian Parliament ratify the START Treaty. Paul Wolfowitz advises US leaders to prevent any rival that could threaten US global hegemony and to be ready to fight several wars simultaneously. President George H. Bush pardons Reagan administration officials involved in the Iran-Contra affair. The World Trade Center in New York is bombed by terrorists. Rwandan farmers uproot thousands of coffee trees because they can no longer make a living from the little money they receive for this export crop. The World Bank's International Development Association orders privatization of Rwanda's Electorogaz and telecommunications company. Multi-party elections held in Kenya. Albania gains independence. The Americans with Disabilities Act becomes law. The world's population is 5.2 bil-

lion. Theodore Roszak's book *Voice of the Earth* popularizes ecopsychology, a new field that studies the health and pathology of human relations with the natural world. Rebecca Walker coins the term "third wave feminism." Paul Shepherd writes *Nature and Madness*. Brian Swimme and Thomas Berry publish *The Universe Story*.

1993:
Czechoslovakia dissolves into Slovakia and the Czech Republic, with Vaclav Havel elected Czech president: "The salvation of this human world lies nowhere else than in the human heart, in the human power to reflect, in human meekness and human responsibility." The Oslo Accords mediated by Norway end the first Intifada between Palestine and Israel. Ghana gains presidential and parliamentary elections. President Clinton submits to a "don't ask, don't tell" compromise on allowing gays in the military. When US federal agents attack religious leader David Koresh's Branch Dividian headquarters in Waco, Texas, a fire breaks out and seventy-two people die. Kim Campbell is the first female prime minister of Canada. A large swath of land in British Columbia receives protection as a world heritage conservation site. UN weapons monitors enter Iraq. Europe's Maastricht Treaty takes effect, creating the European Union. The US Congress approves the North American Free Trade Agreement (NAFTA) to make it easier to purchase products in other countries and to force farmers to grow crops for international trade. Kim Campbell is the first woman prime minister of Canada; Tansu Cillar is first woman prime minister of Turkey. Nigerian leader Major General Babangida declares the country's elections null and void and refuses to give up power. Eritrea breaks from Ethiopia, marking the first successful secession in post-colonial Africa. Russian leaders who believed they had received ironclad US and German promises that eastward expansion by NATO would never be permitted watch in horror as the Clinton and second Bush administrations push NATO right to Russia's borders. Toni Morrison wins the Nobel Prize for literature. James Hillman and Michael Ventura transcribe and publish *We've Had a Hundred Years of Psychotherapy and the World's Getting Worse*. Susan Griffin's *A*

Chorus of Stones: A Private Life of War.

1994:
Rwandan genocide of Tutsis by Hutus slaughters eight hundred thousand in a hundred days. As apartheid ends, South Africa holds its first interracial national election and Nelson Mandela wins the presidency. Ethiopia gains elections and a new constitution. The IRA agrees to a cease-fire in Northern Ireland. An earthquake hits Japan, and over five thousand perish. When NAFTA eliminates the sovereignty of their farmlands, the Zapatistas rise for long-term resistance in Mexico. The US Violence Against Women Act is passed to fight gender-based violent crimes. Russia wages a bloody war against the breakaway republic of Chechnya. Carl Sagan's *Pale Blue Dot: A Vision of the Human Future in Space.*

1995:
The Aum Shinrikyo ("Supreme Truth") cult preaching the end of the world unleashes Sarin nerve gas in a Tokyo subway, killing eight and injuring thousands, and is arrested. Army veteran Ex-Marine Timothy McVeigh bombs the Oklahoma City Federal Building, killing hundreds. Fighting escalates in Bosnia and Croatia. Sweden joins the European Union. A US shuttle docks with Russian space station Mir. Israelis and Palestinians agree on the transfer of the West Bank to the Arabs. The Million Man March draws hundreds of thousands of black men to the US capital. A Jewish extremist kills Israeli prime minister Yitzhak Rabin at a peace rally. United Nations Fourth World Conference on Women held in Beijing. Palestinians are granted limited self-rule.

1996:
France and China agree to end nuclear tests. A product of factory farms, Mad Cow Disease, sweeps Britain. The FBI arrests the "Unabomber" Theodore Kaczynski for planting and mailing numerous bombs. When Iraqis strike a Kurdish enclave, the US enforces northern and southern "no-fly" zones. Islamic Taliban fundamentalists capture the Afghan capital. Clinton appoints Madeleine Albright, the first female US Secretary of State. NATO bombs

Serbia. First and Second Congo Wars flare because of interference in Zaire by Rwanda. Multi-party elections held in Chad. Evidence points to a supermassive black hole in the center of our galaxy. Eve Ensler writes and performs *The Vagina Monologues*. "It seems to me there's this tyranny that's not accidental or incidental, to make women feel compelled to look like somebody they're not. I think the effort is being made to get us to turn our time and attention to this instead of important political issues....Stop fixing your bodies and start fixing the world!" Fritjof Carpra's *The Web of Life*. Howard Clinebell's Ecotherapy: *Healing Ourselves, Healing the Earth*, as research builds confirming the healthful effects of abundant contact with plants and animals. David Abram's *The Spell of the Sensuous:* "The animate earth – this moody terrain that we experience differently in anger and in joy, in grief and in love – is both the soil in which all our sciences are rooted and the rich humus into which their results ultimately return, whether as nutrients or as poisons. Our spontaneous experience of the world, charged with subjective, emotional, and intuitive content, remains the vital and dark ground of all our objectivity."

1997:
The Israeli government's approval of a new Jewish settlement in East Jerusalem predictably escalates violence against Palestinians. When the Hale-Bopp comet makes a close approach to Earth, Heaven's Gate cult members commit mass suicide in California, hoping for a ride with money in their pockets. Hong Kong returns to Chinese rule. Chased by photographers, Princess Diana and two other passengers die in a Paris car crash: an odd and tragic replay, with a twist, to the story of Diana and Acteon. Taliban leaders seize Kabul. Assembling the Project for the New American Century (PNAC) to enforce US control of global resources, William Kristol and Robert Kagan lead neocons into pushing for increased military spending. Jody Williams, co-founder of the International Campaign to Ban Landmines (ICBL), receivesthe Nobel Peace Prize. Scottish geneticists clone Dolly the sheep are eerily surprised by the resulting controversy. Cornel West publishes *Restoring Hope: Conversations on the Future of Black America*. Janine Benyus's

Biomimicry: Innovation Inspired by Nature. Charlene Spretnak's *The Resurgence of the Real: Body, Nature, and Place in a Hypermodern World.*

1998:
US President Clinton is accused of having sex with White House intern Monica Lewinsky and denies it; several of his accusers will get into trouble because of their own sexual dalliances. Thousands dead in an Afghanistan quake. Government forces under new Serbian president Slobodan Milosevic commit war crimes against ethnic Albanians in Kosovo. The Good Friday Accord makes Northern Ireland part of the UK. Indonesian dictator Suharto steps down. A UN tribunal condemns the Rwandan genocide. Iran lifts the death threat against Salman Rushdie. The US budget surplus is the largest in thirty years. A hugely destructive ice storm, the worst in Canada's history, strikes the central and eastern regions of the nation. Matthew Shepard, a gay Wyoming student, is fatally beaten in a hate crime. Tammy Baldwin is the first openly lesbian candidate to be elected to Congress. Former Chilean dictator Pinochet is arrested in London. Construction begins on the International Space Station. A split found in the Antarctic ice cap suggests global warming. The IMF loans money to Brazil and other South American countries to put them in debt via interest, then informs them that instead of going bankrupt, they should sell land to private investors, a move that accelerates the deforestation of the Amazon. Joanna Macy and Molly Young Brown publish *Coming Back to Life: Practices to Reconnect Our Lives, Our World.* Henri Corbin's *Alone with the Alone: Creative Imagination in the Sufism of Ibn 'Arabi.*

1999:
The euro is the currency of the European Union, but not everyone accepts it. The US Senate acquits President Clinton of impeachment charges. The US refuses to accept the Ottowa Treaty against land mine use. NATO launches air strikes on Serbia to end attacks against ethnic Albanians in Kosovo, and the action appears on television almost as it unfolds. Jack "Doctor Death" Kevorkian is convicted of second-degree murder and imprisoned for enabling assisted suicide.

Libya finally hands over for trial two suspects of the 1988 Pan Am jet bombing. Students Eric Harris and Dylan Klebold kill fifteen students, and then themselves, at Columbine High, and years of mass shootings follow. Hugo Rafael Chávez Frías
takes over in Venezuela; he will enlarge presidential powers, cut oil production to drive up prices, install social programs for the poor, and nationalize energy, power, and telecommunications. Nelson Mandela retires; Thabo Mbeki takes over in South Africa and causes international outrage by refusing to believe HIV leads to AIDS. Taiwanese leader Lee Teng-hui angers China by challenging the "One China" policy. Eileen Collins is the first woman to command a space shuttle mission. Second Chechen War, Second Liberian Civil War, Fourth Indo-Pakistani War. The Chinese ban the Falun Gong meditation sect and arrest its members. East Timor votes for independence from Indonesia. A military coup led by General Pervaiz Musharraf takes over Pakistan. Tobacco companies are finally forced to admit that cigarettes are harmful. The US Senate rejects the 1996 nuclear test-ban treaty. Microsoft is ruled to be a monopoly, but nothing substantive is done about it. Violent anti-globalization protests surge around the World Trade Organization conference in Seattle. Natalie Angier's *Woman: An Intimate Geography*.

Year 2000 (Y2K):
Throughout the world, millennial rumors of second comings, visits by messiahs, final judgments, and various Revelations-style end-of-the-world scenarios panic lots of people, some of whom stockpile and arm against a worldwide disaster while others stay home when the clocks change at midnight, but nothing universally catastrophic happens, and earthly life goes on pretty much as it did before.

2000:
Tarja Kaarina Halonen is Finland's first woman president. The Second Intifada explodes. Hawkish Ariel Sharon's catastrophic visit to a joint Jewish and Muslim holy site undoes much previous peace work, and the revolt rages on. AOL buys Time Warner for $162 billion. Torrential, record-setting rains kill eight hundred people in Mozambique. Failed Internet "Dot.Com" companies litter the

Silicon Valley. Vermont approves same-sex unions; other states follow. South Carolina finally removes the Confederate battle flag from its capitol dome. President Alberto Fujimori leaves Peru to avoid corruption and human rights violation charges but is arrested, brought back, tried, and imprisoned. Former Indonesian president Suharto under house arrest, charged with corruption and abuse of power. Presidents of North and South Korea sign a landmark peace accord, but incoming President George W. Bush will warn of an "axis of evil" and drastically increase tensions. The United Nations Millennium Declaration sets an agenda of inclusiveness and freedom from want to be achieved in the years ahead: "We recognize that, in addition to our separate responsibilities to our individual societies, we have a collective responsibility to uphold the principles of human dignity, equality and equity at the global level. As leaders we have a duty therefore to all the world's people, especially the most vulnerable and, in particular, the children of the world, to whom the future belongs." Headed by Vojislav Kostunica, the Yugoslav opposition party wins the elections, but Slobodan Milosevic refuses to step down. Nationwide strikes force him out of power. Saudi royal family-funded Al-Qaida terrorists under former CIA operative Osama bin Laden set off a lethal bomb on the navy destroyer *Cole* while it docks in Yemen. The US pulls out of global warming talks at the Hague. US ambassador to Israel Martin Indyk complains about Israeli targeting of Palestinians: "The United States government is very clearly on the record as being against targeted assassinations. They are extrajudicial killings and we do not support that." During the tightly contested US presidential election, Bush wins by five hundred thirty-seven votes in Florida, where Republican officials under Secretary of State Katherine Harris purged voting lists of supposed felons; without the purge, fifty thousand more African American votes would have counted, undoubtedly ensuring the election of Al Gore. Republican operatives directed by Tom Delay disrupt recount attempts, even assaulting members of the Miami-Dade canvassing board; Harris stops the recount in Florida; and the US Supreme Court—a court of seven out of nine justices appointed by Republican presidents—votes five to four to stop the national recount and give Bush the election. Neocons quickly fill key positions, some taken by oilmen besides Bush. The new US president kills the International Criminal Court treaty, the Kyoto protocol, the ABM Treaty with Russia, and the Comprehensive Nuclear Test Ban Treaty as Vice President Dick Cheney convenes a secret task force to study the possibility of controlling oil piped from the Persian Gulf and the Caspian Sea. Cheney and Bush also work together to push the PNAC agenda for US world hegemony extended into space through plans suggested by Secretary of Defense Donald Rumsfeld.

2001:
Noah is cloned to save his Indian Bison species. The NEAR Shoemaker is the first spacecraft to land on an asteroid (433 Eros). The Taliban pulverize the sixth-century Buddhas of Bamiyan statues in Afghanistan. Mir falls into the Pacific. Dennis Tito goes up in a Russian spacecraft as the first space tourist. Tropical Storm Allison kills twenty-two in Texas. China and Russia sign a defense and cooperation pact. Huge demonstrations mark the G8 meeting of wealthy industrialized nations in Genoa, where police assault anti-globalization protesters. US President Bush receives a daily brief with the title, "Bin Laden Determined to Strike in US" and ignores it; Secretary of State Condoleezza Rice, Attorney General John Ashcroft, and Deputy Defense Secretary Paul Wolfowitz ignore similar warnings. A World Conference against Racism in Durban, South Africa; the US, Israel, and Canada withdraw from discomfort over Zionism being highlighted. On Sept 11, Al Qaida terrorists with strong connections to Saudi Arabia—none were from Iraq—fly stolen airliners into the World Trade Center and the Pentagon. The Bush Administration ignores the Saudis (with whose royalty the Bush family enjoys lucrative ties) and instead blames Iraq, having already begun planning to invade that country to take over its oil supplies; a PNAC letter to Bush states, "...Even if evidence does not link Iraq directly to the attack, any strategy aiming at the eradication of terrorism and its sponsors must include a determined effort to remove Saddam Hussein from power in Iraq." Bush authorizes the CIA to set up detention and torture "black sites" outside the US.

Cheney talks of "working on the dark side" and a war that "may never end." Having lost the presidential election, Al Gore puts together his *Inconvenient Truth* slideshow to warn the world about climate change. Anthrax in letters mailed to various US news agencies. The US and other nations invade Afghanistan (Operation Enduring Freedom) and support opium dealer Hamid Karzai. Iraqis and Afghans are rounded up by bounty hunters and imprisoned without trail at Guantanamo Bay; White House legal counsel Alberto Gonzales maintains that the Geneva Conventions do not apply to these prisoners, some of whom are teens. The PATRIOT Act grants the US Government extraordinary detention and surveillance powers, and an executive order by Bush allows military tribunals to try foreigners suspected of terrorist connections. Telecom companies like AT&T allow the National Security Agency direct access to Americans' phone and email accounts. China joins the World Trade Organization. After years of fraud, the energy company Enron goes under in the largest bankruptcy in US history. Terrorists based in Pakistan attack the parliament of India and kill a dozen people. Boko Haram established in northern Nigeria to fight violently and with terror tactics for strict Islamic governance. Bush withdraws the US from the 1972 Anti-Ballistic Missile Treaty. China and the US normalize trade relations. Manil Suri's *The Death of Vishnu*. Jack Kornfield's *After the Ecstasy, the Laundry:
How the Heart Grows Wise on the Spiritual Path.*

2002:
Mount Nyiragongo erupts in the Congo. A huge chunk of the Antarctic Larsen Ice Shelf melts because of global warming. Serial killer Robert William Pickton arrested in Canada. Rioting in Gujarat between Hindus and Muslims after a train carrying Hindu pilgrims burns. East Timor achieves independence. When President Bush's Nuclear Posture Review claims a US right to use nuclear weapons to destroy buried bunkers, counter weapons of mass destruction, or meet "surprising military developments," the *New York Times* runs an editorial titled, "America as Nuclear Rogue." In response to a suicide bombing in Netanya, the Israeli military enters the West Bank

(Operation Defensive Shield). FBI agent Robert Hanssen imprisoned for life for peddling intelligence secrets to Russia. Dwarf planet Quaoar spotted beyond the orbit of Neptune; the name refers to a tyrannical Tongva god accompanied by a band of avengers who spy on humans. An asteroid just misses Earth. Kevin Warwick of the UK wires two human nervous systems together. A train wreck in Tanzania kills two hundred and eighty-one in the worst rail wreck in African history. The International Criminal Court founded to try perpetrators of war crimes and genocide. The Organization of African Unity becomes the African Union. An outbreak of Severe Acute Respiratory Syndrome (SARS) in Hong Kong narrowly avoids expanding into a pandemic. The crash of a Sukhoi Su-27 fighter jet in Ukraine kills seventy-seven and injures a hundred in the worst air show crash ever. Floods in several European nations drown dozens and displace thousands. Switzerland joins the UN. The US refuses to attend the World Summit on Sustainable Development in Johannesburg, South Africa. The Department of Homeland Security organized in the US. Psychologists connected with the American Psychological Association design torture regimens for use in Abu Ghraib prison in Baghdad, from where a photograph of a hooded man standing with arms spread eerily evokes Jesus on the cross. Jorge Ferrer publishes *Revisioning Transpersonal Theory: A Participatory Vision of Human Spirituality*.

2003:
In Darfur, west Sudan, civil war breaks out when the non-Arab Justice and Equality Movement and the Sudan Liberation Movement fight the Sudanese Arab government and their Janjaweed militant supporters for oppressing non-Muslims. Funded and supplied by the government, the Janjaweed burn entire villages and rape and murder civilians. A Truth and Reconciliation Commission in Peru addresses the rights of people victimized by former president Fujimori. President Bush and Secretary of State Colin Powell make false, disproven claims about Iraq buying uranium from Africa, while Dick Cheney and his Chief of Staff Lewis "Scooter" Libby push CIA analysts to find ties between Iraq and Al-Qaida. The National Security Agency runs an operation to get UN delegates to

support a US war in Iraq. Bush suggests to Tony Blair, Prime Minister of the UK, that a war might be provoked: a defector produced to make WMD claims about Iraq, for example, or a spy plane disguised in UN colors drawing Iraqi fire; retired generals quietly recruited by the Pentagon go on TV and radio as pro-war experts. Ten million around the world protest the war before it even starts. Although Iraq's foreign minister and chief of intelligence confirm to the CIA and British Intelligence that Iraq has no weapons of mass destruction, US and British troops land there and set up base camps with names like Camp Shell and Camp Exxon. A US psychological warfare team stages photographs of a falling statue of Saddam; US forces guard the Ministry of Oil as priceless antiques vanish from museums. Bush administration officials draw up plans to invade Syria, Lebanon, Libya, Iran, Somalia, and Sudan next. Upon reentry the space shuttle *Columbia* blows up over Texas. The human genome is mapped. In the US a record-setting three hundred and ninety-three tornados land in May in nineteen states. Bush administration give optimistic reports about the subjugation of Iraq, whose industries have been privatized to lower tax rates for the wealthy, secure no-bid contracts for firm like Halliburton, and to allow foreign takeovers of Iraqi businesses; bank jobs are reserved for Bush-supporting anti-abortion conservative bankers, one of them a twenty-four-old charged with opening the Baghdad stock exchange even though he had never worked in finance. Security is outsourced to Blackwater, whose soldiers had gained experience fighting for reactionary Latin American governments. Although Iran offers a list of concessions—transparency on its nuclear research, recognition of Israel, suppression of terrorist cells, pressure on Hezbollah—in exchange for access to peaceful nuclear technology and improved relations, it is on the Bush administration hit list, so the offer is turned down. The Indonesian military moves against the Free Aceh Movement seeking the independence of Aceh in Sumatra. Scientists at Texas A&M clone Dewey the deer, and Italian scientists clone Promotea (from "Prometheus") the horse. Hundreds of thousands march successfully on Hong Kong to protest the government's Article 23 order forbidding free speech and protest. In retaliation for former ambassador Joseph Wilson's debunking of the uranium purchase lie, Scooter Libby discloses that his wife Valerie Plame is a CIA agent. The Convention on the Future of Europe works on a European Constitution. The UN sends soldiers to Liberia. China launches its first manned space mission. The collapse of dairy company Parmalat SpA after years of fraud is Europe's biggest bankruptcy. A huge quake kills forty thousand in the Iranian city of Bam. Ruth Ozeki's *All Over Creation*. Richard Heinberg's *The Party's Over: Oil, War, and the Fate of Industrial Societies*.

2004:
The $128 billion surplus inherited from the Clinton administration is now a $413 deficit. Two-thirds of US corporations pay no income tax, but states and counties begin to go under because of insufficient operating funds. Exploration vehicles *Spirit* and *Opportunity* land on Mars. Social media network Facebook goes online. Islamic terrorists kill a hundred and sixteen people by bombing SuperFerry 14 in the Philippines. According to *The Nature and Scope of the Problem of Sexual Abuse of Minors by Catholic Priests and Deacons in the United States* (John Jay Report), more than ten thousand people accused Catholic priests of molestation between 1950 and 2002, but relatively few were ever prosecuted. Haitian president Aristide is forced into exile. Phyllis Lyon and Del Martin are the first same-sex married couple in the US. Cyclone Gafilo, the most powerful ever to form in the Indian Ocean, devastates Madagascar. Hurricane Catatrina, the first known South Atlantic hurricane ever, hits South Brazil. Slovenia, Slovakia, Romania, Lithuania, Bulgaria, Estonia, and Latvia join NATO despite Russian concerns of marginalization. SpaceShipOne lifts off from the Mojave Desert as the first privately funded orbital spacecraft. A series of damaging news disclosures reveals that top Bush officials and the National Security Council's Principals Committee met routinely to discuss and approve torture methods like waterboarding, an invention of the Spanish Inquisition, employed in US prisons holding terror suspects. "History will not judge us kindly," remarks Ashcroft in one NSC meeting. General Barry McCaffrey admits to dozens murdered and tortured "unmercifully." Documents are edited to hide the lack of evidence against

hundreds of suspects detained indefinitely at Guantanamo. Hundreds die when Russian forces storm a school in Beslan where Chechen terrorist hostages are held, most of them children. Brazil launches a rocket into orbit. Remains of Homo floresiensis ("Hobbit Man") found in Indonesia. First European Constitution founded. As part of a conservative backlash, eleven US states ban gay marriage. NASA's *Scramjet* flies ten times the speed of sound. An earthquake in the Indian Ocean that shifts Earth's spin raises up a tsunami that kills two hundred thousand coast-dwellers (Boxing Day Tsunami). Stephen Greenblatt's *Will in the World*.

2005:
Labor Secretary Elaine Chao guts the Mine Safety and Health Administration and the Occupational Safety and Health Administration as US Republicans attack the Environmental Protection Agency and the Department of Labor investigates unions. Around the world, the three hundred wealthiest people own more than the poorest three billion, with the top 1% owning 40% of total global wealth. Dwarf planet Eris ("Discord") detected. Severe storm surges and flooding in Western Europe. The International Criminal Court condemns Lord's Resistance Army leader Joseph Kony of Uganda as a war criminal. Saudi Arabia holds elections—for men. YouTube goes online. Almost a million rally effectively in Lebanon (the Cedar Revolution) to protest Syrian occupation. In Kyrgyzstan the primarily nonviolent Tulip Revolution—the colorful name points back to color-coded revolutions in Portugal, Czechoslovakia, Ukraine, and Georgia—overthrows authoritarian president Askar Akayev. Thousands in Taipei protest China's Anti-Secession Law designed to justify the use of force to stop Taiwan from seceding. Muslims inside and outside Denmark protest cartoons of Muhammad published in a Danish newspaper. Joseph Ratzinger becomes Pope Benedict XVI. Arianna Huffington launches The Huffington Post, an online tabloid fed by an army of mostly unpaid reporters and news story gatherers. In 2011 she will sell it to America Online. An internal Citigroup memo states, "The World is dividing into two blocs—the Plutonomy and the rest." Government troops in Uzbekistan kill several hundred protesters (the Andijan

massacre) after the government puts twenty-three businessmen on trial for terrorism. Live 8 concerts play on behalf of "Make Poverty History" shortly before the G8 meets. Islamic suicide bombers kill fifty-two Underground commuters in four attacks in London. Mumbai, India sags under forty inches of rain in twenty-four hours. Hurricane Katrina hits the US Gulf Coast and floods Louisiana, Mississippi, and Alabama, but President Bush's declaration of an emergency fails to include some of the hardest-hit coastal areas, and citizens languish for weeks without shelter or sustenance. (Filling in of nearby wetlands over time significantly cut their powers as a natural storm surge buffer.) Two banks merge into the Mitsubishi UFJ Financial Group, the world's largest bank. A 7.6 magnitude earthquake in Kashmir. French surgeons give Isabelle Dinoire a face transplant. Robert Bullard publishes *The Quest for Environmental Justice: Human Rights and the Politics of Pollution.* Richard Louv's *Last Child in the Woods: Saving Our Children From Nature-Deficit Disorder:* "Progress does not have to be patented to be worthwhile. Progress can also be measured by our interactions with nature and its preservation. Can we teach children to look at a flower and see all the things it represents: beauty, the health of an ecosystem, and the potential for healing?"

2006:
Russia cuts off natural gas to Ukraine, a primary conduit to the European Union, during a long-standing dispute about Ukraine's contractual obligations to supplier Gazprom. NASA's Stardust probe retrieves material from a comet. Ellen Johnson Sirleaf is president of Liberia and the first woman elected head of state in modern times in Africa. Pope Benedict, an opponent of liberation theology, writes an encyclical to frame the Catholic Church's public role as directed toward charity rather than social justice. Avian Flu surfaces in Scotland. East Timor asks for military assistance from New Zealand and Australia to quell fighting in Tonga between government troops and rebel soldiers. Despite a weary history of military fragmentation of its politics and interference by oil companies, Nigeria pays off all its foreign debt. A 6.3 magnitude in Java kills thousands and displaces millions in Indonesia. Days later, a natural gas well drilled in

East Java blows out to form the largest mud volcano in the world. Israel invades Lebanon again. The Mexican military fights heavily armed drug cartels (Mexican Drug War). Declassified CIA documents reveal that the agency helped set up and train the secret police forces of Cambodia, Colombia, Ecuador, El Salvador, Guatemala, Iran, Iraq, Laos, Peru, the Philippines, South Korea, South Vietnam, and Thailand. Colony Collapse Disorder increasingly eradicates honeybees disoriented and made vulnerable by pesticides. The first International Conference on LGBT Human Rights opens in Montreal. Montenegro wins independence. The International Astronomical Union removes planetary status from Pluto. The film *An Inconvenient Truth* debuts at the Sundance Film Festival.

2007:
In the US, where wages are dropping, the top 1% hold 25% of national income and 40% of the nation's wealth. The Intergovernmental Panel on Climate Change reports that humans "very likely" cause global warming. In response, petroleum companies found front companies posing as citizen's organizations to cast doubt on climate science. South Korean student Seung-Hui Cho kills thirty-two people at Virginia Polytechnic, then shoots himself. Sheikh Mohammed bin Rashid Al Maktoum of the United Arab Emirates donates $10 billion to a children's educational foundation named after him. The People's Power Party restores democracy to Thailand, a country often ravaged by military dictatorships since it tried democracy in 1973. Economist Fakhruddin Ahmed is president in Bangladesh, a nation hit by extreme flooding and a devastating cyclone. A heat wave in Greece kills eleven and ignites many wildfires. Live Earth concerts play in nine cities to draw attention to the environment and to climate change. Cyclone Sidr kills ten thousand in Bangladesh. Benazir Bhutto, former prime minister of Pakistan and leader of the Pakistan People's Party opposing the government, is assassinated in Rawalpindi; riots break out against President Pervez Musharraf. Candis Canyne is the first transgender actress to play on Prime Time. The Universal Forum of Cultures in Monterrey, Mexico; originally opened in Barcelona, the mostly free event promotes cooperation and the arts. The UN Climate Change Conference

in Bali. An Africa-European Union Summit hosted by Portugal in Lisbon. *Terrapsychology* coined to describe a new field and research methodology for studying how the presence of the places where we live and work show up in symbolic psychological form (e.g., congested freeways and congested communications, polluted lakes and polluted moods, healthy heights and peak experiences). Robert McDermott's *Buddha and Christ*. Marc Bekoff's *The Emotional Lives of Animals: A Leading Scientist Explores Animal Joy, Sorrow, and Empathy and Why They Matter*.

2008:
The US sells $37.8 billion in arms: 68% of total world arms sales. Petroleum reaches $100 a barrel. Petroleum company predictions of world oil supply start to agree with those of peak oil advocates: all the oil easy to reach has been extracted. A recession in the US as subprime mortgage foreclosures and delinquencies rise sharply. A record snowstorm kills over a hundred in China and blacks out entire regions. Tornados kill fifty-eight people in the southern US. Kevin Rudd, prime minister of Australia, issues an apology to the Stolen Generations: Aboriginals removed from their homes as children between 1909 and the 1970s and brought up by the state and the church; Canadian prime minister Stephen Harper issues a similar apology to the First Nations people whose children were placed in boarding schools in Canada. Kosovo achieves independence. Raúl Castro is president of Cuba. Allen Andrade convicted of killing Angie Zapata: first US conviction for a hate crime against a transgender person. Internal investigations reveal links between key Colombian government officials and paramilitary forces roaming the country, many involved in the drug trade. A summit deescalates tension between Colombia, Ecuador, and Venezuela after Colombian troops attack rebels gathered in Ecuador across the border. Riots and street protests in Tibet against inflation, high food prices, and immigrants arriving from China. A key chunk of the Wilkins Ice Shelf in Antarctica breaks off. Two blind patients in London receive bionic eyes. More than a hundred and thirty thousand perish in Myanmar when Cyclone Nargis sweeps through. An 8.0 magnitude quake in Sichuan kills almost a hundred thousand and

inflicts massive damage in central China. The Union of South American Nations parallels the European Union. Nepal becomes a republic. An international exposition in Zaragoza, Spain, highlights the theme of "Water and Sustainable Development." Thomas Beatie, whose wife is infertile, is the first US man to give birth. Somalian pirates broaden their attacks on cargo shipping. Hurricanes Gustav, Hanna, and Ike hit the US and the Caribbean. Telecom companies seek immunity from prosecution for releasing their customers' private information to government agencies without warrants; Senator Barack Obama supports their bid. With its books having been cooked since 2007, investment bank Lehman Brothers is the largest-ever bankruptcy in the US. As more banks fail, President Bush signs an act into law to purchase their toxic assets with $700 billion in US Treasury funds. Barack Obama, first African American president in the US, inherits the global crisis, two catastrophic wars, a shredded US Constitution, outcries about government-sanctioned torture tactics, a huge gap between wealthy and poor, schools marginalized by Bush's "No Child Left Behind" policies, a new surveillance apparatus, the Guantanamo Bay prison, and $10 in national debt. Obama turns to Wall Street and the national treasury to bail out banks without prosecuting them for fraud or malfeasance. The shooting of teen student Alexandros Grigoropoulos by police triggers widespread rioting in Greece, where many suffer from unemployment, high educational expenses, and an anemic banking system. Financier Bernie Madoff charged with running the largest Ponzi scheme in history, depriving investors of $65 billion. Citizens of Ecuador pass a law to give rivers, tropical forests, islands, and winds rights similar to those of humans. Colonel Théoneste Bagosora and accomplices receive a sentence of imprisonment for life by the International Criminal Tribunal for Rwanda. Israel attacks Palestinians in Gaza and withdraw. Jane Mayer publishes *The Dark Side: The Inside Story of How the War on Terror Turned Into a War on American Ideals*. Toni Morrison's *A Mercy*.

2009:
Instead of being prosecuted for functioning as debt merchants, the CEOs of Wall Street's thirteen largest banks receive record bonuses

and go on with business as usual. The same with hedge fund managers. President Obama signs the American Recovery and Reinvestment Act to offer a stimulus to the economy and to homeowners with underwater mortgages. Jóhanna Sigurðardóttir, prime minister of Iceland, is the world's first openly lesbian head of state. Bushfires in Australia follow record-smashing high temperatures. A swine flu outbreak in Mexico City. The G-20 summit convenes in London to discuss the global recession. UNESCO (The United Nations Educational, Scientific and Cultural Organization) and the US Library of Congress create the World Digital Library to bring online free cultural and research content from everywhere. The C40 Cities Climate Leadership Group of the world's largest cities convene in Seoul to discuss preparation for the effects of global warming. US company KBR bribes Nigerian officials for the opportunity to construct a liquefied gas plant. The Sri Lanka Civil War ends with the defeat of the Tamil Tigers. A vote in Bolivia gives indigenous people self-government and control over natural resources. Typhoon Ketsana breaks rainfall records in Manila. Belgian prime minister Herman Van Rompuy is the first president of the European Council of the EU. Citizens for European Development of Bulgaria (GERB) comes to power as a minority government. In spite ongoing wars in Iraq and Afghanistan, prisoners at Guantanamo Bay, and escalating unmanned drone attacks against designated enemies of the US, Barack Obama accepts the Nobel Peace Prize. Shortly before the UN's Copenhagen Summit on climate change, hackers break into the research server at the University of East Anglia and distribute thousands of emails purportedly from climate scientists falsifying their data ("Climategate"), but subsequent investigation proves these allegations false despite their continuing use to fortify denial of global warming. Several scientific agencies, including the Union of Concerned Scientists, the American Meteorological Society, and the American Association for the Advancement of Science, reiterate that the scientific consensus firmly supports the conclusion that Planet Earth is overheating. Members of the parliament of Maldives meet underwater in scuba gear to highlight the fact that global warming is sinking their country. Liaquat Ahamed's *Lords of Finance: The Bankers who Broke the World*. Jane Goodall's *Hope for Animals and*

Their World: How Endangered Species Are Being Rescued from the Brink.

2010:
A new constitution for Madagascar. The Burj Khalifa skyscraper opens in Dubai as the tallest building in the world—2,722 feet—but the global economic slump leaves most of it uninhabited until 2012. In the US, 93% of income growth goes to the top 1% of households. Massive quakes in Haiti, Chili, and China, with much loss of life. The erupting smoke from Mount Eyjafjallajökull in Iceland rises so high that flights are cancelled. British Petroleum's Deepwater Horizon oil platform blows up and sinks in the Gulf of Mexico; BP cleanup workers uninformed about the risks of toxicity get sick, and news reporters are blocked from inspecting contaminated shorelines. In *Citizens United v. Federal Election Commission*, the US Supreme Court removes limits to corporate and banking spending in election campaigns. When Greece's credit rating drops to junk status, stock markets and the euro sag worldwide and Ireland faces bankruptcy. Two Chechen women blow themselves up with forty other people in the Moscow Metro. Scientists complete an initial outline of the Neanderthal genome. Kyrgyz president Kurmanbek Bakiyev kicked out and exiled by the Second Kyrgyz Revolution; the first free elections follow. US president Obama invokes state secrets privilege to stop lawsuits for torture, wiretapping, and extraordinary rendition (kidnapping) and vigorously prosecutes whistleblowers like Private Bradley Manning, who released classified information on US military massacres in the Middle East to WikiLeaks, which publishes secret documents online; but no Bush administration official is prosecuted for any of numerous war crimes. Drone strikes personally ordered by Obama remove one militant for every ten to fifteen innocent people killed even while arousing a lust for revenge in the surviving family members, virtually guaranteeing a permanent supply of terrorists to hunt down. According to a four-part series run by the *Washington Post*, eight hundred and fifty people hold top-security clearance as they work out of twelve hundred government organizations and nineteen hundred private companies; the Pentagon runs most of these programs. Meanwhile, the NSA stores 1.7 billion

emails and phone calls a day without using warrants or court orders of any kind, and the FBI seeks an expansion of its own surveillance powers against US citizens. In Afghanistan, where the US invasion to secure mineral interests (lithium, gold, copper, iron ore) and access to Caspian Sea oil and gas has removed drug trade controls, opium production builds until it employs 20% of Afghanis and constitutes 53% of the national economy. President Obama declines to support a national single-payer healthcare program or Medicare expansion and instead invites insurance company representatives to help draft healthcare legislation. He also reneges on a campaign promise to strengthen environmental management and capitulates to Republican demands to slash social services and to extend Bush's tax cuts for the wealthy. Scientists employed by Craig Venter invent a synthetic genome and artificial DNA. The Israeli Navy boards ships sent to bring supplies to Gaza despite the blockade and kills nine activists. In Spain, La Florida, the largest solar energy plant in the world, generates enough electricity to power forty-five thousand homes. Flood waters cover large portions of Pakistan. Biologists discover through DNA analysis that Hitler was part Jewish and African. Miners in Chile are rescued from a collapsed mine. Mount Merapi erupts in Java. South Korea hosts the G-20 summit. The military junta controlling Myanmar frees peace activist Aung San Suu Kyi from house arrest. The CERN particle accelerator in Switzerland collects a small amount of antimatter. North Korea drops shells on Yeonpyeong Island. The UN holds a climate change conference in Mexico. Street vendor Mohamed Bouazizi lights himself on fire in Tunisia to protest having his wares confiscated by the municipal government, and an Arab Spring of revolt spreads rapidly through several Arab countries. Marc Bekoff's *The Animal Manifesto: Six Reasons For Expanding Our Compassion Footprint*. Sean Kelly's *Coming Home: The Birth & Transformation of the Planetary Era*.

2011:
Almost half of US citizens live on low income or are in poverty, and fewer and fewer find the means to make more money. Some remain unemployed for so long that they quit looking for work. Arab Spring uprisings against theocratic authoritarianism and corruption flame

up in Tunisia, Egypt, Yemen, Bahrain, and Libya. South Sudan achieves independence. The opposition Pheu Thai Party wins elections by a landslide in Thailand. The Second Ivorian Civil War on the Ivory Coast between presidential loyalists behind Laurent Gbagbo and president-elect Alassane Ouattara, whose forces take control and eject Gbagbo. Hundreds die in rainstorms and mudslides in Rio de Janeiro. A 9.1 earthquake and tsunami kill almost twenty thousand living on the east coast of Japan and partially melt down reactors at the Fukushima Nuclear Power Plant. News International, a subsidiary of News Corporation chaired by Rupert Murdoch, investigated and closed down for widespread phone hacking and police bribery. SEAL Team soldiers assassinate Osama bin Laden in Pakistan, where he had lived in hiding next to a large military academy. Swedish surgeons give a patient a new artificial windpipe: the world's first artificial organ transplant. Somalia withers under famine. NASA winds down its space shuttle program. Severe flooding in most of Thailand as superstorms grow larger and more frequent across the world. The Egyptian Revolution ousts ailing dictator Hosni Mubarak. Libyan fighters revolt and overthrow and execute Muammar Gaddafi. Helle Thorning-Schmidt is the first woman to be prime minister in Denmark. The Occupy Movement starts with protests in Zuccotti Park near Wall Street and expands across the US as activists occupy campuses, parks, and corporate headquarters to protest greed, corruption, and income inequality: "We Are the 99%." The nationalist/separatist Basque Homeland and Freedom movement ends its campaign. The European Union meets in Brussels to plan bailouts of governments and banks if not of struggling citizens and asks China, holder of over a trillion dollars of US treasury bonds, for billions invested in an emergency stability fund. Severe flooding in the Philippines from Tropical Storm Washi. World population: seven billion. Tim Flannery's *Here on Earth: A Natural History of the Planet*. Curt Stager's *Deep Future: The Next 100,000 Years of Life on Earth*.

2012:

President Obama defeats Mitt Romney in the US presidential election despite widespread Republican attempts to purge voter lists and keep African Americans from voting; Republican efforts to throw the election grow so obvious that the UN sends in election monitors, and the cartoon series *Doonesbury* features the return of a large bird named Jim Crow. Arab Spring protests replace Yemeni president Ali Abdullah Saleh with Abd Rabbuh Mansur Al-Hadi. The *Encyclopedia Brittanica* ends its print edition. Azawad reaches independence. The World Expo in Yeosu in South Korea. The Tokyo Skytree tower that recalls the mythic spear of Izanagi opens in Tokyo. The US shifts naval forces into the Pacific to counter China's presence. According to Joseph Stiglitz, the combined wealth of the six Walmart heirs equals that of the bottom 30% of Americans. *Time Magazine's* Person of the Year is The Protestor. CERN finds a likely candidate for the Higgs boson that gives all particles their mass by setting up an interactive field through which they move. Because of extreme heat and late monsoons, blackouts cross India to leave six hundred and twenty-million people—9% of the world's population—in two days of darkness. After the film clip *The Real Life of Muhammad* (*The Innocence of Muslims*) by Nakoula Basseley Nakoula plays on YouTube, a clip depicting a mob of Muslims slaying Egyptian Christians, rioting erupts in several Arab countries; all actors involved in the piecemeal roles they were hired to perform denounce the film. In Benghazi, Libya, the US consulate and annex come under attack by Islamic militants who slay four Americans, including ambassador J. Christopher Stevens. Norwegian rightwinger Anders Behring Breivik shoots and kills seventy-seven students at a summer camp in Oslo. Australian skydiver Felix Baumgartner breaks the sound barrier on a jump from orbit over Roswell, New Mexico. Hurricane Sandy kills hundreds and reshapes part of the East Coast of the US, and Typhon Bopha kills sixteen hundred in the Philippines. Berkeley, California is the first American city to set aside a day to recognize bisexuals. Krysten Sinema is the first openly bisexual elected to the US Congress, and Mark Takano the first openly gay person of color elected to the House of Representatives. Israel attacks the Gaza Strip again (Operation Pillar of Defense). The US Climate Change Conference held in Qatar extends the Kyoto Protocol until 2020. A court battle won by indigenous activists in New Zealand force the government to grant personhood status to the Whanganui, the country's third-longest river. Misreadings of the Mayan Long Count proliferate as incredulous people sell their homes and stock up on survival items, but nothing universally catastrophic happens and again earthly life goes on pretty much as it did before. Pads and e-readers overtake desktop computers in popularity. Katharine Boo publishes *Behind the Beautiful Forevers: Life, Death, and Hope in a Mumbai Undercity*. Joseph Dodds' *Psychoanalysis and Ecology at the Edge of Chaos*. Susan Cain's *Quiet: The Power of Introverts in a World That Can't Stop Talking*. Voyager 1 leaves the Solar System bearing along a Golden Record of sounds, voices, images from cultures all over Earth, coordinates for our location in space, greetings in fifty-six languages, and a selection of sounds made by nonhuman species living with us on the floating blue globe. The probe will pass within 1.6 light years of a distant star in forty thousand years. It would be interesting to know if anyone will ever intercept our collective human message in the floating interstellar bottle.

Epilogue for a Pale Blue Dot:
Why Are We Here and Where Are We Headed?

Those words appeared in Charles Dickens' new weekly *All The Year Round*, which he launched on April 30, 1859. They begin *A Tale of Two Cities*, his novel of the French Revolution, a novel he wrote in a turbulent time. I sometimes wonder what he would have made of our turbulent time.

It could be argued that the extremes he described are always with us, but, looking back, the impression of an accelerating frenzy persists. And what do we face today?

On February 15, 2013, a meteor exploded over the Russian city of Chelyabinsk, flattening buildings and knocking down trees, at about the time an asteroid made a close passage of our planet. Arthur Clarke had warned about such possibilities in his 1972 novel *Rendezvous with Rama*.

Pope Benedict XVI resigned, the first pope to give up office since Gregory XII in 1415. The new pope, a Jesuit from South America, broke with tradition to take the name Francis after the monk who had fought the Vatican for the right to imitate the poverty of Jesus.

An arm of the Chinese military waged cyberattacks against a wide range of US government agencies, newspapers, and corporations.

Korea's new leader, Kim Jong Un, threatened the US, South Korea, and Japan with nuclear attack by Photoshopped missiles that did not exist.

The US found itself mired in more economic disparity than any other developed nation. The only industrial power lacking an affordable healthcare plan for its people, it continued to spend more on its military than all other nations combined, in part to maintain a thousand bases around the world and its supply of toxic, lethal, and Plutonic petroleum. Thomas Jefferson might never have written, "If there be one principle more deeply rooted than any other in the mind of every American, it is that we should have nothing to do with conquest."

Rebels captured the capital of the Central African Republic and threw out its president, François Bozizé, who flees to Cameroon.

The European Nation offers to bail out Cypress, for a price.

Canada withdraws from the United Nations Convention to Combat Desertification.

At the Svalbard archipelago in Norway, a photographer spots what looks like a weeping face looking out from a wall of ice. The tears of Earth?

In 2013, as this book goes to print, humanity faces accelerating global warming, mass extinction, molecular computers, computerized clothing, experimental cloning, cybernetic implantation, devastated bee populations, mounting evidence of extraterrestrial life, power pushes by companies like Monsanto to patent genes, vanishing freshwater and cropland, genetically modified organisms inadvertently but predictably released into the natural world. Who can keep up with it all? Who can tell where it is headed? Or where it is heading us?

To the sensitized eye, history suggests the power of *idea* behind external workings of method or decree, court or coin. Once upon a time, for example, a boy named Temujin was sold into slavery along with his mother and mate to the clan that had poisoned his father. When he escaped servitude, he set out to shape a band of wanderers into a matchless bow-equipped cavalry. With their help he rescued his loved ones. In time, his following grew. He had an intelligence service so good that his men could be inside a perimeter before his enemies knew of any attack. He had a messenger service similar to the Pony Express nine hundred years before that institution was founded. Backed by the mythic image of the downtrodden lawgiver unifying a wandering people, this enterprising leader is known best by the name his men gave him when he came of age: Genghis Khan.

Every conquest, movement, invention, reformation, regeneration, and renaissance starts as an idea; and every idea embeds itself in myth.

Can there be a mythic image for our time? Joseph Campbell thought so. In his well-known *Power of Myth* interviews with Bill Moyers, he suggested one: Earthrise, photographed by Apollo 8 and transmitted home to the awe and delight of millions. He said:

> Myths and dreams come from the same place... And the only myth that is going to be worth thinking about in the immediate future is one that is talking about the planet, not the city, not these people, but the planet, and everybody on it. That's my main thought for what the future myth is going to be.

Environmentalism, ecofeminism, ecology's coming of age as a science, ecopsychology and deep ecology, virtual currency, Complexity Theory, breakthroughs in trans-species communications research, the sustainability movement, the Environmental Justice movement, climate change research, alternative energy, cleantech, cradle-to-cradle industry, biomimicry research, the World Wide Web: all this and more coincides with and unpacks that image of a shining blue planet floating whole, if shadowed, in the blackness of space. As Carl Sagan wrote in *Pale Blue Dot* while discussing a photograph of Earth snapped from Voyager 1,

> From this distant vantage point, the Earth might not seem of any particular interest. But for us, it's different. Consider again that

dot. That's here. That's home. That's us. On it everyone you love, everyone you know, everyone you ever heard of, every human being who ever was, lived out their lives. The aggregate of our joy and suffering, thousands of confident religions, ideologies, and economic doctrines, every hunter and forager, every hero and coward, every creator and destroyer of civilization, every king and peasant, every young couple in love, every mother and father, hopeful child, inventor and explorer, every teacher of morals, every corrupt politician, every "superstar," every "supreme leader," every saint and sinner in the history of our species lived there – on a mote of dust suspended in a sunbeam.

He continues:

The Earth is a very small stage in a vast cosmic arena. Think of the rivers of blood spilled by all those generals and emperors so that, in glory and triumph, they could become the momentary masters of a fraction of a dot. Think of the endless cruelties visited by the inhabitants of one corner of this pixel on the scarcely distinguishable inhabitants of some other corner, how frequent their misunderstandings, how eager they are to kill one another, how fervent their hatreds....

There is perhaps no better demonstration of the folly of human conceits than this distant image of our tiny world. To me, it underscores our responsibility to deal more kindly with one another, and to preserve and cherish the pale blue dot, the only home we've ever known.

These visions of Earth—as arena for conflict and domination, as Earthrise, as Pale Blue Dot—offer a reminder that the word "spectacle" derives from a root that means "to observe." I suspect that's why we are here: to gaze and hear and touch our planet in profound appreciation, and then articulate its forms, sounds, smells, and textures with ways and means unique to our vocal big-brained species. Perhaps we are Earth's latest experiment—instinctively brought forth, to be sure, rather than deliberately planned—in two-legged planetary self-reflection.

However, the same gifts of agriculturally urbanized civilization that handed us such powerful tools for observation and speculation now threaten to send us down history's drainpipe of extinction with all the other humanoid forms that went before us. If we are to survive to continue our acts of appreciation and articulation, we must accomplish at least three tasks: to prevent dominating, aggressive, and unscrupulous people from gaining control of what the rest of us need to live; to elevate wise, reflective, and courageous women and men to position of cultural leadership and mentorship; and to redesign our communities to be friendlier to Earth and all its inhabitants, lest we go on destroying the places that sustain our very existence. Earthrise offers a beautiful vision of a world free of resource wars and religious opportunism, organized intolerance and industrialized ecocide: a pleasantly evolved world within our reach, for we are the species that visited our moon and that looks in wonder at worlds far beyond. In the past climate shifts initiated by Earth forced us to evolve; today, climate shifts of our own doing demand no less of us.

In ten million years the Rift from which we originated will cleave Africa in two and destroy itself, leaving a new island adrift in a future Afar Ocean. Will any of us be there to see it, or will we remain only as fossils?

If we wish, the study of our own history can fill out empty spaces within where active stories should live. History can show us what to avoid, what mistakes to learn from. And history reminds us that we ourselves are history in the making, and more: that we are history trying to be conscious of itself as we go to and fro over the bright surfaces of our still-verdant homeworld.

Appendix I:
Forty Lessons from History:

1. When in doubt, create.
2. Elitism invites entropy.
3. There is no true self-reliance.
4. The distrustful should not be trusted.
5. Paranoid accusations reveal what the accuser would do in the place of the accused.
6. When power-lovers hold positions of authority, the results are always catastrophic.
7. A group of creative people working together can usually accomplish more than the lone genius.
8. Every tyrant starts out possessed by a drive to improve the world.
9. Retaliation always provokes more retaliation.
10. We eventually become what we violently attack.
11. Force can slow down the spread of evolutionary ideas but cannot prevent it.
12. Every wall invites its own transgression.
13. The closed-minded who think they already know learn nothing of importance until some great shock makes their formerly fixed notions permeable.

14 Systematic denial of the natural human capacity for spirituality lapses into unconscious ritual.
15 Every true act adds something imperishable to collective consciousness.
16 Oppression energizes what is being oppressed.
17 Where there is institutionalized intolerance, someone is benefitting materially from it.
18 What is stopped from coming to voice returns later as a conflict, scandal, or symptom.
19 Artists, poets, mystics, and misfits feel what's on the horizon before anyone else does.
20 Those who wage wars might gain temporarily, but they come out worse in the long run.
21 The preeminent institutionalized evil is controlling what others need to live.
22 Literal-mindedness, certainty, and fear of change are genuine faith's greatest enemies.
23 In a world of constant change, adaptation requires imagination.
24 Refusing to look evil in the face enables it to grow stronger.
25 It is not our faults we fear so much as our possibilities for true greatness.
26 The health and degeneration of thought and language go hand in hand.
27 In the absence of healing, the traumatized tend to repeat their traumatization and the oppressed to become oppressors.
28 Those who sacrifice their freedom for the appearance of security will lose both.
29 Careful self-reflection can limit the harm we do to others.
30 What we fail to grasp of our past we reenact destructively.
31 Clinging to one side of anything invites subtle possession by the other side.
32 Those who repress nature have an inordinate need to repress their own.
33 Powerless people tend to depend on heroes and saviors who will lead them to ruin.
34 Conformists never invent anything worthwhile, but they often jeer at worthwhile inventions.

35 History is moved less by influence or material than by desires, fancies, whims, and dreams.
36 In any conflict between groups, the side with the strongest mythology always wins.
37 There is no such thing as a wise, just, or lasting empire.
38 A people awakened to its own power and solidarity will not abide tyranny for long.
39 The power of sustained love can overcome terror.
40 Nature always has the last word.

Appendix II:
Countries and Regions of the World

Although space and time limitations made it impossible to detail in this book the history of every nation and region, they matter to their inhabitants, so this section gives them a mention:

Afghanistan
Albania
Algeria
American Samoa
Andorra
Angola
Antarctica
Antigua & Barbuda
Argentina
Armenia
Aruba
Australia
Austria
Azerbaijan
Bahamas

Lesotho
Liberia
Libya
Liechtenstein
Lithuania
Luxembourg
Macau
Macedonia
Madagascar
Malawi
Malaysia
Maldives
Mali
Malta
Marshall Islands

Bahrain
Bangladesh
Barbados
Belarus
Belgium
Belize
Benin
Bermuda
Bhutan
Bolivia
Bosnia & Herzegovina
Botswana
Brazil
Brunei Darussalam
Bulgaria
Burkina Faso
Burundi
Cambodia
Cameroon
Canada
Cape Verde
Cayman Islands
Central African Republic
Chad
Chile
China
Christmas Island
Cocos Islands
Colombia
Comoros
Congo, Democratic Republic
Congo, Republic Of
Cook Islands
Costa Rica
Cote d'Ivoire (Ivory Coast)
Croatia
Cuba

Martinique
Mauritania
Mauritius
Mayotte
Mexico
Micronesia
Moldova
Monaco
Mongolia
Montenegro
Montserrat
Morocco
Mozambique
Myanmar (Burma)
Namibia
Nauru
Nepal
The Netherlands
Netherlands Antilles
New Caledonia
New Zealand
Nicaragua
Niger
Nigeria
Niue
Northern Mariana Islands
Norway
Oman
Pakistan
Palau
Palestinian Territories
Panama
Papua New Guinea
Paraguay
Peru
The Philippines
Pitcairn Island

Cyprus
Czech Republic
Denmark
Djibouti
Dominica
Dominican Republic
Ecuador
East Timor
Egypt
El Salvador
Equatorial Guinea
Eritrea
Estonia
Ethiopia
Falkland Islands
Faroe Islands
Fiji
Finland
France
French Guiana
French Polynesia
French Southern Territories
Gabon
Gambia
Georgia
Germany
Ghana
Gibraltar
Great Britain
Greece
Greenland
Grenada
Guadeloupe
Guam
Guatemala
Guinea
Guinea-Bissau

Poland
Portugal
Puerto Rico
Qatar
Reunion Island
Romania
Russia
Rwanda
St. Kitts and Nevis
St. Lucia
St. Vincent and The Grenadines
Samoa
San Marino
Sao Tome and Principe
Saudi Arabia
Senegal
Serbia
Seychelles
Sierra Leone
Singapore
Slovakia
Slovenia
Solomon Islands
Somalia
South Africa
South Sudan
Spain
Sri Lanka
Sudan
Suriname
Swaziland
Sweden
Switzerland
Syria
Taiwan
Tajikistan
Tanzania

Guyana
Haiti
Holy See
Honduras
Hong Kong
Hungary
Iceland
India
Indonesia
Iran
Iraq
Ireland
Israel
Italy
Jamaica
Japan
Jordan
Kazakhstan
Kenya
Kiribati
Korea North
Korea South
Kosovo
Kuwait
Kyrgyzstan
Laos
Latvia
Lebanon

Thailand
Tibet
Togo
Tonga
Trinidad and Tobago
Tunisia
Turkey
Turkmenistan
Turks and Caicos Islands
Tuvalu
Uganda
Ukraine
United Arab Emirates
United Kingdom
United States of America
Uruguay
Uzbekistan
Vanuatu
Vatican City (Holy See)
Venezuela
Vietnam
Virgin Islands (British)
Virgin Islands (US)
Wallis and Futuna Islands
Western Sahara
Yemen
Zambia
Zimbabwe